DEVELOPMENTAL PROBLEMS AND POLICIES IN INDIA

Books from Department of Economics, Osmania University Hyderabad (India)

1. Essays in Political Economics : Selected Papers of Prof. Gautam Mathur
2. Developmental Problems and Policies in India
3. Growth Industrialization and Economic Problems in India

About the Editor

Prof. B. Satyanarayan was born on 10th September, 1938. He has taken his M.A. and Ph.D., Degrees from Osmania University in 1962 and 1973 respectively. He has been working in the University for more than 35 years holding various positions. He is presently working as a Senior Professor of Economics in the Department of Economics, Osmania University. He is simultaneously holding the position of Director/Coordinator, Special Assistance Programme (Sponsored by the University Grants Commission), Department of Economics, Osmania University, during the last six years. Earlier, he worked as Head of the Department of Economics and Chairman, Board of Studies, Osmania University. He is a recognised Research Supervisor guiding M. Phil., and Ph.D., Degrees and a number of Research Scholars are presently working under his supervision, on a variety of problems ranging from Planning, Development Economics, International Trade, Energy, Industry, Family Planning, etc.

He has to his credit more than 100 research papers published in a number of academic Journals, besides more than fifty book-reviews published in various academic Journals of repute. He has participated in a number of National and International Seminars. Professor Satyanarayan has undertaken and successfully completed nearly a dozen research projects, sponsored by the Government of India, U.G.C., Planning Commission, Government of Andhra Pradesh, etc. He has recently completed a major research project on "Regional Co-operation Among SAARC Countries with Special Reference to Trade Prospects" sponsored by the UGC, New Delhi. He had the privilege of being invited as a Visiting Professor by the Illinois Institute of Technology, Chicago, USA (Stwart School of Business) for a period of 3 months during July-October 1994. His name has been published by the Biography International (1992) and Marquis "Who's in the World" (1999). He has authored and edited nearly 10 Books on various aspects of Development Economics.

DEVELOPMENTAL PROBLEMS AND POLICIES IN INDIA
An Appraisal

B. SATYANARAYAN
Co-Ordinatior/Director
Special Assistance Programme (UGC)
Department of Economics, Osmania University,
Hyderabad-7 (India)

CONCEPT PUBLISHING COMPANY, NEW DELHI-110059

ISBN : 81-7022-825-5

First Published 2000

Published and Printed by
Ashok Kumar Mittal
Concept Publishing Company
A/15-16, Commercial Block, Mohan Garden
New Delhi-110059 (INDIA)

Phones : 5648039, 5649024
Fax : 091-11-5648053
E-mail : publishing@conceptpub.com

PREFACE

The present volume consists of the extension lectures delivered by the eminent economists/scholars who have been invited under the auspices of the Special Assistance Programme (Now it is known as Department of Special Assistance), Department of Economics, Osmania University, sponsored by the University Grants Commission. These lectures were spread during the period from 1994 to 1998. We are able to utilise the publication grant sanctioned under the DSA Funds. Our thanks are due to all the Visiting Professors/Scholars who have readily agreed to spare the written matter and send the material for necessary publication.

The Advisory Committee of the DSA has been kind enough to have agreed for the publication of all the extension lectures.

Date : 31 March, 1999 Prof. B. SATYANARAYAN

Hyderabad-7

ACKNOWLEDGEMENTS

At the outset, I wish to thank the University Grants Commission, New Delhi for providing the publication grant. I wish to thank Prof. D.C. Reddy, the Vice-Chancellor and Chairman of the Advisory Committee of the Department of Special Assistance. I wish to express my thanks to Prof. Pannalal, the Registrar and Prof. P. Jaya Prakash Rao, Dean, Development and UGC Affairs, Osmania University and their staff who have helped us in releasing funds. I am also thankful to Prof. V. Ramakishtayya, former Vice-Chancellor, Prof. M. Bhagwanth Rao, former Registrar and Prof. S. Pullaiah, former Dean, UGC Affairs, Osmania University, who have extended their helping hand in completing the task on hand. I also wish to thank all the members of the Advisory Committee of the DSA for their valuable suggestions from time to time.

Finally, I wish to thank all the members of the faculty who co-operated wholeheartedly in the publication of the present volume, particularly the successive Heads of the Department of Economics, Osmania University, *viz.*, Prof. H. Venkateshwar Rao, Prof. M. Narasimhulu, Prof. K. Chakradhar Rao and Prof. V. Suguna. I also thank all the members of the Research and the Administrative staff who have helped me in completing the publication of the present volume.

Date : 31 March, 1999 Prof. B. SATYANARAYAN

Hyderabad-7

CONTENTS

LIST OF CONTRIBUTORS

Prof. G. Parthasarathy, Director, Institute of Development and Planning Studies, Visakhapatnam (A.P.).

Prof. K.N. Reddy, Former Professor, National Institute of Public Finance and Policy, New Delhi.

Prof. D.U. Sastry, Former Professor & Senior Fellow, Institute of Economic Growth, Delhi-7.

Prof. B.S. Sreekantaradhya, Professor of Economics, University of Mysore, Mysore-570006 (Karnataka)

Prof. S.K. Thorat, Professor of Economics, Centre for the Study of Regional Development, Jawaharlal Nehru University, New Delhi.

INTRODUCTION

The paper entitled "The Unorganised Sector in Indian Economy and Public Policy in the Context of Structural Adjustment" by Prof. G. Parthasarathy deals with Capitalist and Marxist theories of organised and unorganised sectors of labour. According to Marxian theory, those who cannot get absorbed, will enter the ranks of immiserised unemployed labour. The author feels that the Indian situation is quite different. The share of unorganised in national income has been declining but the number in the unorganised sector continues to swell. The author, trying to conceptualise the unorganised sector is sometimes identified with the informal sector.

As far as Indian economy is concerned, the share of unorganised labour was as high as 91 per cent while its share in NDP was 36 per cent. The shares of organised and unorganised sectors in 1991 by industry division, *viz.,* Electricity, Gas and Water, Railway Transport, Communications, Public Administration and Defence, etc. are shown in Tables 1.3, 1.4, 1.5, 1.6, 1.7, 1.8, 1.9 and 1.10. These tables are not only informative but useful to the policy makers. The author highlighted the structural adjustments which have been recently taken up. In India, these structural adjustments imply:

1. An increasing flow of foreign direct investment alongwith foreign technology;
2. A decline in the role of the state and an increase in the role of market in industrial growth;
3. An increasing reliance on foreign trade as an engine of growth; and
4. A shift away after subsidies and from protection through tariff.

The author has brought out the *pros and cons* involved in these structural adjustments and their impact on the unorganised and organised sectors. In the end, the paper deals with a number of estimates of unemployed persons in India as a consequence of structural adjustments.

The paper titled "The Role of Finance and Planning in Sustainability of Projects in India" by Prof. K.N. Reddy broadly deals with the role of finance and planning in the sustainability of projects. The paper is divided into four sections. First section discusses the conceptual problems associated with sustainability of projects. The author deals with a number of definitions which take into account not only quantitative factors but also the qualitative factors including the one given by the World Bank. The second section touches upon the process of allocation of funds by finance and planning mechanisms. The author has explained both the Administrative Structure and Inter-Governmental Fiscal Devolution which is prevalent in the Indian Constitution. India has a three-tier federal system, Central Government, State Governments, and local governments. Funds are transferred from central government to state government and from state governments directly to local governments and from state governments through three channels:

1. Planning Commission;
2. Central Ministries; and
3. Finance Commission.

The third section deals with the Magnitude of Funds devolved from the Centre to States. Table 1.3 highlights the details showing the Transfer of Resources from Centre to States. Likewise, Table 1.4 records the Evolution Formulae for Central Assistance evolved over time such as Gadgil Formulae of 1969 and 1980, NDC Formulae of 1990 and 1991. The last section is devoted to discuss various suggestions to tone up sustainability of projects and programmes. The author is of the opinion that attention is to be paid for bringing down the deficits on revenue account of budgets by means of not only increasing the resources but also by curbing down the expenditure. He says that the State should levy appropriate user changes on the provision of social services like education, industry, transport, electricity, communications, etc. According to the author, education and health are "merit" goods and cannot be left to market forces, and the government should always limit its area of intervention in providing them or recover costs from affluent sections. Some of these ideas are relevant in the context of liberalisation and new economic reforms.

Prof. K.N. Reddy in his interesting paper on "Alternative Sources of Financing Health Care in Indian Cities" deals with the National Health Policy with targets to be achieved in respect of infant mortality rate, crude death rate, life expectancy at birth, net reproductive rate, immunisation status, etc. Section I makes an attempt to describe health care provision and health care financing in India and exploration of alternative sources of health care financing with reference to cities in India. Section II deals with the description of health care provision and financing by various government and non-governmental agencies. Section III gives the review of health care financing in some of the efficiently managed countries, such as Canada, Germany, Japan from the Developed World and China from the Developing World. Section IV outlines the alternative sources of health care financing in India. Section V discusses the scope for trying alternate sources of health care financing for cities in India. The final section raises some important issues for consideration while giving some conclusions.

Table 3.1 records the total Expenditure as percentage of GDP of nearly 40 countries (Developed and Developing). Similarly, Table 3.2 records the data pertaining to health care providers alongwith sources of finance, namely, Central and State governments, local bodies, public and private hospitals. The author gives some new ideas as to how government could raise more resources for financing the health schemes. They are;

1. Levying new taxes;
2. Adopting new methods like lotteries;
3. Granting amnesties for those who want to convert black money into white;
4. Appealing philonthropists for liberal donations;
5. Improving efficiency of resources used in health sector as well as in other sectors and there by save some resources and put the same to provide additional health care;
6. Cutting down wasteful and non-productive expenditure;
7. Recovering the costs by levying user charges for the services provided;
8. Introduction of insurance-compulsory or voluntary;
9. Promoting self help organisations in local communities, and
10. Getting more aid from foreign countries.

The author is of the opinion that reprioritization of resource allocation from curative to preventive health care will give better results. According to his study, more than 70 per cent of health care spending in India is on curative while less than 30 per cent is spent on preventive health care measures. While summing up, the author says that although the health status in India during the last 5 decades has improved, but yet in comparison with other similarly placed countries like China, Indonesia, Sri Lanka, it is not impressive. This has to be further probed.

The paper entitled "Health Care Expenditure in India: Is it low?" By Prof. K.N. Reddy makes an attempt to estimate health care expenditure by public and private sectors in India and also examine whether India is spending lower than what other comparable countries are spending. During the past three decades—between 1960 and 1990—life expentancy at birth in India has increased from 47 to 58 years, as compared to China from 43 to 69 years, in Republic of Korea from 53 to 72 years. Three reasons are usually attributed to these disperate achievements:

1. The resources spent on health care expenditure in India are inadequate and comparatively low;
2. The structure and priorities of health care expenditure in India are far different from others; and
3. The system of health care financing is far different and less efficient than others.

It may be noted that India on the whole (public and private sector put together) is spending nearly 3.75 per cent of its GNP on its health care, which is more than that of Indonesia, Sri Lanka, Philippines, Malaysia and Thailand. The share of private sector (households, charitable and private hospitals and private enterprise hospitals) in India constituted about 56 per cent and the rest of 44 per cent accounted by the public sector, *i.e.,* the Central, the State, the Union Territory and the local governments and the public sector enterprises. Finally, the author feels that the allegation adduced for slow progress in India's health status seems to be incorrect. India did spend as much as other developing countries spent. The reason for poor progress in health status was not due to lack of resources for health care, but something else. This study reveals that it could be either inefficiency, misallocation of resources in the health sector, and misallocation of resources between health and other sectors.

The paper on "Pattern of Financing Primary Education in India". By Prof. K.N. Reddy makes an attempt to analyse the pattern of financing Primary education in India during 1974-75 to 1986-87, the period for which comparable and consistent data are reported to be available. It has been found that although primary education was given top priority, over a period of time its share at the national level as well at the level of the states has declined. According to the author, priorities as between different levels of education—primary, secondary, special education, pre-university and higher education, technical education, sports and youth welfare, etc.—in backward/poor states are not much different from that in the rest of the states. As of 1992-93, nearly 1/5th of the states resources were spent on education. But the question posed is what should be the optimum share that should be allocated to primary education. The data produced in Table 5.1 show that the share of expenditure spent on primary education has declined from 46.4 per cent in 1974-75 to 43.6 per cent in 1986-87, while the share of expenditure on university and higher education has slightly increased from 12.9 per cent in 1974-75 to 13.4 per cent in 1986-87.

The author feels that primary education should be made the fundamental right of the people and it must become the obligation of the Union Government to fulfil it. Meeting basic needs—primary education, preventive and essential health care and alleviation of poverty should become the responsibility of the Union government. The author opines that basic needs should not be left to the state governments as not all of them have matured enough to take a long term view and have a tendency to fritter away their limited resources on populist schemes. Moreover, their fiscal capacities are not uniform. And as long as their fiscal capacities are unequal, differences in their levels of literacy and other amenities would persist. The argument, quite often advanced, that citizens of all states, irrespective of their geographical locations, should have equal access to basic needs gains more support as the years pass by. The author raises some important questions. They are:

(a) Why should a citizen of one state or region enjoy poor access to basic needs in comparison to other states or regions when the same citizens are asked to sacrifice equally for the nation?
(b) Are not the citizens, where ever they stay, entitled for a minimum level of social services?
(c) Would it not amount to double standards, for the preservation of sovereignty and for federal polity of the country?

The paper entitled "Social Security for the Elderly in India: Need for Reform" by Prof. K.N. Reddy deals with the problems of elderly (60 years and above) in India. Basically, the problems are four:

(i) Income security;
(ii) Health care security;
(iii) Personal (physical) security; and
(iv) Social emotional security.

As far as elderly people who belong to the organised sector (employees in public and private sector) are concerned, they are covered by various income security arrangements. A majority of elders, who belong to unorganised sector are not covered by any known security measures. The difference between the problems of developed countries and developing countries including India is that the ratio of elderly population to total population (or elderly population to active workers)—called as dependent ratio—is relatively high in them. Day by day, the dependency ratio in almost all the developed countries is reported to be increasing. For example, the dependency ratio was estimated at 37 per cent in Canada, 44 per cent in Germany and 32 per cent in U.S.A.

The author gives the example of South Korea. In South Korea, there are two types of social securities for helping the elderly citizens. They are:

(i) National Pension Programme; and
(ii) National Medical Insurance.

It seems that both these schemes are meeting the requirements of elderly citizens in this country.

The paper on "Need for Reform in Health Sector: Can National Health Insurance be an Alternative?" By Prof. K.N. Reddy traces the progress of the Indian Health Sector, and compares the same with the developing and developed economies. In India, a major chunk of the resources have gone to the curative services rather than to the preventive health services. As of 1990-91, nearly 60 per cent of the resources had gone to curative services, namely; medical relief, medical education and training, the Central Government Health Scheme, etc. However, only 26 per cent had gone to preventive services, namely; prevention of food adulteration, drug control, rural and urban family planning, maternity and child health, etc., and the rest to administrative and miscellaneous services. Similarly, there has been an urban bias in the allocation of resources. Nearly, 67 per cent of the resources spent on health care had gone to the urban sector, which accounts for only 26 per cent of—should be here of the total population, while only 33 per cent of the resources has gone to the rural sector, which accounts for 74 per cent of the total population. In terms of total allocations, the biases are substantial. The per capita expenditure on health care of the urban sector was Rs. 152, as against Rs. 26 of the rural sector. As far as per capita health expenditure is concerned, it is around US$ 1860 in the Established Market Economies, while it is a paltry sum of US$ 41 in the Demographically Developing group including India.

As per the study made by Prof. Reddy in 1989, as far as Andhra Pradesh is concerned the per capita household benefits to the poor were to the tune of only Rs. 20, as against Rs. 40 to the Middle income group, While it was as high as Rs. 726 to the high income group. A wellknown physician lamented that "the fault in our health system lies not in inadequacy of human or financial resources but in their skewed utilisation and distribution."

The quality of service in Indian public hospitals is reported to be deteriorating fastly, partly because of the lack of adequate supply of medicines and equipment and partly because of the faulty manpower planning and selection procedures. According to the findings of some researchers, whether at the sub-centre or at the primary health centre, the health workers remain unaccountable to the community which they are supposed to serve. In the words of a Journalist; "going to a public hospital remains a nightmarish experience, big crowds, long queues, confusing maze-like layouts, incomprehensible instructions, tedious procedures, casual diagnosis, rough handling by sullen staff, rude physicians, bribe-taking touts, complete absence of accountability, and unconscionable delays. Most working people think twice about visiting a hospital OPD, simply because it means missing a day's work and wages. Most public hospitals are inherently patient-unfriendly and hopelessly mismanaged". The author says that there are four alternatives available for any country. They are :

(i) Public financing and public delivery;
(ii) Private financing and public delivery;
(iii) Public financing and private delivery; and
(iv) Private financing and private delivery.

The first-three are in practice in one country or the other. International evidence suggests that the combination of public financing and private delivery—the third model—is relatively superior to the other approaches.

The paper entitled "Factors Affecting Rural Poverty in India: A Review" is by Prof. S.K. Thorat. The author says that there are two norms to decide the poverty level which have been worked out for two reference years, *i.e.,* 1960-61 and 1973-74. As per 1960-61 prices the norm of poverty line in India was fixed at Rs. 20 Per Capita Monthly Expenditure Classes (PCME), while it was fixed at Rs. 49 PCME in 1973-74. Studies on rural poverty in India have addressed two basic analytical issues: One concerning the pattern of long term trend in rural poverty and second relating to the explanation of inter-temporal change either in India as a whole or in different states. The author reviewed a number of studies dealing with various aspects of poverty levels. Some of the important studies are by Ahluwalia, Griffin and Ghose, Mandle, Dharam Narain, Saith, Mathur, Gaiha, Bhattacharya, Sundaram and Tendulkar, etc. Due to discontinuation of Annual Surveys in 1972-73 and their replacement by the Quinquennial Surveys, the studies after 1972-73 are confined to four points of time *i.e.,* 1973-74, 1977-78, 1983-84 and 1987-88. Tendulkar *et al*(1983) highlighted the positive impact of public Employment programmes (including the supply of cereals at subsidised prices through PDS) in alleviating poverty in the short-run. According to Shiela Bhalla, incidence of rural poverty (head-count ratio) was found to be greatest among the agricultural households followed closely by mining and construction, while electricity, gas and water supply categories are reported to be having the lowest incidence of poverty. Sen and Ghose (1993) analysed the poverty and employment link for the years 1972-73 and 1987-88. According to them, the mechanism for poverty reduction in India was the rising trend in the real agricultural wages since the mid-seventies. The improvement in the rural wage rate was largely due to tightening of the labour market because of job diversification. This is due to the movement of the workers from farm sector to non-farm sector. The authors argued that there is an evidence since the mid-seventies that a rise in non-agriculture's share of employment has actually been accompanied by raising the real wage in agriculture and non-agriculture. Higher real wages and sectoral shift would suggest that the shift was largely determined by "pull factors" and hence dynamic in nature.

The paper titled "Reform of Direct Taxation in India" by Prof. B.S. Sreekantharadhya deals with the post-1991 tax reforms. According to him, the following are the broad objectives of tax reforms in India.

(i) Revenue augmentation;
(ii) Enhancing the income—elasticity of tax revenue;
(iii) Minimising the efficiency cost or excess burden;
(iv) Designing an appropriate policy of tax incentives;
(v) Ensuring equity *i.e.,* justice or fairness in taxation;
(vi) Making the tax system as simple as possible;
(vii) Ensuring a combination of flexibility and stability;
(viii) Improving the tax administration.

As far as direct tax system is concerned, the IMF policy advice is as follows:

(a) To overcome the problems like inefficiencies, inequalities, high compliance costs and tax evasion created by a complicated tax system, the existing tax system must be simplified;
(b) Personal income tax must lay emphasis on lowering the marginal rates and broadening the tax base. Top marginal rates should not be more than 40 per cent and tax incentives must be minimised;
(c) Adoption of a single, proportional rate for the corporate income tax within the range of 30-40 per cent is desirable.

All post-1991 reforms are based on the recommendations of the Tax Reforms Committee. Most of the recommendations are meant to raise the revenue resources to the government. The measures which were introduced for widening the tax base are as follows:

1. *Presumptive Tax*: Introduced in 1992-93, the scheme was intended to bring under tax net-retail traders with a turn over of Rs. 5 lakh or less. Of course, the scheme was abolished.
2. *Estimated Income Scheme*: An estimated Scheme was introduced in 1994-95 for contractors and truck owners.
3. *Tax Deduction at Source*: In 1991-92, a scheme of deduction of tax at source in respect of bank interest, income distribution by UTI, etc., beyond Rs. 2500 per annum was introduced. Later on, it was abolished.

4. *Economic Criteria Scheme*: This scheme was introduced in the 1997-98 budget. Those who satisfy any of the two following criteria have to file the income tax returns:

   (a) Ownership of a four-wheel vehicle;
   (b) Occupation of immovable property;
   (c) Ownership of a telephone; and
   (d) Foreign travel in the previous year.

5. *Minimum Alternate Tax*: This was meant to bring all those companies under the tax net which were managing to get into the category of zero-tax companies by making use of all the permitted deductions and concessions.

The paper entitled "Reform of Indirect Taxation in India" by Prof. B.S. Sreekantaradhya deals with major deficiencies which according to the author are as follows:

(i) Indian indirect tax system is a highly unintegrated tax system, *viz.*, The Centre and the States have their own independent policies;
(ii) States' sales tax system lacks harmonisation; and
(iii) Cascading effect is the most important problem of indirect tax system.

The author feels that certain reform measures within the existing system are possible. Firstly, to bring about uniformity in commodity taxation, the Additional Duties of Excise levied on sugar, tobacco and textiles in lieu of sales tax can be extended to more commodities. It is felt that a drastic change in the system is needed and according to the author the real solution lies in the introduction of a full-fledged VAT.

The paper entitled "Industrial Growth in India—Measurement Through Chain Index" by Prof. D.U. Sastry deals with measuring industrial growth as accurately as possible. The objective of this paper is to construct a chain index of industrial production to study industrial growth in India over three decades; 1950-80. According to the author, in 1967 a revised index with 1960 as base has appeared. While the monthly index covered 307 items, the annual index covered a much smaller number of 142 items for which annual data were available. It was argued that periodic revisions of the index with four to five years interval will help to capture changes in industrial structure.

According to the author, construction of the chain index of industrial production involves a number of steps:

(i) Generating value added weights for every year;
(ii) Obtaining quality relatives for each industry group;
(iii) Calculation of primary indices; and
(iv) Constructing the chain index.

In India, the period 1952-78 consists of two distinct phases. The first phase from 1952-65 is a period of industrial expansion and the second period from 1966-78 is a period of Industrial deceleration. At the end, quite a number of tables showing the Value Added Weights in Current Prices for various commodity groups, such as food manufacturing, beverages and tobacco, textiles, leather and rubber products, chemicals, metal industries, machinery, petroleum products are enclosed.

Prof. B. SATYANARAYAN
M.A., Ph.D.
Co-ordinator/Director
Special Assistance Programme (UGC)
Dept. of Economics, Osmania University
Hyderabad-7 (India)

1

THE UNORGANISED SECTOR IN INDIAN ECONOMY AND PUBLIC POLICY IN THE CONTEXT OF STRUCTURAL ADJUSTMENT

—Prof. G. PARTHASARATHY

The Theme

The division of economy into two sectors has a long heritage. Arthur Lewis in a seminal article, back in 1950s, propounded the theory of dualism. His version of dualism differs from an earlier version of Boeke in which a segmented society is explained by fundamental and permanent differences in economic behaviour. This has long been dismissed as untenable by many critics. The socio-economic duality of Arthur Lewis was popular in the 1950s and 1960s. Lewis and others see the cities with their modern industries as dynamic centres from which the static character of the rural order, characterised by stagnating agriculture with very low labour productivity can gradually be overcome. It was assumed in the Lewis model that unorganised sector with surplus labour will gradually disappear as the surplus labour gets absorbed in organised sector.

In the last few decades, the Indian situation at least does not conform to the Lewis model. The organised sector failed to absorb the labour engaged in the unorganised sector. The Lewis model, which is drawn from the experience of the capitalist countries in which the share of agriculture and the share of unorganised sector showed a spectacular decline was not found to be true of many developing countries, including India. The late-comer developing countries faced an entirely new situation of development. Borrowed technology from developed countries was labour displacing. The change in industrial structure was also not favourable to the absorption of labour from unorganised sector. The information and knowledge revolution put a premium on educational skills of the labour force and absorption of blue collar workers as against the white collar workers has been less in the current stage of industrial development. Even in developed countries the share of blue collar workers has been going down.

It is not only mainstream theory that visualised absorption of unorganised sector in the growing urban industrial sector; but, Marxian theory also anticipated the destruction of pre-capitalist structures as a result of aggressive growth of capitalism. In Marxian theory, the small fish is eaten by the big fish. Capitalist accumulation will sweep away the non-capitalist and pre-capitalist village and small industries. The labour in such industries will enter into the ranks of proletariat. Those who cannot get absorbed will enter the ranks of immiserised unemployed labour. Social transformation takes place through a revolution generated by the conflict. Neither in Marxian theory nor in Classical Economic Theory, the unorganised sector has a permanent place in the economy.

The situation we witness currently in India is quite different. The share of unorganised sector in National Income has been declining but the number in the unorganised sector continues to swell. Five decades of post-independent capitalist growth has not been able to absorb the labour force in unorganised sector. There is a need for direct support to unorganised sector besides defending it against appropriation by organised sector for improving employment, productivity and incomes of the poor. We address in the lecture the issues of relative efficiency of the organised *vis-a-vis* the unorganised sector, the exploitation of the unorganised sector by the organised, and the big gap between profession and performance in relation to public support to the unorganised sector. The lecture also focusses on the adverse implications of structural adjustments for the unorganised sector and finally concludes with an appeal for public policy which goes beyond safety nets and adjustments with a human face.

Conceptualization of Unorganised Sector

There is much controversy on the concept of unorganised sector. It is sometimes defined as the sector which is not recorded under any Factory Legislation. In this sense, it is derived as a residual after deducting the registered labour force from the total labour force. Since the small and village industry is not generally registered, the unorganised sector is identified with the small and village industry sector. But this is not appropriate. The method will not cover the unorganised part in service sector. Further, not all industries defined as 'small' by the Government are unregistered. Some are registered under Factories Act. A more meaningful use of the concept of unorganised sector is its identification with pre-capitalistic structure of production while organised sector is related to capitalist structure. In this sense, the unorganised sector is comprised of own account workers, and also casual labour employed in establishments. The latter do not have access to the benefits of social security. The unorganised sector is sometimes also identified with the informal sector though such an identification is not without controversy.

The term 'informal sector' was first launched by Hart (1971). He describes the informal sector as that part of the Urban Labour Force which falls outside the organised labour market. The concept has been further refined by a mission of International Labour Office (ILO), which studied the employment situation in Kenya within the framework of the World Employment Programme (Breman, 1994, pp. 1-4).

In the earlier writings, the approach to unorganised sector was negative. The sector was considered unproductive which would disappear with development. Recent literature shows that activities in the unorganised/informal sector are economically efficient and profitable. Though they are characterised by low capital intensity, low level of productivity, a small and usually poor clientele, a low level of formal schooling, intermediate technology, preponderence of family labour and ownership and ease of entrance and last but not the least lack of support and recognition on the part of Government.

The concept of informal sector is usually applied to urban system. This ignores the production relations within agriculture. The large, medium and semi-medium farms on which modern methods of management have been introduced, may be considered under organised sector within agriculture. Further these need to be distinguished from the self-employed small, marginal farmers and casual labourers. Only the latter category, and not the whole of agriculture needs to be considered under informal sector. Further, the inclusion of modern small scale industry and powerlooms in the unorganised sector may not be considered appropriate.

Magnitude, Trends and Composition of Employment within Organised and Unorganised Sectors

In this paper, as a first step, the employment in the unorganised sector is derived as a residual after deducting the employment in the organised sector from the total labour force given in Census data. The estimates of organised sector employment, are recorded in the Economic Surveys prepared by Finance Ministry. The details of organised sector are available for period 1981 onwards for every year in the pre-budget Economic Surveys. For the years 1961, 1967, 1971 and 1974, the figures are obtained from Fifth Plan draft. The trends of employment in organised and unorganised sector are shown in Table 1.1.

TABLE 1.1: Trends in Employment in Organised and Unorganised Sectors 1961 to 1991

(in millions)

Year	*Organised*	*Unorganised*	*Total*	*Share of Unorganised Sector Employment*
1961	14.60	174.10	188.70	92.26
1971	20.20	206.70	226.90	91.10
1974	22.50	NA		
1981	22.90	214.00	236.90	90.33
1983	24.01	264.00	288.00	91.67
1987-88	25.70	268.00	293.70	91.25
1991	26.70	259.38	286.08	90.66

Note : It may be noted that work participation rates as per the NSS are higher than for Census.

Sources:

1. Five Year Plan Draft, 1978-83, Planning Commission.
2. Economic Survey, 1994-95.
3. Draft Five Year Plan, 1978-83.
4. *Sarvekshana*, Vol. III, No. 1, July, 1979 — Unorganised sector employment is got by deducting the workers in the organised sector from the total workers.

As in 1991, the share of unorganised sector in Indian economy was as high as 90.66 per cent. There has been very little decline in the share since 1961. Employment in the unorganised sector over the period of 3 decades grew at an annual rate of 1.1 per cent. In absolute terms the additions to employment in the unorganised sector per annum during the three decades was 2.68 millions. Employment in the organised sector has not grown at a rate high enough to reduce the rate of growth of organised sector.

The share of employment in organised sector in 1981 was only 9.70 per cent, this may be compared with corresponding share of net domestic product of 30 per cent (Table 1.2). Between 1980-81 and 1990-91, the share of organised sector in NDP increased further from 29.97 to 36.14 per cent. But the share in employment showed a decline from 9.70 to 9.37 per cent. This shows the inability of the organised sector (even in the context of growth) to absorb the growing labour force. Between 1981 and 1991, the annual addition to labour force as per the demographic censuses was 4.9 million. Out of this, absorption of organised sector was only 0.38 millions or around 8 per cent of labour force.

TABLE 1.2: Net Domestic Product by Organised and Unorganised Sectors at Current Prices

(Rs. in crores)

Year	*Organised*	*Unorganised*	*Total*	*Share of Unorganised to Total*
1980-81	33073	77267	110340	70.03
1985-86	72952	134610	207562	64.85
1986-87	84652	145555	230207	63.23
1987-88	96755	164755	261510	63.00
1988-89	114624	199895	314519	63.56
1989-90	131644	228049	359693	63.40
1990-91	151749	268030	419779	63.85

Source : National Accounts Statistics, 1993, pp. 203-04.

We show the share of organised and unorganised sectors in NDP for 1991 by industry division (Table 1.3). Electricity, Gas and Water, Railway Transport, Communications, Public Administration and Defence are exclusively within the organised sector. A major percentage of production in manufacturing, financial services, bank services are within the organised sector. The unorganised sector accounts for much of agricultural production, bulk of trade and construction, major proportion of transport other than railways, and storage.

The preceding analysis is based on data, which show the entire crop production sector and the entire SIS as unorganised. But this position does not seem to be warranted in the light of the changes in rural economy following green revolution. A new class of farmers well integrated with the outside world has emerged following the green revolution. It is appropriate to consider this class under the organised sector, whereas, small and marginal farmers and agricultural labourers are treated under unorganised sector. The organised sector thus covers semi-medium, medium and large holdings. Out of 185 million employed in agricultural sector as per 1990-91, 139 million are in the unorganised sector. Out of these, agricultural labourers form the

TABLE 1.3 : Share of Organised and Unorganised Sectors in the NDP by Industry (1990-91)

(*Rs. in crores*)

	Industry	*Organised*	*Un-organised Sector*	*Total*	*Share of Organised Sector in Total*	*Share of Un-organised Sector*
1.	Agriculture, Forestry & Fishing	4486	135385	139871	3.21	96.79
1.1	Agriculture	3287	126229	129516	2.54	97.46
1.2	Forestry & Logging	1196	5898	7094	16.86	83.14
1.3	Fishing	3	3258	3261	0.09	99.91
2	Mining & Quarrying	7254	767	8021	90.44	9.56
3	Manufacturing	45928	30098	76026	60.41	39.59
3.1	Registered	45928	—	45928	100.00	—
3.2	Unregistered	—	30098	30098	—	100.00
4.	Electricity, Gas & Water	4031	—	4031	100.00	—
5.	Construction	11816	13893	25709	45.96	54.04
6.	Trade, Hotels, Restaurants	4083	53026	57109	7.15	92.85
6.1	Trade	3659	50442	54101	6.76	93.34
6.2	Hotels and Restaurants	424	2584	3008	14.10	85.90
7.	Transport, Storage & Communications	12881	12156	25037	51.45	48.55
7.1	Railways	4368	—	4368	100.00	—
7.2	Transport by other means	4660	11963	16623	28.03	71.07
7.3	Storage	184	193	377	48.81	51.19
7.4	Communications	3669	—	3669	100.00	—
8.	Financing, Insurance, Real Estate & Business Services	19006	13857	32863	57.83	42.17
8.1	Banking & Insurance	18836	2389	21225	88.74	11.26
8.2	Real Estate & Business Services	170	11468	11638	1.46	98.54
9	Community, Social and Personal Services	42264	8848	51112	82.69	17.31
9.1	Public Admn. & Defence	24336	—	24336	100.00	—
9.2	Other Services	17928	8848	26776	66.96	33.04
	Total	151749	268030	419779	36.15	63.85
	Total (Non-Agr.)	147263	132645	27908	52.61	47.39

Source: National Accounts Statistics, 1993.

majority. They are mainly drawn from small and marginal farmer families. Their growth reflects the trends towards the break up of pre-capitalistic structure within agriculture and simultaneously the growth of the capitalist class within agriculture (Table 1.4).

TABLE 1.4 : Trends in the Number of Workers in the Organised and Unorganised Sectors

(Millions)

Item	*1979-80/ 1980-81*	*1990-91/ 1989-90*	*% Change over the Decade*	*% Share of Unorganised Sector*
(1)	(2)	(3)	(4)	(5)
I. UNORGANISED SECTOR				
1. Agriculture:				
a) Marginal farmers	47.00	48.00		
b) Small farmers (*)	15.00	16.00		32.24
c) Agricultural labour	56.00	75.00	33.93	36.76
Total	118.00	139.00	17.80	70.00
2. Non-Agriculture: Traditional: (**)				
a) Khadi	1.12	1.40		
b) Village Industry	1.61	3.21		
c) Handloom	6.15	7.60		
d) Sericulture	1.60	5.00		
e) Handicrafts	2.00	4.21		
f) Coir-Fibre Works	0.60	0.50		
Total	13.08*	21.92*	90.37	11.04
3. Other Non-Agricultural Labour	28.67	25.05		12.62
4. Own Account Workers in Trade and Services	14.33	12.52		6.36
Total	43.00	37.57	12.47	18.98
Total of Unorganised Sector	174.20	198.49	1.32	
II. ORGANISED SECTOR				
1. Agriculture: Medium, Semi-Medium land holding	40.00	46.00	15.00	52.59
2. Non-Agricultural Labour:				
a) Public Sector Employees	15.60	18.00		20.58

(Contd.)

Table 1.4 *(Contd.)*

(1)	(2)	(3)	(4)	(5)
b) Private Sector Employees in Establishments with more than 10 workers	7.40	7.00		8.00
c) Powerlooms	1.10	4.50		5.15
d) Modern Small Scale Industry	6.70	11.96		13.67
Total of Non-Agricultural Labour	30.80	41.46	41.88	
Total of Organised Sector	70.80	87.46	26.69	47.40
Grand Total of Unorganised and Organised Sectors	245.00	286.00	16.53	100.00

* This includes both Household Industry and Non-Factory Non-Household Industry.
Estimated from the household data and the Census data on Cultivation.

** Data from VII Plan Report 1990-91.

Note: The total number of employees in unregistered manufacturing was 18.4 million according to 1980 census. These formed 32 per cent of the total non-agricultural workers. Substantial number of non-agricultural workers are in the tertiary sector. See for details "Employment in Unorganised Manufacturing as per 1980 census, Data Base of the Unorganised Manufacturing Industry : An Appraisal", Small Scale Enterprises in Industrial Development.

If employment in the unorganised sector is classified under pre-capitalist structures of production and the emerging casual labour class (both agriculture and non-agricultural labour), it is equally distributed.

The non-household non-factory industry shows the highest rate of growth during the period 1961-81. The household industry shows a negative rate of growth. Factory sector which showed a high rate of growth during the period 1961-81, shows a deceleration during the period 1981-91.

The entire employment in the public sector is considered under organised sector because of job security and social security benefits that the employees are enjoying. In 1991 employment in the public sector was 18 million as against seven million in the organised private sector. If modern and small scale industries and powerlooms are added to this total, employment in the private organised sector could be around 24 million as against 18 million workers in the organised public sector, making a total of 42 million in the organised sector within non-agriculture as against a total of 54 million in the unorganised sector.

Our adjustments of the components of unorganised sector reduce the share of employment within unorganised sector from around 90 to around 70 per cent in the organised sector from 10 to 30 per cent or roughly 90 million in a total of 285 million.

Within non-agriculture, there has been a shift towards non-factory, non-household sector employment. Household sector's share has steadily declined since 1961. Factory sector employment, which grew at a higher rate of 4.7 per cent per annum from 1961, showed a perceptible decline to 0.04 per cent per annum in the 80s (Table 1.5). Since 1983-84, organised private sector contributed very little to employment. Whatever employment growth we found during this period is attributed to public sector. Thus, the organised sector's capacity to absorb the labour weakened considerably in 1980s.

TABLE 1.5: Distribution of Worker in Manufacturing Establishments 1961-91.

(In 000s)

				Rate of Growth	
	1961	1981	1991	1961-81	1981-91
All-manufacturing	17523	25175	28671	1.83	1.31
	(100.00)	(100.00)	(100.00)		
Household	9651	7743	6804	–1.09	–1.28
	(55.08)	(30.75)	(23.73)		
Factory	3050	7715	7743	4.75	0.04
	(17.40)	(30.65)	(27.01)		
Non-factory & Non-household	4822	9717	14124	3.57	3.81
	(27.52)	(38.6)	(49.26)		

Source : *IJLE*, Vol. 37, No. 3, July-Sept. 1994, See also Ramaswamy, p. 339, *EPW*, Feb. 26, 1994

The preponderance of self-employed in total labour could be seen from Table 1.6A and the trends from Table 1.6B. Regular labour formed over 14 per cent of total labour. When the labour composition is considered by rural and urban, within the rural sector, regular labour formed only 8 per cent as against 40 per cent in the urban sector. As regards the trends, a decline in regular employment in both rural and urban areas for both the sexes, and an increase marked by casualisation are observable in urban areas.

TABLE 1.6A: Absolute Number of Workers by Self-Employed, Regular and Casual Labour Status — 1987-88

(*Millions*)

	Rural			*Urban*			*Total*		
	Male	*Female*	*Total*	*Male*	*Female*	*Total*	*Male*	*Female*	*Total*
Self-Employed	89.31	52.80	142.11	17.75	5.51	23.26	107.06	58.31	165.37
Regular Labour	15.31	3.17	18.48	18.61	3.21	21.82	33.92	6.38	40.30
	(10.04)	(3.66)	(7.73)	(43.65)	(27.46)	(40.17)	(17.39)	(6.48)	(13.73)
Casual Labour	47.85	30.73	78.58	6.27	2.97	9.24	54.12	33.70	87.82
Total	152.47	86.70	239.17	42.63	11.69	54.32	195.10	98.39	293.49
	(100)	(100)	(100)	(100)	(100)	(100)	(100)	(100)	(100)

Note : Figures in brackets are the percentages to toal.

Source : *Sarvekshana.*

TABLE 1.6B : Trends in Employment

Year	*Employment Status*		
	Self-Employed	*Regular Employee*	*Casual Labour*
Rural Males			
1972-73	659	121	220
1977-78	628	106	266
1983	605	103	292
1987-88	586	100	314
Rural Females			
1972-73	645	41	314
1977-78	621	28	351
1983	619	28	353
1987-88	609	37	355
Urban Males			
1972-73	392	507	101
1977-78	404	464	132
1983	409	437	154
1987-88	416	437	147
Urban Females			
1972-73	484	279	237
1977-78	495	249	256
1983	458	258	284
1987-88	471	275	254

Source : *Sarvekshana*, Sept. 7, 1990, p. 92.

Relative Efficiency — Unorganised Sector *vis-a-vis* Organised Sector

The NDP per worker in the organised sector is more than three times the corresponding productivity within the unorganised sector (Table 1.7). Even if agriculture is not considered, productivity in organised sector is much higher than in unorganised sector. Does it imply that organised sector is more efficient? It may not be appropriate to draw such an inference. In a capital scarce economy, capital-output ratios provide a better norm for judging relative efficiency as compared to labour-output ratios.

TABLE 1.7 : Net Domestic Product Per Worker in Organised and Unorganised Sectors — 1987-88 by Industry

Industry	*Organised*	*Unorganised to Unorganised*	*Ratio of Organised*
Agriculture	28100	4435	6.33
Mining and Quarrying	46900	3306	14.19
Manufacturing	46740	7303	6.40
Electricity, Gas and Water	27310	Nil	Nil
Construction	63760	3135	20.33
Trade	95950	3238	29.63
Transport, Storage and Communication	25490	10640	2.40
Finance, Insurance, Real Estate, etc.	93690	71438	1.31
Community, Social and Personal Services	27170	3985	6.82
Total	37640	10110	3.72
All Non-Agricultural Sector	38182	23483	1.63

As we do not have data on capital stock by industry, we could use the data on capital stock for registered and unregistered manufacturing units. The total capital stock used in the organised manufacturing sector is 125118 crores of rupees as against 51141 crores of rupees in unorganised sector in 1987-88. Per worker capital stock is as high as Rs. 201803 lakh in registered manufacturing as against Rs. 20486 lakh in unregistered manufacturing. Thus, the organised manufacturing sector uses 10 times the capital stock per worker when compared to the unorganised manufacturing sector. It is this which gives an advantage to the organised sector. A number of scholars examined the relative efficiency in the past and we may consider their findings.

Dhar and Lydall "Relative Efficiency of Modern Small Scale Industries in India" by Bishwanath Goldar, in K.B. Suri (Ed.) 1988, p. 97] show that capital output ratios in units employing 20 or more persons are not higher. Rather, in certain cases, they are lower. But this is with reference to small scale units in the modern sector. Hajra (1965) in a study, using the data of CMI for 1955-58 came to similar conclusions. Sandesara in his studies and 1969 using CMI data for 28 industries for the period 1953-58 found again negative association between size and capital-output ratios. He concluded that small scale industries neither generated more employment nor more output per unit of capital compared to large scale units. Mehta in a study published in 1969 using the ASI data for 1960-63 however found that capital-output ratios rose with size. The conflict between the results of Mehta and the earlier studies of Sandesara and Dhar and Lydall could be explained in terms of methods used. Mehta used only fixed capital whereas Sandesara, Dhar and Lydall also covered working capital.

A major limitation of the studies based on the CMI/ASI data is that they cover only those small scale units which are registered as factories under Factories Act [p. 99, Goldar (Ed. Suri)]. These cover only 11 per cent of the sample units though they cover 55 per cent of output [p. 61, Suri (Ed.)]. A later study by Bhavani (1980) which uses the census of small scale industrial units comes to conclusions similar to those of Dhar and Lydall [Goldar in Suri (Ed.) p. 100]. Goldar using two factor frontier production functions, arrives at the conclusion that small scale industries are relatively efficient in those industries in which the difference in capital-labour ratio between large scale and small scale units is relatively small. They can not be relied upon to generate large amount of employment under these conditions. Where they had substantial advantage in employment generation, they are relatively inefficient and where they are efficient they do not have much advantage in employment generation [Goldar in Suri (Ed.) p. 111]. Goldar further finds that small scale units are less efficient in the use of capital in almost all (35 out of 37) industries. Estimates of relative efficiency indicate that in a fairly large number of units, small scale units are relatively inefficient compared to large scale units. The relative efficiency index is found to be positively related to size, and the proportion of small scale units using power are negatively related to the ratio of closing stock to consumption of raw materials and the ratio of short term bank credit to inventories [Goldar in Suri (Ed.) p. 117]. The finding of a negative relationship between short-term bank borrowings and efficiency in small scale industries is somewhat surprising suggesting that subsidised credit involves some cost in terms of efficiency.

While there is almost conclusive evidence that modern small scale industry is no different from large scale industry in economising capital use, there is little evidence on the relative efficiency of traditional small industry *vis-a-vis* large scale industry. The virtual absence of serious academic research is altogether intriguing. In fact, there are only two studies of note that have examined this question in the Indian context. One, undertaken by the Project Appraisal Division of the Planning Commission (1979) and the other done for the World Bank by Dipak Mazumdar (1984) (Sanjiv Misra, 1993, p. 90). The Planning Commission study indicated that whereas fixed capital cost per unit of output was the highest in the mill sector and the lowest in the handloom sector, employment per unit of output was the highest in the handloom sector and the lowest in the mill sector. The data also showed that the cost of production of handloom cloth per metre was actually lower than that of mill made cloth by 17 per cent in the case of coarse cloth and 5 per cent less in the case of finer than medium cloth. The Planning Commission linear programming exercise indicated that, at actual factor cost for coarse and lower medium varieties cloth, handlooms were the preferred mode of production. With a low capital constraint, the optimal solution indicated an equal sharing of output between the two sectors, the share of powerloom sector rising as the constraint of capital was progressively eased. As a policy prescription, the study recommended a virtual reservation of all varieties of coarse and lower medium cloth for the handloom and finer varieties for the powerloom sector.

Majumdar's study for the World Bank (1984) presents the data on output per worker and capital per unit of labour and per unit of output for the three sectors, namely, handloom, powerloom and mill. Output per worker per day was 5.4 metres for handloom, 16.8 metres for powerloom and 42.5 metres for mill. Capital cost per metre of cloth works out to Rs. 1054 for handloom and Rs. 467 for powerloom, when fixed capital alone was considered (similar details for mill are not available). If working capital is also included capital costs workout to Rs. 614 for handloom, Rs. 625 for powerloom and Rs. 447 for mill. Dipak's data has shown that production of cloth on powerlooms is the preferred technique over a wide range of interest rates, *i.e.,* between 13.2 per cent and 46.05 per cent. A market interest rate lower than 13.2 per cent would make mill production more profitable than powerloom production, whereas beyond an interest rate of 46.05 per cent, it would be more profitable to produce on handlooms rather than on powerlooms (*Misra*, p. 94).

While the evidence from micro-data on capital-output ratio is fragmented, sketchy and partial, the evidence in the NSA data suggests lower capital-output ratios for the unorganised manufacturing sector as a whole, as compared to the organised manufacturing sector.

It should also be noted that research focus so far has been mainly on technical efficiency but not allocative efficiency. Even if small scale units are inferior in terms of technical efficiency, they may be far superior in allocative efficiency, so that economic efficiency of small scale units may be as high as that of large units.

Earlier Policies to Strengthen the Unorganised Sector: A Critique

Earlier policies to strengthen the unorganised sector may be classified under the following heads: (1) fiscal, *i.e.,* discriminatory excise tax, (2) product subsidies, (3) input quotas, (4) marketing, (5) technical support, and (6) reservations. None of these policies has been a success in strengthening the unorganised sector. Discriminatory excise taxes have failed to benefit the handloom sector. The powerlooms gained at the expense of handlooms and also purchase of hank yarn intended for handlooms was appropriated by powerlooms (L.C. Jain, EPW, August 27, 1983). The importance of tax evasion on powerloom cloth in tilting the scales of competitive advantage in favour of powerlooms vis-a-vis the mills has not received adequate attention (Misra, 1993, p. 101). Discriminatory excise taxes together with the obligation on textile mills to supply controlled cloth have shifted the advantage from textile mills to powerlooms. L.C. Jain commented in 1983 the loss of employment of weavers is unimaginable and one half of those who lost their jobs are women since women are also engaged in handloom weaving industry (*EPW*, August 27, 1983).

Production subsidy has been the other instrument of public policy. The 1985 textile policy has also provided for the production of Janata cloth by the handloom sector through the provision of subsidies devoted to the production of Janata cloth. Overall the total subsidy support to handloom weavers would be of the order of Rs. 200 crore at present (Report of the Committee to Review the Progress of Implementation of Textile Policy of June 1985, January 1990, p. 51). The IRMA (Institute of Rural Management) Report entitled "A Study of Interventions in the Handloom Industry" has the following to say on the Janata scheme "Even in the worst of states, the scheme has helped the weavers get steady earnings, distinctly higher than other state-aided weavers, but not always even a minimum starvation wage — we could not discern any conscious attempt anywhere, to use the scheme to bring relief to the poorest weaver. It is suggested that the organisations could have full freedom to price the Janata products as they find suitable and that the allocation of production should clearly be for the poorest weavers" (IRMA Report, 1989, p. 44) (see also Abid Hussain Committee's Report, p. 66.)

Input quotas have been found necessary in the case of unorganised sector since the sector is found to lose in competition with the organised sector because of aggressive marketing strategies of the latter.

Under the 1985 Textile Policy, spinning mills are required to produce 50 per cent of their total marketable output as hank yarn. But the actual delivery of hank yarn amounts to 40 per cent of total hank yarn produced. This has raised two different kinds of problems. Firstly, there are widespread complaints of diversion of hank yarn to powerlooms. Secondly, the demand for yarn by handlooms is for specific qualities and counts, and there is a mismatch between the yarn supplied and yarn demanded. Further, yarn prices are found to rise to abnormal heights (Abid Hussain Committee Report, pp. 45-46). The role played by the organisations such as the National Handloom Development Corporation (NHDC), the State-Level Handloom Development Corporations and Apex Handloom Organisations in achieving stability of prices leaves much to be desired.

Weavers' Co-operatives have been the chosen agent for assistance in marketing of handloom products. But it is disquieting to note that the weavers co-operatives at various levels in general could not deliver the goods for a variety of reasons. Unfortunately, a major chunk of production and marketing activities in the handloom sector is still in private hands. Further, over half-of-all registered weavers' co-operatives in the country have time and again been reported to have been lagging behind. Broadly speaking, the weavers' co-operative sector registered slow pace of progress *vis-a-vis* the private sector. Lack of co-operative character is said to be one of the main reasons. Further, they do not have the liquid cash for maintaining inventories and they often have inadequate and halting supplies of inputs like, dyes, chemicals, yarn, etc. They are also obliged to depend upon private spinning mills and dyes manufacturers. (Rao A.U., Management of Handloom Co-operatives, Vaikunt Mehta National Institute of

Co-operative Management, 1978, pp. 34-35). One of the main prescriptions of the 1985 Textile Policy is reservation of 22 varieties of fabrics for handloom weavers. This has been rendered null and void by the stay order granted by various High Courts and the Supreme Court (Abid Hussain's Committee Report, p. 93. See also VIII Plan Report, p. 139).

The experience in respect of other traditional industries has not been different. There has been a decline in the growth of handloom and village industries. Changing consumer preferences and produce preference against khadi have been the factors. A large number of artisans' co-operatives engaged in village industries have continued to be dormant. The wages of artisans are found to be lower than those observed for the farm sector (VIII Plan pp. 136-37).

Up to the end of VII Plan, the implementation of various schemes for promotion and development of handicrafts has not been able to provide assistance to large sections of craftsmen insofar as production and related inputs are concerned. Marketing of their produce is still left largely to private trade. Consequently, the programmes have not made any discernible impact on their earnings and standard of living. Their potential in terms of employment and exports are also limited. (VIII Plan, p. 141)

The Political Economy of Unorganised Industry

Organised sector and unorganised sector are not two water tight compartments. In fact, the organised sector exercises its hold on the unorganised sector through several mechanisms. In the Calcutta Sandal Industry, four big companies purchase almost the entire goods produced by 2000 petty producers. The monopoly control on the market has reduced the production sites of Sandal markets into Sweat houses (Manjit Singh, "the Political Economy of Unorganised Industry," 1990, p. 43). The squeezing of coir production in Kerala is carried out by the big merchant-exporters, who impose their own terms on the purchase market. In 1979, only two big merchants controlled 35 per cent of the total market. From the history of the coir mat and matting industry of Kerala, Issac (1982) concludes that as long as there is scope for absolute surplus appropriation, capital will not aim at relative surplus appropriation through increasing labour productivity (Manjit Singh, Ibid., p. 44). The Growth of the Lace Industry of Narsapur, studied by Mies (1982), is reminiscent of the three centuries old British putting-out system, sometimes also termed capitalist domestic industry (Manjit Singh, Ibid., p. 44). The Lace industry has expanded due to boost from the export market. The entire control over workers by the exporters is maintained through agents and their sub-agents. (Manjit Singh, Ibid., p. 45). In the Beedi industry, Mysore, there has been a change over from workshop to put-out system to meet the threat of strike from workers (Manjit Singh, Ibid., p. 46). This development contrasts with the classical development of capitalism in industry, where domestic workers, once brought into the workshops, were pushed into Factory production and not back to domestic work. The carpet industry of Bhadohi is another example of a traditional industry, organised on the basis of putting-out work to domestic weavers and controlled by the merchant manufacturers. (Manjit Singh, p. 47).

The lace, beedi and carpet industry present parallel examples of the putting-out system, carried out under the dominance of merchant-manufacturing capital and characterised by traditional methods of production. On the other hand matchsticks, fireworks and *agarbati* are organised on the basis of workshops. Here the capital-wage relations are more visible. The means of production are owned by the employer while the workers own nothing except their labour power. These workshops constitute the biggest 'slaughter house' of children. (Manjit Singh, p. 48).

The garment export industry of Madras employed three times the workers in the non-factory sector as compared to its employees in factory sector. Here merchant capital is seen to be dominant. The Jari Industry of Surat is another example of putting out system in which independent producers are also found (p. 50). The Cotton Hosiery Industry in Calcutta illustrate the case in which the workers supply not only their labour power but also small machines in the service of capital. (Manjit Singh, p. 50). The merchant-manufacturers bought yarn from the market and advanced this yarn to the knitting units.

Manjit Singh classified the unorganised industries into four broad categories on the basis of the labour process. (1) Industries using traditional skills and traditional instruments of labour; (2) Though the place of work is the home of worker, there is a detailed division of labour and labour is formally subsumed under capital. Merchant-manufacturer plays a key role; (3) Workers are brought to the workshops and are made to work under the direct supervision of the manufacturers; and (4) Those where the production process has changed from manufacture to 'machinofacture' or factory form. Merchant-manufacturing capital thrives owing to the decentralised nature of the production process.

Ancillary industries or sub-contracts have been another method by which organised sector exercises its power over the unorganised sector. Notwithstanding the fact that small industries have gained technical and market support by being ancillaries, the general experience has been that the organised sector used sub-contracts for exploiting the unorganised sector [Sucha Singh Gill, p.173, G.K. Chadha (ed)].

In conclusion, the unique evclution of capitalism in the colonial context has resulted in lack of progress of industries in the unorganised sector to organised sector. Further, industries in the organised sector have failed to step up labour productivity.

Inadequate Public Support to Unorganised Sector

If organised private sector is found to squeeze the unorganised sector through appropriation of absolute surplus, public support to the unorganised sector has been inadequate and there has been a big gap between profession and implementation. We show in Table 1.8, Plan Outlay, value of output, employment and export for small, medium and large industries. It is evident that Plan Outlay for small industries does not correspond either to its share in employment or share in output or exports.

The position seems to be much worse when modern small scale industries are not considered. The share of Plan Outlay for traditional industries does not match their share in employment, output and exports (*see* Table 1.9). Even gross bank credit is not proportionate to the share of small scale industries in output, employment and exports.

As regards, IDBI refinance to small scale industries (Patvardhan's Study for 1983) [(Ed. Suri), p.243] only one-sixth of the small scale units are benefitted from refinance. Moreover refinance was found unequally distributed across the states. The RBI's survey on Credit to Small Scale Industry Sector was done in 1977-78 and the results are rather out of date. But, in view of the reliability and its systematic nature we drew upon the results of the survey for insights particularly into the variation between backward and other districts (Table 1.10). Backward areas are marked by much worse position. Patvardhan concluded "the SFC's thrust towards a relatively small scale among SSI enterprises has not yielded satisfactory results."

We may conclude that public support by way of Plan allocations and institutional credit to SSI sector has been inadequate and within the sector, traditional industries got little support.

TABLE 1.8: Bank Credit, Output, Employment and Exports by Type of Industry

(Crores)

Type of Industry	*Employ-ment (1989-90) (millions)*	*Percen-tage*	*Plan Outlay*	*Per-centage*	*Value of Output (1989-90)*	*Per-centage*	*Exports (1989-90)*	*Per-centage*	*Net Domestic Product (1990-91)*	*Percentage Outstand Gross Bank Credit as on March 22, 1991***	*Per-centage*
1	2	3	4	5	6	7	8	9	10	11	12
Small Scale Industries	38.45	84.04	6334.2*	13.50	114314	30.76	14807	62.38	30098	37.60 17181	27.85
Medium and Large Industries	7.3	15.96	40587.5*	86.50	257284*	69.24	8929	37.62	49959	62.40 44508	72.15
Total	45.75	100.00	46921.7	100.00	371598	100.00	23736	100.00	80057	100.00 61689	100.00

* Economic Survey, 1994-95, pp. S-51, S-49.

** Currency and Finance Report, 1992-93, p. 204.

Output — National Accounts Statistics, p. 169.
Eighth Five Year Plan, p. 149.

Exports — Economic Survey, p. S-93.

Plan Outlay — Eighth Plan Outlay (1992-97)

Output of manufacturing and electricity and gas comprise medium and large industries.

TABLE 1.9 : Output, Employment, Exports and Plan Outlay by Type of Industry in 1989-90 within VSI Sector

Type of Industry	*Production (crores)*	*Percentage*	*Employment (millions)*	*Percentage*	*Exports (crores)*	*Percentage*	*VII Plan Outlay (crores)*	*Percentage*	*Productivity Per Worker*
Modern small scale industries	92080 (15478)	80.55	12.0	24.77	7626.00	51.50	1120.51	40.71	76,733.33 (12,898.33)
Powerlooms	9865	8.63	4.5	9.29	—	—	11.77	0.42	21,922.22
Khadi cloth	203	0.18	11.41	23.55	1.39	0.01	636.25	23.11	1,439.72
Village industries	1101	0.96	3.21	6.63	3.66	0.02			3,429.91
Handlooms	3377	2.95	7.60	15.69	342.00	2.31	512.26	18.61	4,443.42
Sericulture	493	0.43	5.00	10.32	400.61	2.71	309.96	11.26	986.00
Handicrafts	7067	6.18	4.22	8.71	6400.00	43.22	122.86	4.46	16,746.45
Coir fibre	128	0.12	0.50	1.03	33.32	0.23	39.13	1.43	2,560.00
Total	114314 (35717)	100.00	48.44	100.00	14806.98	100.00	2752.74	100.00	29,769.00
Registered Manufacturers	219304 (39247)**		7.00		7830.00		19662.80		9,300.00** (56,070)**

Source : Eighth Five Year Plan, p. 149. Small Scale Industries in India, p. 14. (Dr. D. Nagaiya)

Note : For the same year, net domestic product from unregistered manufacturers was 30098 and net domestic from product registered manufacturers in 39247, while value of output, manufacturers registered is Rs. 219304.

TABLE 1.10 :Small Scale Industries in Backward and Other Districts 1977-78

		Backward	*Others*	*Ratio of others in Backward*
1.	Per unit value of gross output	1,72,839	6,62,000	3.83
2.	Market value of fixed assets.	43,924	1,41,184	3.21
3.	Per unit loan outstanding	34,802	1,38,897	3.99
		Registered	Unregistered	Ratio
4.	Value of gross output per unit	1.68	0.17	9.88

Source : Patvardhan [Suri (ed.)].

Structural Adjustment and Impact on Unorganised Sector

Structural adjustment in the Indian Economy implies

1. An increasing flow of foreign direct investment alongwith foreign technology;
2. A decline in the role of the State and an increase in the role of market in industrial growth;
3. An increasing reliance on foreign trade as an engine of growth; and
4. A shift away from subsidies and from protection through tariff.

We will examine the implication of each of these for unorganised sector. One could expect that since direct foreign investment supplements domestic investment, its effects should give a stimulus to industries in the unorganised sector through (i) growth effect, (ii) output linkage effects. But such a conclusion is unwarranted when we consider the technology impact in the specific industry and on overall economy. Technology development has been concentrated in the advanced countries. The vast bulk of world's capital goods manufacture is also concentrated here. This means that Third World Countries have no choice but to use technologies of the developed countries. This will be all the more so in the case of foreign direct investment. There is a strong tendency for more capital intensive technologies to be selected. Technology designed in advanced countries does reflect their climatic conditions with a concentration of increased cost when it is transferred. The use of advanced country techniques also means the use of advanced country's organisation. This rules out the possibility of local development and local entrepreneur's talent. Managerial dependence follows from technological dependence. The transfer of technology involves transferring advanced country's investment per head to the underdeveloped economy; but available savings per head is much lower because of the lower labour productivity in the poor countries. As a consequence, most investment resources have to be concentrated in the sector receiving the advanced country technology, so that required investment levels per employee in this sector may be achieved. Since savings per head in India are much lower, only a small fraction of the labour force could be employed in the advanced sector by using the technology designed for US and UK (F. Stewart, Inappropriate Technology and Underdevelopment, Macmillan Press, London, 1978, p. 72).

The heavy investment demands imposed by advanced country technology result in concentration of country's resources in the organised sector to the neglect of the unorganised sector. The organised sector is associated with high labour productivity, and the unorganised sector suffers from lack of resources and poor efficiency as a result of lack of scientific and technological research. The huge gap in labour productivity between the two sectors has a parallel in a gap between the wage levels in the two sectors. The possibility of high wages encourages foreign training facilities. The net effect is disbursal of expenditure on education and training of a few in advanced sector, while neglecting the majority. The educational requirement imposed by advanced technology alters also the style of life in developing countries. Alternative life styles are closely associated with patterns of demand for consumer goods. Two effects ensue out of the transfer of products designed for consumption of much richer society to the poor. Unequal incomes creates markets for high income products, while unbalanced consumption patterns extend these markets.

The links between techniques and other parts of the economy extend to requirements for particular types of transport such as roads, of legal and administrative services and so on, as well as for particular products as inputs.

In brief, the inflow of direct foreign investment is likely to deprive the unorganised sector of resources, skilled workers, etc. It can be seen that a dualistic pattern of development is an inevitable consequence. The origin is to be found in the characteristics of advanced country technology. Concentration of resources in the advanced sector, high labour productivity and high incomes in this sector in relation to rest of economy (Steward, p.74). The emerging pattern of foreign investment and the capital investment techniques by the MNCs contribute to accelerated growth of dualism in the labour market, reduce the linkage effects between the industrial sector and the rural/ agricultural sector and arrest the growth of local autonomous small scale industry Parthasarathy, G. and Chalam, K.S. (Ed.), "Readings in Political Economy", p. 331]. Further, there is an irreconcilable conflict between the social objective of decentralised, participatory and sustainable integration, local development and the pattern of growth achieved when transnationals enter into agro-processing (Parthasarathy, G. "Neocolonialism", Ibid., p. 333).

Subramanyam, who examined the relationship between economic liberalism and development of technological capability of the country finds that the Import of Foreign Technology has an adverse effect on the R&D effort in the country [Subramanyam pp. 13-27; Yoginder. K. Alagh & others (ed.)].

The second implication of structural adjustment is the declining role of the State. In Indian situation, this reflects more in a decline in capital and planned expenditure of the State in Human Resource Development. While the current revenue expenditure continued to be maintained (see G. Parthasarathy, Janus Faced 5th Budget of Manmohan Singh, IDPS, 1995.) such decline in capital expenditure particularly in agriculture has adverse effects on the entire rural sector. As capital formation in agriculture declines, incomes of the masses in agriculture tend to decline particularly in the context of rising capital-output ratios. The falling income of the mass of people in agriculture have adverse effects on the unorganised non-agricultural sector, as the demand for their products shrink. A recent study on the transformation of South Korea (OECD, Paris, 1995) challenges the view that economic success was simply based upon sensible macro economic policies. It argued that the role of government far surpassed that of simply adopting and implementing these policies. It explains why an activist role favouring enterprise, prioritizing education and reducing rural inequalities makes sense in terms of economic efficiency for a country in economic transition. The study concludes that economic transition can be accelerated by such an activist role of the State.

Removal of all trade restrictions and reduction of import duties is considered to bring domestic prices in alignment with international prices. By removing factor price distortions, these are expected to stimulate labour intensive exports. One may argue that liberalisation will benefit the labour intensive unorganised sector as it will be in a position to export its products at competitive prices. The case of garment industry is often cited. While this may be true, this ignores another aspect of the problem. Most of the industries in unorganised sector depend upon raw material supplied by the organised sector. If there is a free export of such products, the prices of raw materials rise. Since the unorganised sector is unable to shift the higher price on to the consumers, the burden of high price of raw material has to be borne by the producer. This will mean further reduction in his meagre earnings. Two feature articles in a popular fortnightly magazine, *Frontline*, one in the issue of December 6, 1991, entitled "Starvation Deaths in Andhra Pradesh", (p. 47); and another published in a later issue (Vol. 12, No. 7, March 7-25 April, 1995) under the title Special Feature, "Troubled Tirupur" bring out tellingly how an export-led growth, unmindful of its consequences could ruin the handloom weavers. The journal provided a list of starvation deaths, 31 in Guntur District and 22 in Prakasam District of A.P. The impoverished weaver of Andhra Pradesh has been forced to pay dearly for a range of policies—in particular steps tailored to promote a policy of export oriented growth. Steady export of cotton yarn from 40 million kgs. in 1987-88 to 62 million kgs. in 1988-89 and then to 90 million kgs. in 1989-90 and to 100 million kgs. in 1990-91 resulted in abnormal prices. Another reason behind the rise in yarn prices is an increase in cotton exports. Stocks piled up with master weavers and co-operatives since they could not sell domestically nor export the same. Both the organisations had to count down the employment of weavers, and also pay lower wages. The Government could neither control the prices of inputs like yarn, dyes and chemicals nor organise the market to protect the handlooms from unequal competition with powerlooms and textile mills. On top of all this, the government in acute financial crisis withheld Rs. 20 crore payment. It also cut down its own purchase of cloth from the sector. The APCO, an apex co-operative body has transferred this burden of arrears to primary co-operatives, resulting in domestic decline in production. Further, the continuing cut for the production of Janata Cloth, earmarked exclusively to the handloom sector, has been cut by a hefty 25 per cent.

The weaver has traditionally resorted to the following to cope with crisis—(a) borrowing, (b) migration, (c) occupational diversification, and (d) sale of assets. All these coping mechanisms have been only of limited help. The weaver resorted to sale of cloth at lower prices and the handover of his membership card in the primary co-operative society. The middlemen collects the wage on behalf of the weaver, pays him less and makes a profit. This is the price that weavers pay for primary societies becoming sick and inactive. History repeated again in 1995; this time at Tirupur, a centre for cotton hosiery, Coimbatore District in Tamil Nadu. The first symptoms of trouble came in 1993 when yarn prices began to rise with Union Government's decision to allow exports of cotton and cotton yarn. Early in 1994, yarn prices were up by Rs. 12 per kg. There was enormous pressure on hosiery units with prices going up by 30 per cent. At one shot, the margin scheme came under pressure, production dropped, and the number of shifts came down drastically. The situation worsened when prices rose by another Rs. 12 per kg. For the industry, the situation was fatal. Small units stopped, production and the exports came down slowly by nearly 40 per cent and reduction in jobs followed.

Protection to unorganised sector by way of subsidies, input quotas and reservations have been found necessary, because of handicaps of the unorganised sector in the product, input, credit and labour markets. Further, such subsidies were found increasingly necessary for regionally backward areas which are subject to severe disadvantages due to backwash effects while spread effects are small. Further, while advanced regions have economies of agglomeration investments in backward regions are found to be risky. For this reason, capital instead of flowing to backward areas with high interest rate flows in reverse direction. State intervention by way of subsidies to industries in backward areas are found to be necessary. The ideology of structural adjustment looked with disfavour at all such measures of protection including reservations. Yet popular pressures from handloom weaver organisations have contributed to the continuance of several such schemes, Janata Cloth Scheme, Modified Workshed Housing Schemes, and invariable design collection programmes (*see* for details, Detailed Reports of Commissionerate of Handlooms, Ministry of Textiles, Govt. of India,). But the impact of the schemes in protecting the handlooms has been negligible in the absence of upgradation of technology, improved labour productivity and adaptation of handloom products to the shifting consumer preferences.

Much reliance has also been placed on agricultural exports in the light of structural adjustment. The GATT provisions, to which India is now a signatory, are expected to contribute to growth of agricultural exports as subsidy revision in the developed countries is likely to raise international prices and make Indian agricultural exports more competitive. While such circumstances may benefit the large farmers among agriculturists, the rise in price of the foodgrains due to structural adjustment will certainly affect the poor, the real wages of casual labour is likely to be pushed down [H.S. Sidhu, p. 153, G.K. Chadha (ed.)].

The issue of reservation to products of unorganised sector is important. They have been stalled by High Court Decisions in the past and it is therefore being pleaded that such reservations should be included in the IX Schedule of the Constitution keeping this out of judicial purview. The IRMA Report suggests that the consensus in handloom circles is that the existence of a reservation order, even with partial enforcement has a salutary effect (p. 12). They also present the view that the entire cotton production should be reserved for handlooms. But the economic consequences of this on the cost and price of cloth, which the IRMA Report did not examine (p. 54), are likely to be adverse.

The Abid Hussain Committee which examined the reservation issue, however, did not view reservations with favour. It preferred promotional measures to reservations. We are inclined to agree with Abid Hussain Committee.

Policy Directions

Structural adjustments programmes are likely to have a significantly adverse impact on employment both within the organised as well as unorganised sectors. The organised sector is likely to witness retrenchment and casualisation of employment opportunities. The unorganised sector will be forced to accept persons released by the organised sector and in the process wage and self-employment opportunities for the unskilled and the semi-skilled are likely to deteriorate further. Industrial firms may shift to capital intensive technologies requiring higher skills and push relatively unskilled to declining traditional industries with prospects of income losses and eventual loss of employment [Ashok Chandra in Rizwanul Islam (ed), p. 91)].

Sudipto Mundle (Rizwanul Islam (ed), pp. 164-68) estimated the unemployed as a consequence of structural adjustment at 5 to 8 lakhs for the organised sector. He does not cover the impact of structural adjustment on the unorganised sector. A consequence of structural adjustment is the increase in the number in the unorganised sector. Since the 80s, there has been no additional employment in the private organised sector despite increase in investment. Given this experience, the disinvestment of public sector, and the shift to private sector are likely to close even the meagre opportunities for entry into the organised sector specially for blue collar workers. They will drift into unorganised sector and into self-employment or casual labour. The need for improved access to institutional credit will be greater than in the past. One important aspect of institution building is building of credit institutions to meet the requirements of the poor and unorganised. In this context, the Thrift and Credit Societies organised on group basis for women (see Parthasarathy, "Economic Impact of Women's Thrift and Credit Societies," 1995), have been found to serve a useful function. In the dark environment of credit indiscipline, the Women's Thrift and Credit Societies have emerged as torch-bearers of thrift and self-reliance. In performing this function, they also emerge as training grounds for economic democracy for women. But, their success essentially depends upon commitment with which the sponsoring organisation establishes a system and makes it successful. Government assistance may help, but it is not the key factor. The key factor is the role of voluntary organisation which sponsors the group, nurtures it and makes it a self-reliant Thrift and Credit Society. The role of enlightened citizens in promoting such voluntary organisations becomes important. But, there is a limit to the success of these organisations in the absence of income-generating activities. Income-generating activities for the members have to meet the constraints of marketing [see Parthasarathy "Group Lending by Mahila Mandals in the BCT Area, Yelamanchili, Visakhapatnam Dt," (mimeo) 1993]. The tie-up of group activities of women with organised purchasing agencies has been found to be helpful. It is here that government could help promote marketing products of unorganised sector. It should be made obligatory on the part of all public sector employees, who form the privileged section, to purchase part of consumption requirements from unorganised sectors. Similarly, it must be made obligatory on schools to use the products of unorganised sector for uniform material. This may sound unnecessary and wasteful interference with market and consumer preferences. But, where the trade-off is joblessness and starvation for the many petty producers *versus* a little discomfort to the privileged sections in the organised sectors, this has to be accepted as a measure towards redistribution of incomes from organised to unorganised sectors.

Small and petty producers suffer from constraints of not only marketing, but also production. Water management has to be a group activity even while each peasant cultivates his own plot because of externalities involved. Similar externalities are involved in pesticide spraying. A small peasant with less than a hectare will not gain from pesticide spraying if he alone sprays and the neighbours do not spray. This becomes critical in view of the shift to crops like vegetables, fruits and flowers, in which both water management and pesticide spraying become important. The gains from globalisation could be got from small farmers only with institution building based on group activity.

Structural adjustments have resulted in pressures from certain sections for relaxing all constraints on land market. There is a plea for relaxing ceiling laws and for unlimited flow of private investments into agriculture and land acquisition. This may be considered desirable if the labour has opportunities outside agriculture and land. In the absence of such opportunities, revoking the ceiling law is bound to displace many marginal and small peasants and accelerate the trends towards casualisation of labour. Such trends will result in a situation where less than 25 per cent alone within agriculture (the present position is 25 per cent of the holders belong to the semi-medium, medium and large farms category) could benefit from the changes brought about by structural adjustment. The success of structural adjustment in Korea, Taiwan, People's Republic of China, etc. is attributed to the successful land reforms preceding the New Economic Policy. A widely dispersed agricultural growth benefiting the mass of peasants shifting their consumption patterns to higher levels will be necessary for the emergence and growth of non-farm activities. Even if there is no programme for a fresh piece of land reform, it will be necessary to ensure that current programmes on the statute books are not disturbed. This is also important from the viewpoint of political stability which is necessary for the progress of economic reforms. Given the huge and rising pressures on land, programmes in agriculture alone will not be found to be adequate. They need to be supplemented by development of non-farm activity for the benefit of bulk of marginal farmers and agricultural labourers. The products of traditional industry could be distinguished into the following groups : (1) products with national demand and catering to the elite class, (2) products with local demand and depending on local raw material for their sustenance, (3) products catering to the mass market and competing with the organised sector. The structural adjustments and globalisation are likely to step up the demand for the first type of products. But, this will bring relief to only a small percentage within the unorganised sector. The second type of products depending upon local raw material and catering to local markets will face the competition of the organised sector, especially in the input market. The unorganised sector is not likely to win the race in the raw material market. A similar situation arises in the third type of market also. The unorganised sector might seek to overcome this constraint by arranging tie-ups with the organised sector in production and marketing. As we have seen earlier, such a tie-up system often tends to be exploitative. Non-exploitative relations could be established if group strength of the unorganised sector is promoted through public support. The overall situation of traditional industry is not found to be favourable with structural adjustments. We should expect the current trends of deceleration to continue, within the rural sector. More numbers could be expected to be casualised and drift into urban informal sector.

In the light of not too optimistic position of traditional industries, massive public investments in modern energy, transport and communication infrastructure, public civil engineering projects and social services will be found necessary. This will create massive number of new jobs while at the same time conserving, upgrading and increasing the technological capabilities of workers. But, this needs to temper market fundamentalism and a release from the hegemony of the IMF and World Bank combine (*Bhagawan, Economic and Political Weekly*, Feb., 18-25. 1995).

Countries with massive proportion of workers in the unorganised sector have to reckon with the fact that the numbers of these are likely to rise as a consequence of structural adjustments. Safety nets and structural adjustment with human face could hardly bring solutions to their problems. A new approach to development in which the petty producers are made the agents of social transformation through their own organisations which will bring them economies of scale of production, technology, credit and marketing will be found necessary. The newly set up Panchayati Raj Institution should help promote this process. It is unfortunate that in the euphoria of liberalisation and globalisation we are made to forget the most fundamental tasks, *i.e.*, institution building for mobilisation of the rural, urban masses within the unorganised sector for growth, employment and poverty alleviation.

REFERENCES

Breman Jan & Sudipto Mundle (ed.) *Rural Transformation in Asia*, Oxford University Press, New Delhi-110001, 1991.

Chadha , G.K. (ed.), *Sectoral Issues in the Indian Economy : Policy and Perspectives,* Har-Anand Publications, New Delhi, 1994.

Chung, H. Lee, *The Economic Transformation of South Korea : Lessons for the Transition Economies,* Development Centre Studies, Development Centre of the Organisation for Economic Co-operation and Development, Paris, 1995.

Islam Rizwanul (ed.), *Social Dimensions of Economic Reforms in Asia,* International Labour Organisation, 1994, New Delhi.

Manjit Singh, *The Political Economy of Unorganised Industry : A Study of the Labour Process,* Sage Publications, New Delhi, 1990.

Parthasarathy, G. "Neo-Colonialism, Transnational Corporations and Basic Developmental Issues," *Readings in Political Economy*, Chalam, K.S. (ed.), Book Centre, Visakhapatnam, 1991.

Parthasarathy, G. "Economic Impact of Women's Thrift and Credit Societies," Institute of Development and Planning Studies, Visakhapatnam, 1995.

Parthasarathy, G. "Janus-Faced Fifth Budget of Dr. Manmohan Singh," Occasional Paper, Institute of Development and Planning Studies, Visakhapatnam, 1995.

Rao, S.B., Datar, D.R. & Deshmukh, M.A. (ed.), "Management of Handloom Co-operatives : Policies, Programmes and Perspectives," Vaikunth Mehta National Institute of Co-operative Management, Pune-16, 1978.

Schumacher, E.F., *Small is Beautiful: Economics as if People Mattered*, Harper Colophon Books, Harper & Row Publishers, New York, 1975.

Suri, K.B. (ed.), *Small Scale Enterprises in Industrial Development : The Indian Experience*, Sage Publications, New Delhi, 1988.

Sanjiv Misra, *India's Textile Sector : A Policy Analysis,* Centre for Policy Research, Sage Publications, New Delhi, 1993.

Uma Kapila (ed.), "Economic Status of Handicraft Artisans," National Council of Applied Economic Research, New Delhi-110002, 1993.

Vijayagopalan, S., "Economic Status of Handicraft Artisans," National Council of Applied Economic Research, New Delhi, 110002, 1993.

Yoginder, K. Alagh, Raghuvir. J. Mody & Rohit. D. Desai (ed.), *Sectoral Growth and Change : Essays in Honour of D.T. Lakdawala,* Har-Anand Publications, New Delhi, 1993.

REPORTS

Central Statistical Organisation, Dept. of Statistics, Govt. of India, New Delhi, "Annual Survey of Industries, 1983-84," 1987.

Central Statistical Organisation, Dept. of Statistics, Govt. of India, New Delhi, "Annual Survey of Industries, 1985-86," 1989.

Central Statistical Organisation, Dept. of Statistics, Govt. of India, New Delhi, "National Accounts Statistics," 1993.

Central Statistical Organisation, Dept. of Statistics, Govt. of India, New Delhi, "Economic Census, 1980, All India Report," 1985.

Reserve Bank of India, "Report on the Currency and Finance — 1992-93," Bombay.

Ministry of Labour, Labour Bureau, Chandigarh, "Report on the Working and the Living Conditions of Workers in the Powerloom Industry in India, 1988," 1991.

Ministry of Labour, Labour Bureau, Chandigarh, "Report on the Working and the Living Conditions of Workers in the Handloom Industry in India, 1986-87," 1990.

Institute of Public Enterprises, Hyderabad, "Technology and Underdevelopment by Stewart, F. in "Technology and Development, Vol. III of Selected Readings for the Course on Policy Planning and Analysis for Civil Servants."

National Institute of Small Industry Extension Training, (A Govt. of India Society), Hyderabad, "Small Scale Industries in India, Handbook of Statistics," 1989.

Govt. of India, Planning Commission, "Draft Fifth Five Year Plan," 1978-83, New Delhi.

Govt. of India, Planning Commission, "VII Five Year Plan," 1990-91, New Delhi.

Govt. of India, Planning Commission, "VIII Five Year Plan Outlay," 1992-97, New Delhi.

Govt. of India, Ministry of Finance, "Economic Survey—1994-95," New Delhi.

Ministry of Textile, Govt. of India, New Delhi, "Textile Industry in the 1990s Restructuring with a Human Face, Report on the Committee to Review the Progress of Implementation of Textile Policy of June 1980," 1990.

Institute of Rural Management, Anand, "A Study of Interventions in the Handloom Industry—Final report," 1989

Institute of Development and Planning Studies, "Group Lending by Mahila Mandals in B.C.T. Area, Yellamanchili, Visakhapatnam District, Andhra Pradesh" by Parthasarathy, G., (Mimeo) Visakhapatnam, 1993.

2

THE ROLE OF FINANCE AND PLANNING IN SUSTAINABILITY OF PROJECTS IN INDIA

—Prof. K.N. REDDY

An attempt is made in this paper to delineate the role of finance and planning in sustainability of projects. In the first section, conceptual problems associated with sustainability are discussed. In the second section, the process of allocation of funds by finance and planning mechanisms are described. In the third section, magnitude of funds devolved at the behest of the Finance Commission, the Planning Commission and the Central ministries to States from Centre are presented. And, in the fourth section, suggestions to tone up sustainability are attempted.

SUSTAINABILITY OF PROJECTS

From the literature available so far, there is no unique definition of sustainability. It ranges from a narrow definition that takes into account quantitative factors to that of broad definition that takes qualitative as well as quantitative factors into account. A few definitions would be helpful in this context. Honadle and Vansant (1985) defined project sustainability as:

> The percentage of project-initiated goods and services that is still delivered and maintained five years past the termination of donor resources, the continuation of local action stimulated by the project, and the generation of successor services and initiatives as a result of project built local capacity.

According to the Operations Evaluation Department (OED) of the World Bank (1986) :

> 'Sustainability' as the ability of a project to maintain an acceptable level of benefit flows through its economic life. While this may often be expressed in quantitative terms involving the internal economic or financial rates of return, benefits may also be qualitatively assessed. For projects in the productive sectors such as industry, the principal measure of performance is output, generally expressed in terms of capacity utilization but World Bank supported projects normally have other objectives such as sub-sectoral policies, technology transfer and intuition building which must be assessed qualitatively.

Bamberger and Cheema (1990) opined that "sustainability is a relative concept and has to be assessed in terms of a set of indicators which combine different quantitative and qualitative aspects of project performance." According to them, a distinction has to be drawn between whether a project has been sustained up to the time it is studied (often around five years after it has begun to operate) and whether it is likely to be sustainable over its intended life time.[1]

In whatever way (narrow or broad) sustainability is defined, several factors influence it and the degree of its success depends on the trade off that takes place among them. According to a report prepared by the Economic Development Institute, project design and implementation, project organization, macro-economic policy factors, trade unions, business associations, changes in governments, political factors, response of actual and intended beneficiaries, community participation and diversion of resources influence sustainability. To what extent each factor affects sustainability is a matter for detailed examination, case by case.[2]

For the purpose of this paper, it is intended to go alongwith the definition of the World Bank, and define sustainability as the ability of a project or programme or service, financed by Central Government or State Government or local body—urban or rural—or jointly by Central and State Governments or state and local governments to maintain an acceptable level of benefits through its economic life. It matters little from where resources come as long as efficiency of project or programme or service is ensured in terms of its output.

THE PROCESS OF ALLOCATION OF FUNDS TO PROJECTS AND PROGRAMMES

The process of allocation of funds to different projects and programmes is a complex matter and delineation of it in detail may form a separate study by itself. However, for the purpose of this paper, it is sufficient if we knowhow funds flow from one level of government to that of another and interconnections thereof in ensuring sustainability.

India has a three-tier federal system—Central government, state governments and local governments—with judiciary as a separate entity but responsible to the President of India who is the constitutional head of legislature, executive and judiciary at both Central and State levels (Fig. 2.1). Funds are transferred from central government to state Governments and from State Governments directly to Local Governments through three channels: (i) Planning Commission, (ii) Central ministries, and (iii) Finance Commission (Fig. 2.2).

Allocation of Funds at the Behest of Planning Commission

The Planning Commission (a body constituted in March 1950 by the Government of India) is guided by the National Development Council (NDC), with Prime Minister as its Chairman and Ministers of Central Cabinet, Chief Ministers of the states, the members of the Planning Commission and administrators of the union territories as its members. It draws up Five Year Plans in consultation with the central ministries and State Governments and oversees their implementation. Its functions *inter alia* are to:

- make an assessment of the material, capital and human resources of the country, including technical personnel, and investigate the possibilities of augmenting such of these resources as are found to be deficient in relation to the nation's requirements;
- formulate a plan for the most effective and balanced utilization of country's resources;
- on a determination of priorities, define the stages in which the plan should be carried out and propose the allocation of resources for the due completion of each stage;
- indicate the factors which are tending to retard economic development, and determine the conditions which, in view of the current social and political situation, should be established for the successful execution of the plan;
- determine the nature of machinery which will be necessary for securing the successful implementation of each stage of the plan in all its aspects;

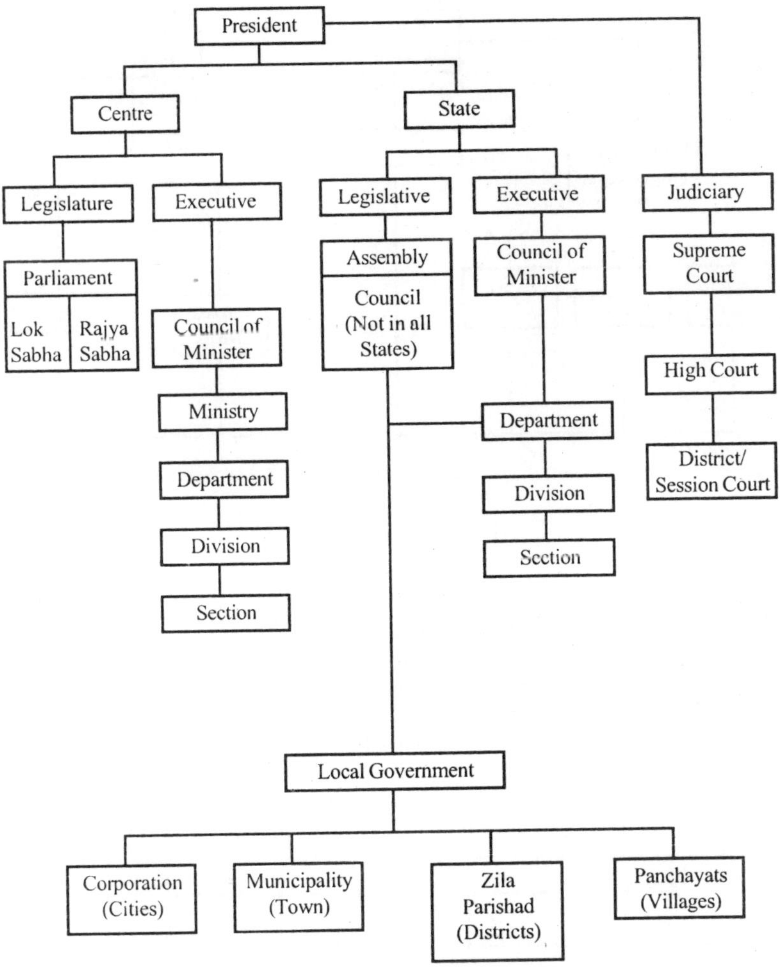

FIG. 2.1 : India : Administrative Structure under the Constitution

Note : Structure of local bodies differs across states.

Soruce : United Nations, Economic & Social Commission for Asia and Pacific, Bangkok, 1991, Fiscal Decentralization and the Mobilization and Use of National Resources for Development: Issues, Experience and Policies in the ESCAP Region, Development Paper No. 11, p. 98.

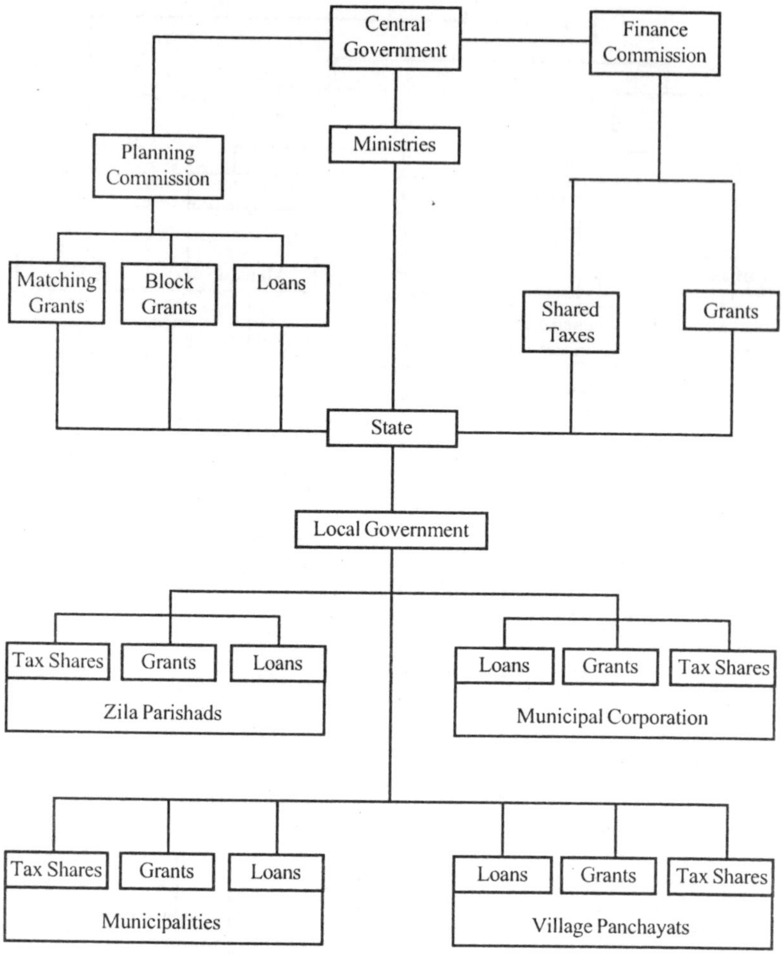

FIG. 2.2 : System of Inter-governmental Fiscal Devolution in India

Note : Structure of local bodies differs across states.

Soruce : Same as Figure 2.1.

— appraise from time to time the progress achieved in the execution of each stage of the plan and recommend the adjustment of policy and measures that such appraisal may show to be necessary; and

— make such interim or ancillary recommendations as appear to it to be appropriate either for facilitating the discharge of the duties assigned to it or on a consideration of prevailing economic conditions, current policies, measures and development programmes or on an examination of such specific problems as may be referred to it for advice by central or state governments (Government of India, 1991).

After formulating the overall macro framework for the national plan, it attempts to indicate to each state both financial magnitudes of the outlay for the state plans and guidelines regarding the formulation of the sectoral proposals. The states then formulate their plan proposals together with their financial requirements and send the same to the Planning Commission. The difficulty here is that there is a mismatch between the physical programmes and financial needs with the suggested financial magnitudes generally falling short of plan proposals of the states. In many cases, the plan outlays proposed by different departments and districts put together add up to an outlay which is much in excess of the plan suggested by the Planning Commission for the state.

Then, the macro-economic framework as well as policy proposals are placed before the NDC, and its formal consent obtained after an extensive debate and discussion. Unfortunately, the consent obtained is not in clearcut terms. For, it is obtained out of heated debate and allegations made by Chief Ministers against the Centre for smaller allocation of plan outlay to them. The Chief Ministers want more central assistance to the states and hope to undertake more schemes. At the same time, they are reluctant to make any clear commitments about their share in the proposed mobilization of resources. In regard to the central government also, the picture is not clear. In the early stages of the formulation of the plan (Five Year Plan), the centre is unclear about the magnitude of financial mobilizations it would undertake. The tussle between the Planning Commission and the states about the contemplated size of the public sector outlay continues right up to the beginning of the Five Year Plan Period (Paranjape, 1990). In fact, there have been instances of the Five Year Plan not getting a final shape until it is about half way through. Take, for example, the Eighth Five Year

Plan; its size and financial implications have not yet emerged clear, although the Plan is stated to have started from April 1992. An element of unrealism is thus built in, right in the formulation of Plan.

Further, a distinction is made between plan and non-plan expenditure which is artificial and the transfer of resources from the Centre to States on this count adds to unrealism. The Constitution provides for transfer of resources from the Centre to States both through tax-shares and grant-in-aid in need of assistance. It does not mention about plan or non-plan. While plan expenditure is developmental and investment-oriented, non-plan expenditure usually refers to house-keeping activities and also maintenance of assets created. The element of artificiality gets compounded with the maintenance of a plan scheme at the end of the plan period becoming what is called committed expenditure and, therefore, a liability on the non-plan account. For example, expenditure on development schemes funded under the Seventh Plan (1985-90) and the Annual Plan (1990-91), suddenly becomes non-plan expenditure from the beginning of the Eight Plan (*i.e.*, from 1st April, 1992). Over the years, a system has got evolved that the Planning Commission provides funds for plan purposes, while the Finance Commission, which is a Constitutional body set up to sanctions transfer of resources through a twin system of tax-sharing and grant-in-aid to states for non-plan needs. These are generally known as statutory transfers. The assistance provided by the Planning Commission is expected to supplement the States' resources on account of plan expenditure, whereas, for the non-plan requirements of states the funds provided on the basis of the award of the Finance Commission are expected to cover any gap in the states' finances on non-plan expenditure on revenue account.[3] Thus, the requirements of states for funds from the centre are fully taken care of.

Allocation of Funds at the Behest of Central Ministries

Various ministries of Central Government also transfer substantial sums for implementation of Central sector projects and the centrally sponsored schemes, *e.g.*, Accelerated Rural Water Supply Programme, Jawahar Rozgar Yojana, Biogas Programme, Malaria Eradication Programme, T.B. Control Programme, Leprosy Control Programme, Family Welfare Programme, Maternity & Child Health, Operation Black Board, Non-Formal Education, Vocationalization of Education, Integrated Child Development Services, Supplementary Nutrition for Additional Beneficiaries, Nehru Rozgar Yojana, Special Central

Assistance for Scheduled Castes Component Plan, Liberation of Scavengers, and so on. The objectives of these schemes are of national character, welfare-oriented and, therefore, laudable. But, in practice, these schemes have not produced the desired results. In fact, the Ninth Finance Commission has pointed out that Centrally sponsored schemes created a number of problems to states. (a) in respect of norms for staffing, and (b) in respect of providing accommodation, vehicles, equipment, etc. Justice A.S, Qureshi, a member of the Ninth Finance Commission, observed that "Centrally sponsored schemes became a permanent liability to states after the expiry of the period of the schemes; the wastage left heavy financial burden on the states after the Centre had withdrawn from these schemes. The states could not do away with the surplus staff and had to maintain the costly establishments.[4]"

Allocation of Funds at the Behest of Finance Commission

The Finance Commission is a quasi-judicial body, appointed once in five years or earlier under Article 280 of the Indian Constitution, to recommend transfers from Centre to states to correct fiscal imbalances between Centre and States on the one hand and amongst states on the other. So far, nine Finance Commissions have been appointed and their reports have been accepted by and large.

The point is that the Finance Commissions for the past forty years have been concerned with the sustainability of projects in one way or the other. The last four (sixth to ninth) Finance Commissions (Government of India, 1973, 1978, 1984 and 1989 respectively) were asked specifically to make recommendations regarding adequate maintenance and upkeep of capital assets such as major, medium and minor irrigation works, flood control works, maintenance of roads buildings, etc. They made provision for maintenance expenditure based on certain engineering norms, but expenditure incurred in actual practice by the states has been far too low relative to the norms as well as the requirement for the maintenance of the assets even on a minimum basis. The Ninth Finance Commission pointed out :

> "There is strong preference for the creation of additional assets with little attention being paid to the maintenance of assets already created. In the process, the quality of the assets and their useful life span declined steeply. The neglect of maintenance is an unhealthy practice and must be discouraged. The amount

> required for the maintenance of the existing assets should be the first charge on the resources of the states. We would even suggest that the Planning Commission should be given a special responsibility for ensuring that the maintenance of the existing assets in the states is in no way compromised. At the time of assessing the resources for the state plan, the Planning Commission should take special care to ensure that the maintenance expenditures are fully provided for (Government of India, 1989)."

Further, the Finance Commissions have been asked to look into efficiency aspects of certain projects also which include State Road Transport Corporations, State Electricity Boards, state-owned enterprises, departmental undertakings like water supply schemes, milk schemes, etc. While assessing returns from departmental undertakings and public sector enterprises, different Finance Commissions assumed different rates of return based on certain norms and expert opinion. The Ninth Finance Commission made the following assumptions: (i) in the case of water supply schemes the losses should be reduced gradually by 1994-95 to one-fourth of those in 1986-87, (ii) in the case of milk supply schemes there should be break even atleast, (iii) in the case of industrial schemes a positive return of 5 per cent by 1994-95 (iv) in the case of power projects a return rising gradually from 3 per cent in 1990-91 to a maximum of 7 per cent in 1994-95, and (v) in the case of road transport undertakings, a return of at least 1 per cent in 1990-91, 2 per cent in 1991-92, 3 per cent in 1992-93, 4.5 per cent in 1993-94, and 6.5 per cent in 1994-95 in the non-hill states. Likewise, in respect of the Central government projects also, the Finance Commission assumed an annual rate of return of 6 per cent on investments in public sector undertakings and an increase of 5 per cent per annum over the level in 1989-90 in respect of other investments.

But the fixation of norms has had little effect on the performance of departmental undertakings and the working of various projects and programmes both at the Central and State levels. For example, the *Economic Survey*, 1991-92 noted as under:

> "Net profits of Central government enterprises declined from Rs. 3,789 crore in 1989-90 to Rs. 2,368 crore in 1990-91. The rate of return as measured by the ratio of net profits to capital employed, declined from 4.5 per cent in 1989-90 to 2.3 per cent in 1990-91, the lowest since 1984-85. The working results of

> departmentally run commercial undertakings of state and Union territories have continued to be poor. Of all departmentally-run enterprises, only forest and mines have been generating net surpluses. While the profits from forest and mines registered a modest increase between 1985-86 and 1991-92, the losses of non-profit making enterprises more than doubled during this period. On the whole, the losses of departmentally-run enterprises are estimated at a staggering level of Rs. 1,827 crore during 1991-92 budget estimates (BE) (*see* Table 2.1) The two major non-departmental undertakings, *viz.,* the State Electricity Boards (SEBs) and the State Road Transport Corporations (SRTCs) continued to incur substantial losses in their operations. The commercial losses of all SEBs taken together amounted to Rs. 4,104 crore in 1989-90 and Rs. 4,169 crore in 1990-91. The performance in terms of rate of return on capital (after depreciation and interest) was negative, being (–)16.4 per cent in 1989-90 and (–)13.8 per cent in 1990-91. The rate of return is estimated to deteriorate to (–)14.8 per cent in 1991-92 (Government of India, 1992)."

The performance is no better at the Central level. This is described thus, net profit (after tax) to capital employed declined from 4.4 per cent in 1988-89 to 2.3 per cent in 1990-91 (*see* Table 2.2).

MAGNITUDE OF FUNDS DEVOLVED FROM CENTRE TO STATES

As of 1991-92 revised estimates (RE), total funds devolved at the behest of the Finance Commission, the Planning Commission and the Central ministeries amounted to Rs. 39,290 crore and if we add the share of states from small savings collections total transfers net of repayments of loans jump to Rs. 41,641 crore. In the budget for 1992-93, the correspondence figures are Rs. 42,928 crore and Rs. 44,964 crore respectively. It will be seen from Table 2.3 that in 1991-92 (RE) 52.6 per cent of total gross transfers were made at the behest of the Finance Commission. But, such a statement will mean that states are getting funds at the mercy of central government. A fair way of looking at it is to exclude the share in central taxes by virtue of their right as per the Constitution of India which are under Articles 270 and 272.

TABLE 2.1: Financial Results of Departmental Commercial Undertakings of States and UTs [Profit (+)/Loss (–)]

	1985-86	*1986-87*	*1987-88*	*1988-89*	*1989-90 (RE)*	*1990-91 (BE)*	*1991-92*
Dept. Com. Undertakings*							
(i) Forest	497.70	516.21	543.69	414.35	540.24	372.46	528.3
(ii) Power Projects	–75.04	–93.81	–116.40	–84.19	–34.83	–54.56	–42.9
(iii) Road & Water Tpt. Services	–25.65	–36.59	–110.76	–56.51	–93.21	–75.78	–64.1
(iv) Dairy Development	–99.29	–40.45	–43.91	–52.38	–106.99	–72.23	–77.1
(v) Industries	–14.10	–16.46	–20.51	–10.09	–159.66	–112.91	–40.0
(vi) Mines and Minerals	40.06	35.05	27.02	51.83	60.62	60.43	75.2
(vii) Irrigation Projects (Commercial)	–871.60	–1225.95	–1344.50	–1840.79	–1916.85	–2002.63	–2206.6
(viii) Multipurpose River Project							
Profit of Profit Making Undertakings	537.76	551.26	570.71	466.18	600.86	432.89	603.5
Loss of Loss Making Undertakings	–1085.68	–1413.26	–1636.08	–2043.96	–2311.54	–2318.11	–2430.9
Net Financial Results of Departmental Undertakings	–547.92	–862.00	1065.37	–1577.78	–1710.68	–1885.22	–1827.3

* These do not include State Electricity Boards and State Road Transport Corporations.
Source : Government of India, *Economic Survey 1991-92* , Part II, Sectoral Department, p. 21.

After excluding the share in central taxes, the quantum of statutory transfers effected at the behest of the Finance Commission (*i.e.*, grants-in-aid under Article 275, and grants in lieu of railway passenger fare and others) amounted to only Rs. 3,472 crore as against Rs. 12,318 crore at the behest of the Planning Commission and Rs. 6,301 crore at the behest of the central ministries in 1991-92 (RE) (Table 2.3). In other words, transfers at the behest of the Planning Commission and central ministries, which are generally termed as ad hoc transfers, have far exceeded the statutory transfers. The situation could have been more distressing if the Ninth Finance Commission had not transferred some portion of plan grants to states. This pattern of devolution has led to a lot of bitterness between the Centre and the States (and particularly when some states are ruled by the parties other than the party ruling at the Centre). The point is that while transfers effected at the instance of the Finance Commission come under specific constitutional arrangements, and are, therefore, free from political bargaining, transfers effected at the instance of the Planning Commission and the Central ministries come out of hard bargaining and number of visits to New Delhi by state officials. Sometimes ad hoc transfers are used as arm twisting techniques of Central government to make states realize their dependence on centre. This attitude has never been liked by states.

TABLE 2.2 : Profile of Centre's Public Enterprises

		Unit	*1980-81*	*1983-84*	*1984-85*	*1985-86*	*1986-87*	*1987-88*	*1988-89*	*1989-90*	*1990-91*
1.	Number of Running Public Enterprises	No.	163	201	207	211	214	221	226	233	236
2.	Capital Employed	Rs. crore	18207	29851	26382	42965	51835	55554	67629	84869	101779
3.	Turnover	Rs. crore	28635	47272	54784	62360	69088	81271	93137	106069	118335
4.	Gross Margin (profit before depreciation interest and tax)	Rs. crore	2401	5771	7386	8230	9897	11134	13438	16412	18510
5.	Depreciation*	Rs. crore	983	2205	2758	2983	3376	4150	4866	5790	7151
6.	Gross profit Before Interest and Tax	Rs. crore	1418	3565	4628	5287	6521	6984	8572	10622	11359
7.	Interest	Rs. crore	1399	2086	2529	3115	3420	3595	4167	5329	7539
8.	Net Profit Before Tax	Rs. crore	19	1480	2099	2172	3101	3389	4405	5293	3820
9.	Tax	Rs. crore	222	1239	1190	1000	1330	1329	1411	1504	1452
10.	Net Profit Before Tax	Rs. crore	-203	240	909	1172	1771	2060	2994	3789	2368
11.	Internal Resources Generated (gross)	Rs. crore	1225	3278	4251	5068	6014	6947	8915	10774	11372
12.	Net Profit (after tax) to Capital Employed	Per cent	-1.1	0.8	2.5	2.7	3.4	3.7	4.4	4.5	2.3

*Includes deferred revenue expendiure

TABLE 2.3 : Transfers of Resources from Centre to States

(*Rs. in crore*)

	1991-92 (RE)	*1992-93 (EE)*
A. Statutory Transfers/Transfers at the Behest of Finance Commission (1 + 2)	20.67	23,811
1. Share in Central Taxes		
(a) Income Tax (Article 270)	5,106	5,868
(b) Union Excise Duty (Article 272)	12,093	14,124
Total (a + b)	17,199	19,992
2. Grants-in-Aid		
(a) Under Artice 275 – Plan Grants	1,333	1,780
– Non-Plan Grants	1,964	1,864
(b) Grants in Lieu of Tax on Railway Passenger fares – Non-Plan	150	150
(c) Other (Grants to M.P. for Bhopal Gas Tragedy-Non-Plan)	25	25
Total (a + b + c)	3,472	3,819
B. Transfers at the Behest of Planning Commission	12,318	12,494
C. Transfers at the Behest of Central Ministries (1 + 2)	6,301	6,623
1. For Central & Centrally Sponsored Plan Schemes	5,874	6,096
2. For Other Non-Plan Items	427	527
D. Transfers at the Behest of Finance Commission, Planning Commission and Central Ministries (A+B+C)	39,290	42,928
E. Loans to States from Small Savings Collections (Gross)	5,500	5,700
F. Recoveries of Loans from States	3,149	3,664
G. Total Transfers to State Government (net) (D+E+F)	41,641*	44,964*

* This does not include payment of interest by states on central loans.

Source : Government of India, Ministry of Finance, *Budget at a Glance. Expenditure Budget,* Volume 1 and 2, 1992-93.

It may be noted in this context that Centrally sponsored schemes compete with the strategy of welfare and populism worked out by the states and, therefore, diminish the states enthusiasm in implementation. It is true that Central ministries contribute to the programmes launched. But, not all the programmes are 100 per cent funded by Central government; some are 50 per cent funded and still some others are marginally funded. Take, for example, the following schemes under the Ministry of Rural Development:

1. Accelerated Rural Water Supply Scheme
2. Integrated Rural Development Programme (IRDP)
3. Jawahar Rozgar Yojana
4. Rural Housing Scheme

The Accelerated Rural Water Supply Scheme has to be implemented by the state under the state sector Minimum Needs Programme (MNP). However, to supplement the state resources, Central assistance is being provided as 100 per cent grant under this programme, subject to a matching provision being made by the state governments under MNP. The expenditure under IRDP is equally shared between the centre and the states. The Jawahar Rozgar Yojana (JRY) is being funded by the Centre and the States on 80:20 sharing basis whereas, the rural housing is funded in the ratio of 50:50. Sometimes names of the leaders of a particular party are attached to certain programmes. Both the matching share expected from the states and the names attached to the programme aggravate disinterestedness in the programmes.[5]

Another point to be noted is the way pattern of central assistance is decided, the *inter se* allocation made among states and the type of impact it has on the implementation of certain plan schemes. During the past one decade, net inflow of assistance to states has been declining and in the case of some states it has been tending to be negative. Such a situation has never been expected. Central assistance for state plans has been given partly in the form of grants and partly in the form of loans, *i.e.*, 30 per cent in the form of grants and 70 per cent in the form of loans to non-special category states, *viz.*, (1) Andhra Pradesh, (2) Bihar, (3) Goa, (4) Gujarat, (5) Haryana, (6) Karnataka, (7) Kerala, (8) Madhya Pradesh, (9) Maharashtra, (10) Orissa, (11) Punjab, (12) Rajasthan, (13) Tamil Nadu, (14) Uttar Pradesh, and (15) West Bengal; and 90 per cent in the form of grant and 10 per cent in the form of loans to special category states, *viz.*, (1) Arunachal Pradesh, (2) Assam, (3) Himachal Pradesh, (4) Jammu & Kashmir, and (5) Manipur. These states are given the special status in view of their very poor and even negative resource base. But, this should not go on for all time.

More importantly, the very basis of allocation of Central assistance to states is being questioned. No satisfactory formula has been evolved so far, although in the last NDC meeting in December 1991, a consensus formula has been evolved. Though formula-based as it looks *prima facie*, the distribution of Central assistance is unable to shake off the discretionary character. To compound the procedure which is already complex some states are given a special category status. A glance at Table 2.4 will convince that how a modified Gadgil formula has been further modified in NDC meetings held in October 1990 and December 1991. Some states want to be considered as special category states, so that grant-loan component might undergo change to their advantage. It appears that gradually, list of special category states will increase and the concept of so called special category will lose its importance over a period of time. The distinction between non-special and special is a manifestation of policies pursued by Central government and why should the rest of the states sacrifice their interests? It is time that the special category states make attempts to raise resources to stand on their feet.

The end-result is that resources that become available to finance projects do not match with requirements, as a consequence of which time and cost over-runs take place. The sustainability of the projects becomes questionable. Worse still, funds are diverted for meeting other expenditure which are unforseeable and also unforeseen for which sufficient cushion is not made. Maintenance of assets created is the main casualty in this situation. Often at times, borrowed money is used for meeting revenue expenditure requirements, instead of being used for investments in viable capital projects.

TABLE 2.4 : Evolution Formulae for Central Assistance Over Time

		Original Gadgil Formula 1969	*Modified Gadgil Formula 1980*	*NDC Oct., 1990*	*NDC Dec., 1991*
1.	Population (1971)	60	60	55	60
2.	Per Capita Income Below National Average	10	20	—	—
3.	Per Capita SDP	—	—	(a) (b) 20+5	(a) (b) 20+5
4.	Per Capita Tax Effort/Fiscal Management	10	10	5	(c) 7.5
5.	Outlay on Continuing Irrigation & Power Projects	10	—	—	—
6.	Special Problems as Perceived by Planning Commission	10	10	15	(d) 7.5

(a) Deviation method – only to states below National average.

(b) Distance method – all states.

(c) Performance in matters relating to tax effort, fiscal management, performance in national priorities such as population control, literacy, completing externally aided projects and land reforms.

(d) Special development projects.

SUGGESTIONS TO TONE UP SUSTAINABILITY OF PROJECTS AND PROGRAMMES

In the light of foregoing analysis, sustainability of projects and programmes is absolutely essential. Otherwise fiscal health of the country, states, and local bodies will suffer and even the rate of growth of the economy will be impaired. There is no doubt if this difference, between non-special and special category states, continues and the number of the latter increases, our children and grand children will have to pay heavy price and they will not forgive us for our indolence. What concrete steps have to be taken up to tone up sustainability is a matter for careful thinking and detailed investigation, case by case. Pending such investigation, some steps may have to be thought of for immediate implementation.

The first and foremost thing is to pay attention to deficits on revenue account of budgets. There are two ways to correct it, one is by increasing resources through tax and non-tax sources and the other is by way of curbing expenditure growth on revenue account. Still another way is a combination of both the methods. As far as raising of resources through the first method is concerned, further taxation has to be ruled out, as tax levels have already reached maximum limits. The only option is that of tapping non-tax revenue sources further. Contributions from departmental undertakings (such as railways, post and telegraph, power projects, irrigation projects—commercial—multipurpose river schemes, water supply schemes, milk schemes and industrial schemes), non-departmental undertakings (such as State Electricity Boards, State Road Transport Undertakings), and state-owned enterprises should be increased by raising their efficiency levels and by levying appropriate user charges on the provision of social services like education and health and economic services like agriculture, industry, transport, electricity and communications.

It may be noted that receipts from public undertakings which were positive at Rs. 308.51 crore till 1986-87, turned out to be negative at Rs. 260 crore in 1987-88 and increased much further to Rs. 1011.41 crore in 1990-91 (RE) (Table 2.5). Equally worth noting is the fact that receipts from social and community services, such as education, medical and public health have declined from Rs. 930 crore in 1986-87 to Rs. 720 crore in 1990-91 (RE).

To put it differently, education and health have been subsidized substantially. Can this subsidization continue for ever? It will be luxury for a poor country like ours if we do so. Assuming that education and health are 'merit' goods and cannot be left to market forces, the government can always limit its area of intervention in providing them or recover costs from affluent sections. A study conducted by the author for Andhra Pradesh revealed that benefits from expenditure on education and health accrue largely to high income groups (Reddy and Sudhakar, 1989). Therefore, attempts must be made to recover costs from upper income groups. Not only this, indirect beneficiaries of these services, particularly education, should be tapped appropriately (Reddy, 1992).

Attempts at improvements have to be made on the expenditure side as well. It is wellknown that expenditure of government has increased rapidly, and government itself has urged on a number of occasions that expenditure growth should be curtailed. But to everybody's surprise little evidence is seen to that effect. One important reason is that the scope for reducing expenditure is getting limited. Two items, namely, interest payments and defence, cannot be touched at all. Wage hike of government employees is increasing beyond expectations. Attempts at containing its growth have not borne fruit. The only item that can be touched is that of subsidies. Here again, food subsidies cannot be touched being essential. But, there is scope for reducing them by targeting the public distribution system to lower income group only (Reddy and Selvaraju, 1972). Fertilizer subsidies is a complex matter and has to be studied carefully. The point is, growth of government expenditure cannot be easily curbed, unless overall philosophy of government changes towards its intervention in developmental and non-developmental activities.

To start with, attempts should be made to decentralize planning and finance. What programmes and what projects be taken up should be left to the state and local governments. The Planning Commission should confine itself to the determination of financial assistance to state plans, preferably in the form of block grants, and not monitor the implementation of programmes, which they have failed miserably.

In any case, sustainability as a concept both at macro level as well as micro level has tremendous relevance and ways and means have to be explored to disseminate the mechanics of its application. The simplest way would be to ensure completion of a concerned project on time and endeavour to obtain adequate return therefrom. Therefore, both finance and planning would need to be dovetailed to secure a fair deal.

TABLE 2.5 : Receipts from Selected Non-Tax Revenue Sources for Centre, State and Union Territories Combined

	1986-87	1987-88	1988-89	1989-90	1990-91
1. Net Contribution of Public Undertakings	308.51	–260.00	–667.06	–1121.17	–1011.41
(A) Net Contribution of Departmental Undertakings	–11.90	–682.28	–980.53	–1652.31	–1624.50
(i) Railways	—	—	—	—	—
(ii) Post & Telegraphs	–216.43	–190.87	–169.74	–262.99	–159.38
(iii) Profits of RBI	210.00	210.00	210.11	210.11	210.00
(iv) Forest	526.92	553.16	427.31	544.55	377.55
(v) Power Projects	–250.61	–335.15	–287.31	–390.64	–180.31
(vi) Irrigation Projects (commercial)	—	—	—	—	—
(vii) Multipurpose River Projects	-1126.50	-1344.50	-1840.79	-1916.85	-2002.63
(vii) Profit from Exports of Edible oil	—	—	146.41	—	—
(ix) Discount Royalty on Crude Oil	943.04	449.78	474.53	387.86	511.55
(x) Others	98.32	24.70	58.95	224.35	81.28
(B) Dividends from Non-departmental Undertakings	320.41	422.28	313.47	531.14	613.90
2. Interest Receipts	4284.65	4555.39	5588.22	6626.02	6576.25
3. Fiscal Services	731.95	783.34	728.56	835.74	663.68
4. General Services	1014.00	1124.32	1324.30	1579.89	2289.02
5. Social and Community Services	929.97	562.75	517.13	744.09	720.14
6. Economic Services	1625.47	2425.59	2123.51	4864.98	2382.11
7. External Grants	436.18	492.06	599.99	754.10	822.06

* Includes road and water transport services, dairy development (including Delhi Milk Supply Scheme), industries, mines and minerals, overseas communications services, and defence services canteen stores department

NOTES

1. For some kinds of projects like housing or road construction, the intended project life time may be "as long as thirty years or considerably shorter for others."
2. For elaboration and excellent description of the determinants of sustainability, see, *The Management Report on the Sustainability of Social Sector Programme in India* prepared by the Economic Development Institute in co-operation with the Lal Bahadur Shastri National Institute of Public Administration and the Department of Personnel and Training, January 1992, pp. 8-9.
3. However, there was exception in this regard; that was in regard to the Ninth Finance Commission; they were asked to assess the "entire revenue expenditure including plan expenditure". But the result of their analysis was that "to deal with committed

liability in an isolated manner without a linkage to new plan revenue expenditure can be misleading. What is worse is that such an exercise could lead to wasteful expenditure.

4. See the note of dissent by Justice A.S. Qureshi, Member of the Ninth Finance Commission, appended to its Second Report (1989), p. 55.
5. It may be noted that there is no way of knowing the exact number of programmes sponsored by various central ministries unless one goes through the demands for grants. Similarly, it is not easy to know the matching contributions. A quick estimate of centrally sponsored programmes tells us there are about 290 programmes and some of them are as old as three decades and could not be dispensed with.

REFERENCES

Government of India (1973), *Report of the Finance Commission*, p.2.

Government of India (1978), *Report of the Finance Commission*, p. 2.

Government of India (1984), *Report of the Finance Commission*, p. 2.

Government of India (1989), *Second Report of the Ninth Finance Commission*, p. 1.

Government of India (1989), Ninth Finance Commission, p. 12.

Government of India (1992), *Economic Survey*, 1991-92, pp. 20-22.

Government of India, *Planning Commission Annual Report*, 1990-91, pp. 4-5.

Honadle, George and Jerry, Vansant (1985), *Implementation of Sustainability Lessons from Integrated Rural Development*. West Hartford, CT, Kumarian Press, p.2.

Operations Evaluation Department (1986), *Sustainability of Projects Review of Experience in the Fertilizer Sub-sector*, Washington, D.C., World Bank, p.1.

Paranjape, H.K. (1970), *Centre-State Relations in Planning*, The Indian Institute of Public Administration, New Delhi, pp. 6-11.

Reddy, K.N. (1992), "Utilization of Resources in Education: Some Issues", presented at a discussion meeting held on 3-5 March, at NIEPA, New Delhi .

Reddy, K.N. and Sudhakar (1989), "Who Benefits from Government Expenditure? A Case Study of Andhra Pradesh," *Journal of the Indian School of Political Economy* Vol. 1, No. 1 , January-June, p. 123.

Reddy, K.N. and V. Selvaraju (1992), "Containment of Food Subsidy in the Context of Revenue Deficit" NIPFP, Working Paper No. 1 January, 1992.

3

ALTERNATIVE SOURCES OF FINANCING HEALTH CARE IN INDIAN CITIES

—Prof. K.N. REDDY

Ever since the launching of Five Year Plans, India has been making strenuous efforts to improve health status. Investment outlay of government on health, family welfare and water supply has gone up from Rs. 763 million in the First Plan (1951-56) to Rs. 137,749 million in the Seventh Plan (1985-90) and is likely to reach up to Rs. 307,869 million (in 1991-92 prices) by the end of Eighth Plan (1992-97). Achievement of "Health for All by 2000 AD" has been committed through the universal provision of comprehensive primary health care services. The National Health Policy (1983), alongwith specific targets to be achieved in respect of infant mortality rate, crude death rate, life expectancy at birth, net reproductive rate, immunization status, etc., has been announced. On account of all these steps, perhaps life at birth (an important indicator of health status) moved up from 31.66 years (per 1,000 population) in 1951 to 58.96 years during 1986-91; infant mortality rate (another important indicator of health status) has gone down from 146 (per 1,000 live births) during 1951-61 to 91 in 1989. But, in comparison to other developing countries like China, Indonesia and Sri Lanka, this improvement is not impressive (Table 3.1). Questions arise as to what went wrong with our policies? Was it on account of inadequate resources devoted to health care? Was it on account of the organizational weaknesses? Was it on account of misallocation of resources? To go into these questions in detail will form a separate study by itself and therefore, no attempt is made in this paper to answer them.

What is attempted here is the description of health care provision and health care financing in India and exploration of alternative sources of health care financing with special reference to cities in India. Section

TABLE 3.1:Total Health Expenditure as Percentage of GDP (Selected Countries)

	Life Expectancy at Birth (Years)		*Total Health Expenditure (as percentage of GDP)*		
	1960	*1990*	*1960*	*1990*	
Canada	71.0	77.0	5.5	8.6	
Japan	67.9	78.6	2.9	6.8	
Norway	73.4	77.1	3.3	7.5	
Switzerland	71.2	77.4	3.3	7.7	
Sweden	73.1	77.4	4.7	9.0	
USA	69.9	75.9	5.2	11.2	
Australia	70.7	76.5	4.6	7.1	
France	70.3	76.4	4.2	8.6	
Netherlands	73.2	77.2	3.9	8.5	
United Kingdom	70.6	75.7	3.9	6.1	
Ireland	73.2	77.8	3.5	7.8	
Germany	69.5	75.2	4.7	8.2	
Denmark	72.1	75.8	3.6	6.0	
Finland	68.4	75.5	3.9	7.4	
Austria	68.6	74.8	4.6	8.4	
Belgium	70.2	75.2	3.4	7.2	
New Zealand	70.9	75.2	4.4	6.9	
Israel	68.6	75.9	1.0*	2.1*	
Italy	69.2	76.0	3.3	6.9	
Ireland	69.6	74.6	4.0	7.4	
Spain	69.0	77.0	2.3	6.0	
Greece	68.7	76.1	3.2	5.3	
Czechoslovakia	69.9	71.8	2.9*	4.2*	
Hungary	68.1	70.9	2.3*	3.2*	
Poland	67.0	71.8	3.5*	4.0*	
USSR	68.3	70.6	3.5*	3.2*	
Bulgaria	68.4	72.6	2.0*	3.2*	
Yugoslavia	62.9	72.6	3.2*	4.3*	
Portugal	63.3	74.0	0.8*	6.4	
Romania	65.5	70.8	2.0*	1.9*	
Sri Lanka	62.0	70.9	1.3*	1.7*	(1987)
Pakistan	43.1	57.7	0.3*	0.2*	(1987)
India	44.0	59.1	0.5*	0.9*	(1987)
				1.0**	(1991)
				3.8***	(1991)
Indonesia	41.2	61.5	0.3*	0.5*	(1987)
Colombia	56.6	68.8	1.1*	0.7*	(1987)
Bangladesh	39.6	51.8	—	0.6	(1987)
China	47.1	70.1	1.3*	1.4	(1987)

* Public expenditure only.

** Central, state and union territory governments' combined expenditure on medical, public health and family welfare as estimated by us.

*** Public and private sector agencies' expenditure as estimated by us.

Sources: 1. UNDP, *Human Development Report,* 1992, p. 189, pp. 134-35 and pp. 150-51.

2. *Ibid.,* 1990, pp. 148-49.

II starts off with the description of health care provision and financing by government and non-government agencies. Section III presents the review of health care financing in some of the efficiently managed countries, *e.g.*, Canada, Germany, and Japan among the developed countries and China among the less developed countries. Section IV outlines the alternative sources of health care financing in India. Section V discusses the scope for trying alternative sources of health care financing for cities. And finally, Section VI draws conclusions and raises issues for consideration.

II

HEALTH CARE PROVISION AND FINANCING IN INDIA

As of now, several agencies provide health care in India, *e.g.*, central government, state governments, union territory governments, local bodies, public enterprises (departmental and non-departmental), autonomous bodies (fully or partly) funded by government, insurance companies, private corporations, private hospitals, charitable hospitals, private dispensaries and clinics, physician consultants and native doctors such as *Vaids, Hakims, Naturophaths, Tantrics* and the like. The financial sources of each agency differ from the other (Table 3.2).

Government (central, state and union territory governments and local bodies) finances health care through taxes and other sources like non-tax revenues, fees received for the services rendered, grants and/or donations from international and domestic agencies, profits from public sector enterprises—departmental and non-departmental—it runs, and deficit financing. It is difficult to quantify the contribution of each source. By and large, taxes are the main source. Fees received for the services rendered to patients account for less than 5 per cent. It varies from state to state.

Public enterprises and autonomous organization funded by government (fully or partly) provide health care to all their employees and dependents of their employees through their own hospitals (if they have any) and through reimbursements of medical expenditure to a limited extent in certain cases and unlimited extent in some other cases against the submission of certified medical bills and prescriptions from unregistered private doctors. Similar is the case in respect of autonomous and semi-autonomous institutions. The sources of finance for these agencies are their own profits or budgetary support from government if they are not earning profits. In either case, their sources of finance are traceable to government.

TABLE 3.2: Health Care Providers and their Sources of Finance

	Health Care Providers	*Medium Through which Health Care is Provided*	*Receipts of Health Care*	*Sources of Finance*
	1	2	3	4
1.	Government: C.G. S.G. U.T.G. L.G.	1. Public hospitals. 2. Primary health centres.	All people subject to the availability of resources to rationing by queue	Taxes, non-tax revenues deficit financing , foreign aid capital receipts, gifts and fees for services rendered profits, grants from governments, gifts, fees for services rendered
2.	Public enterprises	Hospitals owned by them and reimbursement for treatment in private hospitals	Restricted to their employees	Profits, grants from governments, gifts, fees for services rendered
3.	Autonomous institutions fully or partially funded	Hospitals owned by them and reimbursement for treatment in private hospitals	Restricted to their employees	Profits, grants from governments, gifts, fees for services rendered
4.	Insurance companies a) Social insurance:			
	CGHS	CGHS clinics	Restricted to central government employees	Central government revenues and employees' contributions
	ESIS	ESIS hospitals	Restricted to workers of ESIS	Employee, employer and government contributions
	b) Private insurance	Public hospitals/ private hospitals/ physician consultants/private dispensaries	No restriction-open to all who can afford	
5.	Private corporations	Hospitals owned by them and reimbursements for treatment in private	Restricted to their employees	Profits, tax concession, grants from government, fees for the services rendered
6.	Charitable hospitals/research laboratories	Hospitals owned by individuals trusts/ philanthropers	No restriction-open to all who can afford	Contributions from philanthropists, fees for the services rendered

(*Contd.*)

TABLE 3.2 (*Contd.*)

	1	2	3	4
7.	Private hospitals	Owned hospitals by individuals/groups of individuals	No restriction-open to all who can afford	Fees for the services rendered
8.	Private dispensaries, clinics, nursing homes	Owned hospitals by individuals/groups of individuals	No restriction-open to all who can afford	Fees for the services rendered
9.	Physician consultants	Private hospitals and through their own consultancy clinics	No restriction-open to all who can afford	Fees for the services rendered
10.	Native doctors such as *Vaids, Hakims, Naturophaths, Tantrics,* etc.	Own clinics	No restriction-open to all who can afford	Fees for the services rendered
11.	Pharmaceutical companies/surgical equipment/manufact uring companies/ opthalmological equipment manufacturing companies, etc.	Medical stores and dispensing chemists/hospitals (private and public)	No restriction-open to all who can afford	Fees for the services or supply of goods in question

Insurance companies are another important category providing health care; some are of government and others are of private. The examples of the former are Central Government Health Scheme (CGHS) and Employees State Insurance Scheme (ESIS) which, for all practical purposes, are government funded. In fact, expenditures on these agencies are met from respective government revenues only. But there is a difference in the sense that there are contributions from employees to the scheme. A little elaboration of these schemes may be useful.

The CGHS provides Comprehensive medical care to Central government employees based at Delhi and nineteen other cities, in addition to three peripheral towns of Delhi, *i.e.,* Gurgaon, Faridabad and Ghaziabad. The scheme also covers certain other specified sections of population like employees of autonomous organizations, retired Central government employees, MPs, ex-MPs, ex-Governors, retired Judges of Supreme Court and High Courts, freedom fighters and members of their family and members of public in fourteen specified areas in Delhi. The facilities under the scheme include free medical care provided through the network of allopathic dispensaries as well as ayuverdic, homeopathic, unani, siddha dispensaries/units and supply of medicines, laboratory and X-ray investigations, domiciliary visits, emergency treatment, ante-natal care, confinement and post-natal care, advice on family welfare, specialist consultation and hospitalization facilities in government hospitals as well as in hospitals recognized under CGHS. The scheme covered 3.95 million Central government employees and other entitled persons in 1991-92.[1] The rate of contribution is extremely low.

The ESIS, slightly different from the CGHS, is a kind of social security scheme in which risks are pooled, resources are pooled, and relief made available to the insured worker as and when needed. "It provides for sickness, medical care, maternity and employment injury benefits. All factories, other than seasonal factories and establishments in the notified centres, are included in the notified class of establishments in which ten or more employees are employed and in any part of which a manufacturing process is being carried on with the aid of power or is ordinarily so carried on or in which twenty or more employees are employed and in any part of which a manufacturing process is being carried on without the aid of power or were working on any day in the last twelve months are covered under this Act and scheme. But mines under Mines Act, 1952 or railway running-shed are not covered. Shops, hotels, restaurants, cinemas including preview theatres, road motor transport and newspaper establishments employing twenty or more persons have been covered.[2] Employees of covered factories and establishments in receipt of wages not exceeding Rs. 3,000 per month are covered.[3] The scheme is financed by contributions from employers and employees. The employers contribute 4 per cent of the wage payable to the coverable employees and the employees contribute at the rate of 1.5 per cent of their wages. The employees, who are in receipt of average daily wages up to Rs. 15 per day, are not required to contribute; the employers, however, contribute their share in respect of such employees also. The state governments contribute a minimum of 12.5 per cent of the expenditure on medical care. As of 1991-92, a total number of 6.5 million persons were insured and Rs. 2,409 million were spent on their medical care by states. It means that an amount of Rs. 370.41 per head was spent on medical benefit which was several times more than what the insured employees must have contributed to the scheme.

Private corporations and numerous private companies also provide health care to their employees and dependents of their employees, depending on the contractual arrangement they enter into with them. The health facilities may sometimes far exceed the facilities provided in public sector enterprises. How much on the whole is spent by them is difficult to know. Approximately, it can be around 9 per cent of the emoluments of the employees.

Private hospitals are the largest category nowadays, providing health care; they range from small hospitals to super speciality hospitals and sometimes comparable to those in developed countries; for example, Apollo Hospitals in Madras and Hyderabad; CDR, Medinova, and Medwin Hospitals in Hyderabad; and Escorts, Batra, Gangaram, St Stephen, Tirath Ram, B.L. Kapur Memorial, Khera, Mohinder, Aashlok and Jaipur Golden Hospitals in Delhi.

The private hospitals finance health care through fee-for-service, and in some cases through grants from governments, subsidies from governments and aid from international agencies and pharmaceutical companies. There is no set pattern of financing for them. The pattern differs from hospital to hospital. But by and large, fee-for-service is the principal source of finance.

Private dispensaries, clinics, nursing homes, physician consultants, native doctors and pharmaceutical companies are another category providing health care. They finance health care through fee-for-service and very rarely free of cost to poor people.

Charitable hospitals provide health care to numerous persons— free of cost to certain sections of the society, concessional or full cost to some others. They are supposed to work on no profit-no loss basis. But rarely, they work like that as expansion and technical improvement have to be carried on for their survival. The sources of finance for all these hospitals/institutions are: (a) charity from philanthropists, (b) grants from government, and (c) donations from international and domestic agencies.

Except for government (for which budgetary data are available), no reliable information is available on financing health care for non-government agencies. Some guestimates and some estimates have been made from time to time, but they add very little to our knowledge on health care financing. According to an estimate, 44.17 per cent of health care expenditure in the country is funded by public sector (*i.e.*, central government, state governments, union territory governments, local bodies, public enterprises/quasi-governments) and the rest, 55.83 per cent, is financed by private sector.[4]

III

HEALTH CARE FINANCING IN SELECTED COUNTRIES

While it is true that health care financing is largely based on fee-for-service, and 56 per cent of health care expenditure is met by non-government agencies, it must be interesting to know what actually are the practices in Canada, Germany, Japan and China whose health care provisions and financing have been acclaimed for efficiency and equity. Perhaps a reflection on their practices may help devise appropriate policies for our country.

Canada

According to Prof. William C. Hsiao of Harvard University, the Canadian system scores the highest marks from the point of universal coverage, equal access, cost control, efficient use of resources, equity in financing, consumer choice, and innovation. The German and Japanese systems of health score the next highest marks.[5]

In Canada, all residents are fully insured for all necessary hospital and medical services. Access is universal and complete, in the sense that there are no financing barriers to care. Hospitals, with very rare exceptions, are not for profit, and are run by community boards with ownership by charitable municipal or religious organization. Physicians are rarely employed by hospitals and gain access to hospital facilities through the granting of privileges. "As in the US physicians practise privately and are paid on a fee-for-service basis. Provincial fee schedule deletermines the price for each service and physicians are not allowed to bill patients directly for changes in exceses of these prices. There are no public subsidies for private care at least in the hospital and medical sector. Briefly speaking, Canada has *socialized insurance* superimposed on private delivery system.[6] About 76 per cent of health care expenditure in Canada is funded by public and shared between federal and provincial governments. In respect of physician and hospital services public funding goes beyond 90 per cent. The relative shares of federal government and provincial governments for important services may be seen from Table 3.3.

TABLE 3.3: Statistical Break Down of Federal and Provincial Funding in Canada

	Federal	*Provincial*	*Total Public*
Hospital and others institutions	1.7	84.1	88.4
Physician	0.6	92.5	94.3
Dentists	1.9	10.9	13.5
Drugs and appliances	0.6	21.9	23.0
All other	11.2	57.3	76.3
Total	3.1	70.1	75.9

Source : R.G. Evans, *The Canadian Health Care System : A King's Fund Interrogatory*, The University of Britannia, Columbia, March 1989.

Germany

According to Siegfriend Eichhorn, health care system in Germany consists of all the institution and persons which are supposed to promote, support and restore the health of the population. Because the system is a vital component of the society's infrastructure, it is primarily financed by public funds. The government is responsible for seeing that medical services are offered to the entire population on as equal terms as possible. Even so, the state left the provision of all kinds of medical care to private initiative and to voluntary and non-profit self-help organization; it only acts as offerer of medical services in cases where voluntary self-help and private initiative will not be sufficient.[7]

In Germany, there is a variety of private doctors and other health personnel, hospitals as well as other medical institutions, which are supported either by local authorities or by different voluntary associations. Moreover, there are many professional organizations—the general medical councils, the dentist's and pharmaceutical societies, and a number of professional associations for other health personnel—that supply medical services, as well as numerous societies for the promotion to certain areas of social health care.

> "Social sickness insurance is the cornerstone of the German health care system. The sickness insurance is based upon compulsory insurance. All who are employed, have been employed (retired persons), are trained for employment, or are unemployed, are compulsorily and automatically insured. Manual workers are insured irrespective of the size of the wage packet, but non-manual workers are insured only if their salary is below a certain amount; however, employees whose salaries exceed this limit are entitled to continue their insurance voluntarily. Nearly 93 per cent of the population enjoys the benefit of the 'sickness funds' 5 to 6 per cent (soldiers, prisoners and receivers of national assistance for example) have other legal rights for health services; the remaining 1 to 2 per cent are privately insured."

An interesting feature of the German health care system is that doctors in private practice are paid by the physicians' organization and not by patients directly. Physicians in private practice must join an association of sickness funds physicians.

Japan

Japan's system of health is somewhat complex in terms of organization and financing. One of the reasons for such a complexity was its continuous search for better health care system to its people. The last time it made major amendments to its system was when it adopted German health care system as its model in 1961 and revised its National Health Insurance Law. This revision provided universal coverage.

According to Masami Hashimoto[8] medical services are supported, for the most part, by health insurance. The health insurance programmes in the country fall into two categories; (i) health insurance for employees and their dependents, and (ii) the national insurance programme for others. The format category is subdivided into several programmes. One is the government managed health insurance, which is established for each specific type of large enterprise through a special insurance society for the employees of the enterprise. There are also insurance programmes for specific groups of workers.

The national health insurance programmes for the citizens are managed by the primary local authorities (cities, towns and villages) throughout the country. These programmes also include specific national health insurance associations that are organized exclusively for a profession or a trade. Table 3.4 shows the coverage of social health insurance scheme as of March 1979.

In regard to finance and contributions, "health insurance is supported by local governments. As a rule, the premium of the employee's health insurance is shared on a 50-50 basis by employee and employer, and the amount is determined by multiplying the wage of the insured by a fixed rate. In the government managed health insurance, the rate was raised to 8 per cent standard remuneration in February 1978. The rate of the association managed health insurance varies among association but is generally low as compared to the government managed health insurance."

As in 1979, percentage contribution of funds to national medical expenditure by government, social health insurance and direct patients' pay was 12.6 per cent,75.8 per cent and 11.5 per cent, respectively. Of the 75.8 per cent of social health insurance, employees insurance was 45.5 per cent, national health insurance was 28 per cent and other was 2.5 per cent.

TABLE 3.4 : Coverage of Social Insurance by Programmes in Japan as on 31st, March 1979

	Per Cent
I. Employers' insurance	61.3
Government managed health insurance	25.9
Society managed health insurance	23.5
Day labour health insurance	0.5
Seaman's health insurance	0.6
Mutual aid association	11.1
II. National health insurance	38.7
Total	100.00

Source: Hashimoto Masami "Health Services in Japan" in Raffel, Marshall. W (ed.), *Comparative Health Systems*. The Dennsylvania State University Press, University Park and London, 1989.

China

Even though China is a socialist country, its health care system is "less socialized than that of Canada."

According to Teh-Wei-Hu,[9] there are three types of health care insurance coverage in China: (i) public expenses medical insurance, (ii) labour medical insurance, and (iii) co-operative medical services. Public expenses medical insurance covers the medical expenses of the state cadres and the students are fully covered without any contribution from them to the insurance premium. About 2 per cent of population is covered by this insurance plan excluding family dependents. Insurance coverage includes visits to clinics and cost incurred during hospitalization, although hospital meal costs are excluded. Labour medical insurance covers workers as staff members in factories and state-owned firms. This is funded by factory employer's contribution— about 2 to 3 per cent of the total factory income before salaries are distributed to workers. About 10 to 12 per cent of population is covered by this insurance fund including the dependents of the factory workers. These people are located primarily in urban areas. It should be noticed however, that this type of insurance provides 100 per cent coverage only for the workers themselves, and not their dependents who must pay about 50 per cent of their medical expenses under this system. The co-operative medical services are intended for rural agricultural areas. The main forces for establishing the co-operative medical services are poor and lower middle class peasants. Participation is voluntary—in the early years of service commune members had the option of joining the system; in recent years the decision is made at the commune level. Once a commune decides to join, everyone on the commune must participate.

There are no free medical services or unlimited amounts of medical services in China. Hospital charges vary according to the location of the hospital and types of illness.

IV

ALTERNATIVE SOURCES OF FINANCING HEALTH CARE IN INDIA

As noted in Section II, the Government in India is the single biggest provider of health care accounting for 44 per cent of total health care expenditure (34 per cent by the central, state and union territory governments and 10 per cent by local governments and quasi-governments). It can supply more health care, provided additional resources are raised. The usual sources of government to raise resources are taxes, and all other sources, receipts from which are charged to the Consolidated Fund of India. To what extent these usual sources are exploitable depends upon the politico-economic conditions. As of now, there exist persistent deficit in the central, state and union territory governments with poor scope for additional taxation, and keen competition from other services (like education, housing, environment, infrastructure) for additional allocation of resources. Under such circumstances, it is difficult to expect much from usual sources. In order to raise resources, new avenues have to be found out. The following are some of the new avenues that may be tried.

1. levying new taxes;
2. adopting new methods like lotteries;
3. granting amnesties for those who want to convert blackmoney into white;
4. appealing philanthropists for liberal donations;
5. improving efficiency of resources used in health sector as well as in other sectors and thereby save some resources and put the same to provide additional health care;
6. cutting down wasteful and non-productive expenditure;
7. recovering the costs by levying user charges for the services provided;
8. introduction of insurance—compulsory or voluntary;
9. promoting self-help organization in local communities; and
10. getting more aid from foreign countries.

Alternative 1 may take the form of levying cess on sales tax for medical (as was done in certain provinces of Canada) or earmarking a particular percentage of taxes levied and spending locally for health care (as was done in Senegal) or imposing a special new tax on agricultural products at the point of marketing earmarked for the improvement of rural health services (as was done in Brazil).[10]

Alternatives 2 to 4 are wellknown and self-explanatory.

Alternative 5 is not a new one. It has been in force in one form or the other ever since long term fiscal policy was announced in 1985 by V.P. Singh, the then Finance Minister of India, and subsequently pursued through zero base budgeting and economy measures by the finance ministers who succeeded him.

Alternative 6 again is not new. it has been talked about throughout 1980s and is even now. Its success is not known.

Similarly, alternative 7 has been in the air, and efforts have been made to recover costs from the general wards and special wards in almost all the public hospitals.

Alternative 8 has not yet been tested, although voluntary insurance is already in force and several well-off sections have already been availing of it.

Alternative 9 has not yet been tried and needs speical consideration.

Alternative 10 is beset with a number of political strings attached. It may burden future generations.

More alternatives are possible. But, which of them are the most suitable is a big question. Detailed investigations into the feasibility of each of the alternatives are needed. Pending such investigations, for which considerable time and resources are required, we should concentrate on alternative sources of health care financing for cities only. Three reasons prompt us to do so:

(i) Cities form a separate entity by themselves with their peculiar problems of congestion. filth, unhygienic conditions, slums, fast growth of population, exposure to contagious diseases, pollution, etc.

(ii) Cities have the potential of rising up to the occasion, with its vast network of professional associations, welfare organizations, voluntary associations and well staffed local bodies.

(iii) Cities by and large, have been neglected presuming that their proximity of public and private hospitals would help solve the problem. That is why, perhaps it has been mentioned in the Eighth Plan document that "health status of urban slums is as much bad as, if not worse than, in rural areas; infrastructure for primary health care hardly exists."[11] Moreover, cities are getting more and more crowded with more and more slums coming up. According to the Planning Commission, 40 to 50 per cent of urban population is slum population. Therefore, any neglect of slum population may affect rest of the society adversely and badly. No civilized society can brush it aside. Already there exists more than 17 per cent of untreated sickness in urban areas due to non-availability of medical facility, long waiting, financial difficulties and other reasons.[12]

V

ALTERNATIVE SOURCES OF FINANCING HEALTH CARE IN INDIAN CITIES

Although most of the alternatives suggested above apply for the country as a whole and for the cities in the country, a few of them deserve implementation in metro cities like Delhi, Bombay, Calcutta, Madras, Hyderabad, Ahmedabad and Bangalore on an experimental basis. They are:

1. social insurance;
2. earmarked taxes at the local bodies level;
3. reprioritization of health care financing;
4. promotion of non-profit self help organizations;
5. cost recovery in hospitals and medical education; and
6. multi-pronged approach.

Social Insurance

It is an irony that when majority of people are groaning under poverty, unemployment, filth, sickness, and lack of shelter, a few privileged (3.9 million employees of central government under CGHS and 6.5 million employees under ESIS) are enjoying medical benefits at a negligible cost. It is iniquitous and uncivilized. It is high time to go in for social insurance—compulsory if possible—on the lines on which China and Japan have done. It may be recalled from Section III that China has had three types of insurance, and one of them was specially meant for workers or staff members in factories and state-owned firms. It was funded by factory employers through contributions. Similarly, in the case of cities in India, employers may be asked to deduct 2 per cent of the factory income before profits are distributed or wages are paid and the same may be sent to insurance company specially created. If this gets accepted, government will have to contribute its own share. Social insurance may be voluntary but the success of it cannot be ensured. For, public finance theory tells us that people have a tendency to undervalue the need for medical care.

Before opting for this alternative, all issues relating to social insurance have to be sorted out. Who should foot the medical bill? Who should fund capital costs? What should be the relationship between patient and doctor? Who should make the payment to doctor? How to counter moral hazard of doctors? Why not national insurance as in UK? Cannot we have the insurance partly by government and partly by beneficiaries? What should be the role of the state governments in social insurance? What should be the financial implications for Central government, state governments and local bodies? What would happen to the existing formal system? Should the insurance system be complementary to the existing system?

Earmarked Taxes at Local Bodies Level

As of now each city is being provided with civic amenities by the local bodies which, in turn, raise funds from taxes like property tax, octori, education cess, etc., and grants from state governments. Local authorities responsibility to provide health care is onc of their obligatory functions and they have special obligation to people who cannot provide health care for themselves. To augment their own resources, a specific tax— health care tax— may be completely earmarked for health care. If they do not want to take responsibility for providing health care to people, the proceeds from specific tax may be handed over to health insurance fund/corporation as their contribution.

A cess on one of the existing taxes like property tax, octori, entertainment tax, and profession tax, may also be levied and the proceeds from it may be spent on health care. But the point is, earmarking of the funds of a specific tax may invite competition from other social sectors, *e.g.* education, housing, poverty alleviation, employment guarantee, and power supply, pressing for similar taxes to be levied. Therefore, quite a few issues arise and have to be sorted out?

Can the levy of specific tax for health care be practicable? What would be its implications for local bodies? Would it be politically acceptable? Cannot the levy be made by state governments and its proceeds be distributed among cities for the purpose? Above all, should these funds be supplementary or complementary? These issues need close examination.

Reprioritization of Resource Allocation

Another alternative source of financing health care, not explored fully, is the savings that might arise on account of reprioritization. In order to do so, one should be convinced that the present priorities are not in the right direction. It seems allocation of resources is highly biased towards curative health care. According to a study made by us, 71 per cent of health care spending by governments (Central, State and Union territory governments combined) in urban areas in 1990-91 was allocated to curative service[13] and 24 per cent and 5 per cent were allocated to preventive[14] and others[15] respectively. This high bias towards curative services may be diluted by allocating more resources to preventive health care, which means better primary health care and sanitary conditions. But this assertion needs close examination. Perhaps a detailed discussion on the following issues may provide clues for it.

Does reduction of resources to curative services help improve health status? What is the empirical evidence on it? How do we define preventive health care? Should we not include services like water supply and sanitation, nutrition and child, and handicapped welfare in the preventive services? Empirical findings suggest that women's education has a strong positive influence on health status. Then, should we not look at preventive health care from a broader perspective?

Promotion of Non-Profit Self-Help Organizations

Sometimes help from government and employers may not be forthcoming for one reason or the other. In such cases self-help societies by patients themselves may go a long way in providing health care. Patients themselves may form a health co-operative and contribute by way of premium for recurrent expenditure on health care and capital expenditure may come from government. Experience of Germany, Japan and China in running such organizations and society managed health insurance programmes will be helpful. As noted earlier in Section III, different societies may be encouraged to come up for each type of profession, trade and occupation.

Financing by self help organizations is a kind of community financing. It is advocated for several valid reasons : (i) Households, as we all know, spend substantial amounts of money in purchasing health care from the private sector, both modern and traditional. According to an estimate made by us, about Rs. 81,820 million were spent on medical care by households in India in 1990-91. Assuming that a sizeable portion of it is spent by households in cities, it would be economical for households in cities to come together and finance health care, (ii) Resources (labour, land and contribution in kind) not exploited fully may be put to better use, (iii) Right type of priorities for resource allocation may be possible. But as against these some negative points also are there:

1. community financing may not promote equity;
2. resources cannot be raised on a sustained basis;
3. community financing may tend to favour the creation of those kinds of health facilities for which there is high local demand rather than meeting professionally perceived needs; and
4. a high degree of external support is needed to mobilize and sustain community efforts.

Assuming that positive points far outweigh the negative points, the following issues need be thrashed out: How do we define concept of self-help organization? What should be the mode of contribution to the organization or community? Should not the finances come from other sources? How to ensure efficiency of community? How to tackle equity aspects? Does the community financing displace funds or does it supplement the aggregate resources available for health care? Would it be successful in the present political context?[17]

Cost Recovery in Hospitals and Education

It is wellknown that medical facilities in public hospitals are underpriced to better-off sections. Recently, policy analysts of the World Bank who visited India hinted partial or full recovery of cost hospitals and education. To quote their own language; "Higher health budgets are essential, but spending should be targeted towards programmes with greater country wide health impacts. Without doubt, the result will be lower public spending on hospitals and medical education, two areas where the private returns are high and the social returns relatively low. However, these programmes lend themselves, for the very same reasons to cost recovery. Cuts in government support to them do not have to mean to cuts in budgets, because they have the ability to charges for their services. Sensible policy developments require that preparation (analytical, regulatory and legal) begin so that these facilities can start to generate revenues to cover at least a fraction of their operating costs."[18] I am afraid that such a recovery of cost in hospitals may be extremely difficult politically. Partial recovery is already in existence, *i.e.*, there are free wards, general paying wards and special paying wards in public hospitals. Free wards are generally meant for poor people. According to the NSS (42nd round), in 1986-87, about 55 per cent of the hospitalized cases in urban areas are treated in free wards, 32 per cent and 13 per cent of in paying general wards and paying special respectively.[19] Had the facilities been so cheap as they have been made out, percentage of cases treated in the latter category must been much more. Nevertheless, it is an empirical question to be examined, hospitals by hospital, state by state, extent of subsidy enjoyed by the better off section, and additional revenue expected from the cost recovery.

There is ample justification for recovery of cost from medical education. The presence of high capitation fee in private medical colleges, in spite of the Supreme Court verdict, is a clear indication that there is scope for doubling up of the fee for medical education. Here again, under the present dispensation of scholarships and concessions to socially and economically backward classes, doubling of the fee may be a problem. In short, mobilization of resources through cost recovery is a slow process and much depends upon the political will of the party in power.

However, it must be noted that without proper investigation into the possibilities raising resources through cost recovery methods, it is premature to presume large inflows of receipts to the exchequer. Cost recovery methods have to be viewed in socio-political context. The following issues merit attention in this context. Are the public hospitals underpricing their services? Are government medical colleges subsidizing the rich? What should be the optimum fee structure for medical colleges? Should not the medical education and research be entrusted to private sector? What should happen to equity objective, if cost recovery principle is implemented? Are there no ways for reducing operating costs, except through the hike in the rates charged for the services in hospitals?

Multipronged Approach

There are quite a few other alternative sources of financing health care in cities. They are; (a) licencing policies (*e.g.*, location of health facilities, practice of health provider, regulation of fees for service, approval of drugs for the market); (b) giving loans or subsidies or financial support to community health programmes; (c) saving money by increasing efficiency and improved co-ordination (*e.g.*, delegation of certain routine tasks to personnel with less training, development of less elaborate hospitals, replacing inpatient care by ambulatory care, cheaper home care, day-care and self-care using traditional methods in constructing health buildings, bringing proper co-ordination between hospitals run by different levels of government—Central, State, Local and military—and improving administration and management of hospitals by proper training; (d) instituting revolving funds for health care; and (e) encouraging *yoga* and proper dissemination of information on the cleanliness, etc.

Now, given the above alternative and complementarity of resources for financing health care, a consensus has to emerge, particularly regarding which alternatives are most feasible and what permutations and combinations have to take place. It may be noted that a mere identification of alternative sources is not sufficient; organizational structure, delivery system, rate of contributions, centre-state and state-local government linkages in funding have got to be worked out before any alternative systems of financing health care is commended.

SUMMARY AND CONCLUSION

To sum up, during the past forty-seven years, health status in India has improved, but in comparison to other countries—notably China, Indonesia and Sri Lanka—it is not impressive. Reasons are not transparent as to why such slow progress has been there.

Assuming that lack of enough financial resources is one of the important reasons, a search has been made to find out alternative sources of financing health care in India. Before doing so, health care provision and health care financing as they exist today are reviewed. It has been found that government is the single biggest provider and financier of health care in India. The share of government (Central, State and Union territory governments combined) is 34 per cent, of local bodies and quasi-governments combined is 10 per cent, and of non-government agencies is 56 per cent in total health care expenditure.

It is interesting to know that there are several non-government agencies providing health care. Not paying attention to the increase in provision of health care by the government may compel the public to go to non-government agencies who are "notorious for profit-making and exploitation of patient's helplessness".

The practices prevailing in health care provision and health care financing in Canada, Germany and Japan among developed countries and in China among the less developed countries are worth going through. Insurance schemes that are practised by them are instructive.

There is no need to be panicky about the shortage of funds for health care in India, as it is not always necessary to depend upon traditional budgetary methods for raising resources. Several non-traditional alternatives may be thought of for the country in general and cities in particular.

As far as financing health care in cities is concerned, the following alternatives appear most suitable:

— social insurance;
— earmarked taxes at the local bodies level;
— reprioritization of health care financing;
— promotion of non-profit self-help organizations;
— cost recovery in hospitals and medical education;
— saving money by increasing efficiency and improved co-ordination;
— instituting revolving funds for health care; and
— effective use of licencing policies.

It is recommended that a mere identification of alternative sources of health care financing is not enough. It must be accompanied by an appropriate organizational system for delivery of health care, balanced combination of modern and traditional systems of medicine, dissemination of information on the importance of cleanliness in house, neighburhoods and public places and efficient civic administration.

NOTES

1. Government of India, Ministry of Health and Family Welfare, *Annual Report*, 1991-92, p.11.

2. Pardman Singh, *A Manual of Social Security in India*, AITUC Publication, p.83.
3. Employees State Insurance Corporation *Annual Report*, 1991-92 p.61.
4. K.N. Reddy, "Economic Foundations of Health Care; Issues in Resource Allocation and Resource Mobilization," Platinum Jubilee Conference Number, *Indian Economic Journal* February 19-21, 1994.
5. William C. Haiso, "What Lessons Can Less Developed Countries Learn from the Experiences of Developed Nations About a Comprehensive Health Financing Strategy", International Seminar on Comparative Financing Strategy in Selected Asian Nations, December 10-14, 1990 (mimeo) Table 6.
6. Jonathan Lomas, Catherine Fooks, Thoma Rice, Rebert I. Labelle, "Minding Our Ps and Qs: Simultaneous Control of the Price and Quantity of Physician Services in Canada," Centre for Health Economics and Policy Analysis McMaster University, Hamilton, Canada 1989 pp. 3 and 4 R.G. Evans, "The Canadian Health Care System: A King's Fund Interrogatory," The University of British Columbia, 1989, and R.G. Evans, "Accessible, Acceptable and Affordable; Financing Health Care in Canada," The University of British Columbia, 1990.
7. Siegfriend Eichhorn, "Health Services in the Federal Republic of Germany" in Marshall W. Raffel (ed.), *Comparative Health Systems*. The Pennsylvania State University Press, University Park and London, 1989, pp. 287-334.
8. See Masami Hashimoto, "Health Services in Japan" in Marashall W. Raffel, *op. cit,* pp. 335-70.
9. Teh-Wei-Hu, "Health Services in the Peoples Republic of China" in Marshall W. Reffel (ed.), *op. cit.* pp. 141-46.
10. For elaborate discussion of these new types of taxes prevalent in different countries, see E.P. Mach. "The Financing of Health Systems in Developing Countries: Discussion Paper," *Social Sciences and Medicines*, Vol. 12, 1978, pp.3-11.
11. Government of India, Planning Commission, *Eighth Five Year Plan* (1992-97) Vol II, p. 323.
12. Government of India, National Sample Survey Organization, Sarvekshana, Vol. XV No. 4 April-June 1992, p. 75.
13. Largely includes medical relief ESIS, CGHS, medical education and training research and other systems of medicine. See K.N. Reddy and V. Selvaraju, *Health Care Expenditure by Government in India: 1974-75 to 1990-91* National Institute of Public Finance and Policy, New Delhi, 1993.
14. Largely includes prevention and control of diseases, prevention of food adulteration, drug control, family planning and maternity and child health.
15. Includes international co-operation, medical stores department, department of drugs, school health schemes, other health schemes and tribal areas training and health statistics, public health transport and laboratories and transport, etc.
16. See Note 4 above.
17. For detailed discussion of these and other related issues, see Brian Abel-Smith and Ajay Dua, "Community Financing in Developing Countries: The Potential for Health Sector," *Health Policy and Planning*, 3(2):95-108, Oxford University Press, 1998.
18. World Bank, "India Health Finance, Coping With Adjustment Opportunity for Reform," *Economic Times* April 5, 1993.
19. Government of India, National Sample Survey Organization, Department of Statistics, Ministry of Planning, *Sarvekshana*, Vol, XV, No. 4, April-June, 1992, p. 55.

4

Health Care Expenditure in India : Is It Low*?

—Prof. K.N. REDDY

Introduction

It is of common knowledge that India has achieved considerable progress in health status (in terms of life expectancy at birth and child mortality rate—the two most widely used indicators of health status), but in comparison to other countries, notably to those of developing countries, there is not much to be proud of. For example, during the past three decades—1960 to 1990—life expectancy at birth in India has increased by 23.40 per cent only (from 47 to 58 years) as against 60.46 per cent in China (from 43 to 69 years), 24.13 per cent in Sri Lanka (from 58 to 72 years), 30.76 per cent in Thailand (from 52 to 68 years), 32.08 per cent in Republic of Korea (from 53 to 72 years), 28.26 per cent in Indonesia (from 46 to 53 years) and 36.96 per cent in demographically developing group (from 46 to 63 years) and child mortality rate has decreased by 45.96 per cent in India (from 235 to 127) as against 79.52 per cent in China (from 210 to 43), 84.29 per cent in Sri Lanka (from 140 to 22) 75.84 per cent in the Thailand (from 149 to 36) 76.69 per cent in Republic of Korea (from 133 to 31), 48.13 per cent in Indonesia (from 214 to 111) and 53.10 per cent in demographically developing group (from 226 to 106)—*see* Table 4.1. Three reasons are usually attributed to these disparate achievements :

(i) The resources spent on health care in India are inadequate and comparatively low,
(ii) The structure and priorities of health care expenditure in India are far different from others, and

---

* Largely based on a study *Health Care Expenditure by Government of India* (1993) completed a few month ago. The views expressed here are personal.

(iii) The system of health care financing is far different and less efficient than others.

To test the validity of these reasons, empirical studies have to be conducted. An attempt is made here to test the validity of the first one, leaving aside the second and the third for the present.

TABLE 4.1 : Health Status Indicators for Selected Countries

	General Mortality life expectancy at birth		*Percentage increase in 1990 over 1960*	*Median age at death 1990*	*Child Mortality Rate*		*Percentage decrease 1990 over 1960 child mortality*
	1960	1990			1960	1990	
Sub-Sahara Africa	43	52	20.93	5	251	175	30.28
India	47	58	23.40	37	235	127	45.96
China	43	69	60.46	64	210	43	79.52
Other Asia Islands	50	62	24.00	12	182	97	46.70
Sri Lanka	58	72	24.13	73	140	22	84.29
Philippines	59	64	8.47	49	103	62	39.81
Thailand	52	68	30.76	71	149	36	75.84
Malaysia	58	72	22.41	63	106	20	81.13
Korean Republic	53	70	32.08	71	133	31	76.69
Indonesia	46	59	28.26	47	214	111	48.13
Latin America and the Caribbean	54	70	29.63	55	161	60	62.73
Middle Eastern countries	44	61	38.64	24	242	111	54.13
Formerly Socialist Economics of Europe (FSE)	66	72	09.09	72	68	22	67.65
Established Market Economics (EME)	70	76	08.57	75	36	11	69.44
FSE and EME	69	75	08.70	74	46	15	67.39
Demographically Developing group	46	63	36.96	39	226	106	53.10
World	53	65	22.64	35	195	96	50.77

Source : World Bank Development Report 1993, pp. 200-01.

The first task in this endeavour is to estimate the volume of expenditure on health care in the country and the second task is to examine weather India is spending lower than what other countries are spending. Let us take up the first one and describe the methodology by which it is estimated.

Estimate of Expenditure on Health Care-Methodology

As of now several agencies are spending on health care in India. They fall broadly into categories : (i) Government and its agencies, and (ii) Non-Government agencies quite often called as public sector and private sector respectively. The former consists of the Central Government, the State and the Union Territory Governments, the local bodies which are constitutionally responsible for health care and innumerable number of enterprises, institutions and autonomous bodies which are under the control of governments or answerable to Parliament. The non-government agencies consist of private households, charitable hospitals/institution, private sector enterprises and institutions.

Government and its Agencies (Public Sector)

The Central Government : The Central Government—the apex layer in a federal set up on India—lays down health policies for the whole country, spends substantial sums on its own on health care through the Ministry of Health and Family Welfare and other Ministries and transfers considerable sums to the States and the Union Territories for health care. The Ministry of Health and Family Welfare is responsible for implementation of a number of programmes of national importance like family welfare, primary health care, prevention and control of major diseases, etc. It has several centrally sponsored schemes which are implemented through the states. At the same time, it has also central sector schemes.

The Ministry of Health and Family Welfare organisationally, consists of (i) the Departments of Health, and (ii) the Department of Family Welfare, each of which is headed by a Secretary to the Government of India. The Department of Family Welfare operates vertical structures and meets the requirements of the programme. The Department of Health deals with medical and public health matters including drugs control and prevention of food adulteration and functions through the Directorate of Government of Health Services—an attache office—which renders technical advice on all medical and public matters and in the implementation and monitoring of various health schemes. It may be noted that expenditure on medical; public health and family welfare is incurred not only by the Ministry of Health and Family Welfare but also by other Ministries—Railways, Defence, Communications, Energy and Labour—and Union Territory governments without legislature, namely, Andaman and Nicobar Island, Chandigarh, Dadra and Nagar Haveli, Daman and Diu, Delhi and Lakshadweep—whole demands for grants are presented under the Ministry of Home Affairs.

In estimating the expenditure on health care, the Detailed Demand for Grants of the Department of the Health is needed, which contains information on health care under the following heads:

(i) Secretariat, social services;
(ii) Council of Ministers;
(iii) Medical and Public Health;
(iv) Grants-in-aid to State governments;
(v) Grants-in-aid to Union Territory governments;
(vi) Aid materials and equipments on Revenue Account;
(vii) Capital outlay on medical and public health;
(viii) Loans for medical and public health; and
(ix) Loans and advances to State Governments on capital account.

The sum total of these 9 major heads constitute gross expenditure of the Department of Health under the Ministry of Health. But, a part of that gross expenditure, though shown in the Demand of the Department of Health, is financed by other Ministries such as Defence, Railway, etc., and as such the former (Department of Health) gets reimbursed that part of expenditure from the latter as recoveries. So, when recoveries from other Departments are accounted for, net expenditure (or actual expenditure) of the Department of Health is arrived at.

However, neither the expenditure of the Department of Health represents the total expenditure on health nor recoveries of the Department of Health represent the total Ministries/Departments of Health. The amount of the recoveries is not only included in the gross demand of the Department of Health, but is also reflected in the expenditures of other Ministries/Departments. So to avoid double counting of the amount of recoveries, while adding the expenditures of other Ministries to that of the Department of Health (*i.e.,* the amount of recoveries has been deducted from the gross expenditure of the Department of Health and arrived at net expenditure. One important reason for deducting the recoveries from the gross expenditure of the

Department of Health is that, other Ministries/Departments spend much more than what they reimburse to the Ministry of Health and Family Welfare. By taking the full amount of expenditure on health of other Ministries and adding it to net expenditure of the Department of Health, health expenditures are reflected truly; otherwise they would have been understated/overstated. While adding the gross expenditure of the other Ministries to the net expenditures of the Department of Health, expenditures on Revenue Account only have been taken into account (as they are available). It was not possible to take into account as it was part and parcel of overall capital expenditure of that Ministry. However, it would have been extremely negligible even if it had been possible to do so.

Then to obtain total Central government expenditure on health, expenditure on health of the two entries — *i.e.* (1) Net (or actual) expenditure of the Department of Health/Ministry of Health and Family Welfare, and (2) Gross expenditures of other Ministries/Departments — have been added.

In the *Department of Family Welfare* unlike in the case of Department of Health (where net expenditures was taken) gross expenditure has been taken into account. The reason is that the whole of expenditure on family welfare in other Ministries is shown under the demand for grants of the Department of Family Welfare. That is the recoveries, if any received by the Department of Family Welfare from other Ministries are equal to the expenditure of the latter.

State Governments : Under the Indian Constitution, health sanitation, hospitals and dispensaries are in the state list. Naturally their responsibility for health care of the people is much more than that of Central government. The delivery system is roughly the same as that in Central government. The Department of Health and Family Welfare of the State government is assisted by the Directorate of Health Services headed by a director. Within the directorate, the organized structure varies from state to state. In most cases, the district level administration functions directly under the state health and family welfare department. However, in some states, the district administration is linked to the state through a set up at the divisional level headed by Additional/Joint Directors as in the case of Madhya Pradesh, Uttar Pradesh, Bihar and so on.

The State and Union Territory Governments have separate budgets, and their expenditures on medical and public health and family welfare, have to be separately shown for meaningful analysis.

Hence, data for these have been collected separately using the same methodology as adopted for the Central government.

Aggregation of the Central, the State and the Union Territory Governments' Expenditures : To obtain the combined total health expenditure, expenditures of all the three governments have been added. Due care has been exercised in adding them up to avoid double counting, for, transfers do take place from the Centre to the States and the Union Territories in the form of grants-in-aid and loans and advances. These grants and loans, although financed by the Central government, are really put to use by the States and the Union Territory governments and as such are reflected in the expenditures of the latter governments. Therefore, while combining the Central, the State and the Union Territory governments' expenditure on health (*i.e.* total expenditure on Medical Public Health and Family Welfare), expenditures on grants-in-aid to the State governments, grants-in-aid to the Union Territory governments, and loans and advances to the State governments of the Central government have been deducted from the total expenditure.

Local Bodies : Under the Constitution of India, local bodies are autonomous and have been assigned their own revenues and functions. They incur expenditure on health care since public health, the sanitation is the obligatory function. It is interesting to know that in metropolises and in other larger cities, local bodies run hospitals and dispensaries on their own. In the States of Andhra Pradesh, Gujarat, Maharashtra, Tamil Nadu, Uttar Pardesh and Delhi, a seizable number of hospitals are run by local bodies. The hospitals and dispensaries run by these organizations are similar to those of the State government. These provide medical facilities to the general population which include free consultation, free clinical tests and free medicines that are available with them. But information about health expenditure of local bodies is very scanty and not easily available and whatever collected by some individual scholars and institutions (National Institute of Urban Affairs) is either old or derived from some other estimates. After careful consideration based on our own experience with local bodies in Karantaka and elsewhere, data available from the Statistical Abstract of India have been used to estimate expenditure on health care in local bodies. The following is adopted for estimation.

At first, the data on health expenditure of the 30 major local bodies —Hyderabad, Patna, Ahmedabad, Baroda, Surat, Shimla, Bangalore, Hubli—Dharwar, Calicut, Cochin, Trivandrum, Bhopal, Gwalior, Indore, Jabalpur, Raipur, Ujjain, Bombay, Nagpur, Pune, Sholapur, Madras,

Agra, Allahabad, Kanpur, Lucknow, Varanasi, Calcutta, Chandranagore and Delhi, available from the Statistical Absract of India 1989, has been taken as given. Then using the growth rate of preceding 10 years, data have been adjusted or updated for all the 30 corporations. For the rest the municipalities, it has been assumed, that per capita health expenditure (in them) has been similar to that of the municipal corporation/municipalities whose population has been 1 lakh and above but below 30 lakhs. Next, per capita expenditure of these municipal corporations/municipalities have been multiplied by the respective populations of cities and town to arrive at aggregate expenditure of major corporations and municipalities and added the same to the expenditures of mega municipal corporations of Bombay, Calcutta, Delhi, Madras, Hyderabad, Bangalore and Ahmedabad. In regard to the small municipalities and Panchayats, whose populations are below 1 lakh, it has been assumed that the per capita expenditure on health must have been at least one-third of the per capita expenditure of the municipal corporations/municipalities whose populations are between 1 lakh and 30 lakhs and multiplied it by the relevant population. Next, expenditures of all the three types of corporations — (i) corporations; (ii) major corporations/municipalities; and (iii) small municipalities have been added to arrive at total health expenditure of local bodies.

Public Sector Enterprises/Institutions : Corporations in public sector engaged in manufacturing and service activities spend substantial amounts on the health of their employees and their family members—by providing medical facilities through their own hospitals. In major public sector projects, a town or a township is created through the location of a public sector undertaking and quality of hospital services tend to be quite satisfactory. Certain numbers of non-employees population in these townships and their surrounding area also get served by these facilities. Facilities created at Dhanbad for Coal India Ltd., at Korba for National Thermal Power Corporation (NTPC), at Bhııai for Steel Authority of India and at Piplani for Bharat Heavy Electricals Ltd. (BHEL) are some important examples. In other cases, where the employees with the undertakings constitute only a small fraction of the town population arrangements are made with the State governments. For the employees of small undertakings that do not have their own dispensaries/hospitals, medical facilities are provided through reimbursements. But information about how much they are spending is not just available.

In the absence of information, we have assumed that per capita health expenditure in public sector enterprises may be on par with the per capita health expenditure of Central government employees under C.G.H.S. This assumption seems to be reasonable since the level of reimbursements must have been worked out on the basis of some norm by the government for their employees in Administrative Departments. If at all there is any deviation, the expenditures on health care by the enterprises/institutions would more than what the employees in Administrative Departments must be getting through C.G.H.S. on per capita basis.

Non-Government Agencies (Private Sector)

Household : Households spend considerable sums on health care over and above the free services they get from government hospitals and institutions. How much each household, and how much all households together in the country, under private consumer expenditure, spend on health and medicine is difficult to estimate, afresh without conducting a survey. It costs time and resources heavily. Hence, data available from national accounts statistics, published by the central statistical organisation, Government of India have been used.

Charitable Institutions and Private Hospitals : Apart from households, quite a few private hospitals and charitable institutions also spend on health care. But, not all of them free of cost. A major part of the cost is recovered through appropriate pricing—that is by charging no fee to the poor and lower income groups, normal fee to middle income groups and slightly more than normal fee to upper middle and high income groups. In these hospitals, we come across free wards, 'paying general wards' and 'paying special wards' as are found in government hospitals for in-patients. It amounts to double counting, if the entire amount spent by them on providing health care is taken into account. We have therefore included only that portion of money that is devoted to free provision of health care, and excluded the remaining as the latter has reflected already in the private consumer expenditure of households on health care. Unfortunately, no reliable data on them are available. As a crude approximation, we have estimated it on the basis of N.S.S.O.'s data for 1986-87 (42nd round) and published in Sarvekishana, April- June,1992 (Department of Statistics, Ministry of Planning, Government of India) and adjusted for inflation, using All India Consumer Price Index.

Private Sector Companies : Large private companies—for example Modis, Tatas, Jyoti and Alembic — provide medical facilities to their employees through a network of a hospitals/ clinics. They offer certain facilities to non-employees also. Similarly, smaller companies also provide medical facilities through their hospitals/dispensaries for their employees and family members. But most of them are provided either through reimbursement of medical expenses, or through fixed medical allowances. The problem here is, no information is available on the amounts they spend or reimburse to their employees. On enquiry from various organisations, it has been understood that they spend about one month's salary of the employees on health care. Hence, we have assumed accordingly.

Volume of Health Care Expenditure

The estimates volume of expenditure devoted to health care is presented in Table 4.2 by government and non-government agencies—item-wise for 1990-91. It can be seen that government (public sector) is the single largest provider of health care (44.17 per cent) and within this, the state government contributed the major share (62.44 per cent), followed by the local bodies (21.96 per cent), the Central government (11.84 per cent) and public sector enterprises (1.49 per cent). Within the non-government agencies, households bear the brunt of healthcare expenditure (83.97 per cent), followed by private companies (15.41 per cent) and private institutions (0.61 per cent). And as a per cent of GNP (at factor cost) health care expenditure by public sector was 1.65 per cent and by private sector was 2.09 per cent and by both public and private sectors was 3.75 per cent.

It may be noted that this estimate of health care expenditure is at variance with other estimate, the reason being that (a) definition of health care adopted and (b) the coverage of expenditure under as well as private sectors are different. As for example, in a study completed by us (*Reddy, K.N.* and *V.Selvaraju* (1993) a few months ago, health care expenditure in government was defined to include expenditure on (1) medical and public health (2) family welfare (3) nutrition (4) water supply and sanitation and (5) child and handicapped welfare cutting across several Ministries/ Departments to be 2.18 per cent of GDP in 1990-91[4], Ravi Duggal (1986) covering public and private sectors, but including expenditure on nutrition and family welfare in public sectors, estimated to be 8.33 per cent of GDP in 1983-84. FRCH (1987) covering public and private sectors but excluding nutrition, water supply and sanitation and other non-health Ministry programmes in government estimated to 2.9 per cent of GDP in 1982-83 I.I.M.(1987) covering public and private sectors, but including nutrition, water supply and sanitation, other non-health Ministry programmes and local government spending in government estimated to be 5.1 per cent of GDP in 1984-85 combined World Bank studies, Ravishankar and Subbarao (1989) covering public and private sectors but excluding spending by local government and including expenditure on nutrition, medical, public health, family welfare, water supply and sanitation estimated to be 3.1 per cent of GDP in 1986-87. The World Bank (1993) covering public and private sectors, but excluding water supply and sanitation, and other non-health Ministry programmes and including outlays for prevention, promotion rehabilitation and care, population activities, nutrition activities, programme food aid, and emergency aid specifically for health in government, estimated to be 6.0 per cent of GDP in 1990 (Table 4.2). The point is, the definition used here and items included in it, refer to be expenditure relating to medical, public health and family welfare only, which by and large, are of the same nature at various levels of government and in various public and private sector institutions. Further a kind of consistency is followed here in the type of items covered in public and private sectors, which I am afraid others have done so, therefore, the estimate made by us appear more reliable than others and relevant for policy purposes.

TABLE 4.2 : Comparative Statement of our Estimates and other estimates on Resources Devoted to Health Care in India

Sector/Agency	*Our Estimates This estimates*	*earlier estimates*	*I.I.M.*	*FRCH Annual Average for Sixth Plan*	*Duggal*	*Ravi-Shankar and Subbarao*	*World Bank*
	(90-91)	*(90-91)*	*(90-91)*	*Period (82-83)*	*(83-84)*	*(86-87)*	*(90)*
	(1)	(2)	(3)	(4)	(5)	(6)	(7)
I. **Public Sector**							
1. Central government	91306	160570	69400	255560	191050	49100	--
2. State government	481302	836340	201670				
3. Union territory government	17474	33210	NA	NA	NA	NA	--
4. Local government	169300	NA	58160	NA	84910	NA	--

(*Contd.*)

	(1)	(2)	(3)	(4)	(5)	(6)	(7)
5. Public sector enterprises/ quasi-governments	11468	NA	NA	NA	NA	NA	—
Total Public Sectors (1+2+3+4+5)	770850	1030130	329230	255560	275960	521900	—
II. **Private Sector**							
1. Households	818200	—	529120	229580	989050	380400	—
2. Charitable institutions and private hospitals	5971	—	29160	NA	327700	NA	—
3. Private sector companies	150190	—	NA	NA	NA	NA	—
Total Private Sector (1+2+3)	974361	—	558280	229850	1361750	380400	—
III. **Public and Private Sector** (I+II)	1733795	—	887510	485140	1637710	902300	—
IV. **As Percentage of GDP/GNP**							
Public sector	1.61	2.18	1.58	1.61	1.48	2.01	1.30
Public sector	2.09	—	2.68	1.45	7.32	1.46	4.70
Public and Private sectors combined	3.75	2.18	4.26	3.05	8.81	3.47	6.00

Sources : 1. Text of this paper 2. K.N. Raddy and V Selvaraju (1993), Health Care Expenditure Government in India, National Institute of Public Finance and Policy, New Delhi (mimeo). 3. IFM : Indian Institute of Management, Ahmedabad (1987), Study of Health Care Financing in India (Based on Care Studies in Maharashtra and West Bengal), Report submitted to Asian Development Bank, Manila. 4 FRCH : Foundation for Research in Community Health (1987), Health Status of the Indian People, A supplement to the ICSSR/ICMR Report Health for All : An Alternative Strategy, Bombay. 5. Duggal, R. (1986), "Health Expenditure in India", *FRCH Newsletter*, Vol. I. 6. Ravishankar, V. and K. Subbarao (1989), Combined World Bank Studies quoted by Peter Berman (1991), Health Economics, Health Financing and the Health Needs, Poor Women and Children in India, Ford Foundation, January New Delhi. 7. World Bank (1993), World Development Report, Oxford University Press, p. 210.

Is Health Care Expenditure Low?

The question is so to what extent this expenditure on health care (a) in the country (public and private sector combined) in general and (b) in public sector in particular is low, in comparison to other countries and more particularly to China, Sri Lanka, Indonesia, Philippines, Republic of Korea, whose health status (defined either in terms of life expectancy at birth or child mortality rate) was around, the same level as that of India about three decades ago. It can be seen (Table 4.3) that India on the whole (public sector and private sector combined) is spending 6 per cent or 3.75 per cent depending on the estimate one

TABLE 4.3 : Heath Care Expenditure in India (1990-91)

	Sector	*Volume (Rs. lakh)*	*Per cent share in total*
	A. Health Care Expenditure by Public Sector in India 1990-91		
1.	Central government[a]	91,306	11.84
2.	State governments[a]	4,81,302	62.44
3.	Union territories[a]	17,474	2.27
4.	Local bodies[b]	1,69,300	21.96
5.	Public enterprises/quasi-governments[b]	11,468	1.49
	Total[a]	7,70,850	100.00
	B. Health Care Expenditure by Private Sector in India 1990-91		
1.	Households[d]	8,18,200	83.97
2.	Charitable Institution and private hospitals	5,971	0.61
3.	Private companies[e]	1,50,190	15.41
	Total	9,74,361	100.00

C. Health Care Expenditure in India by Public and Private Sectors and as Percentage of GNP : 1990-91

		Volume (Rs. lakh)	*Per capita (Rs.)*	*Per cent share in total*	*As percentage of GN P at factor cost*
1.	Public sector	7,70,850	91.30	44.17	1.65
2.	Private sector	9,74,361	115.45	55.83	2.09
	Total	17,45,211	206.71	100.00	3.75

Notes :

a. Expenditures on medical public health and family welfare only (for methodology of estimation see the next).

b. For methodology see the text.

c. Expenditure by public enterprises is =
Number of employee in quasi-government organisations i.e. 61 lakh × Per capita expenditure in CGHS (Rs. 188) = Rs. 1,148 lakh

d. Expenditure by households is the private final consumption expenditure on medical care and health services published in NAS by CSO, 1992 p. 40.

e. Expenditure by charitable institutions, nursing homes and private hospitals is —
Number of parties treated (as in patients) in private hospitals nursing homes and hospitals run by charitable institutions in free wards × Total expenditure per treatment (*i.e.* payment to hospitals if any + other incidentals) for free ward service in private hospitals

For want of relevant information, the expenditure on outpatient treatments has not been included.

f. For the assumption made see the text.

would like to put faith—and is spending on par or higher than most of the developing countries in the World. Confining ourselves to public sector alone, it can be seen that India is devoting more resources than that of Indonesia, Sri Lanka, Philippines, Malaysia and Thailand in terms of percentage of GDP (Table 4.4).

TABLE 4.4 : Health Expenditure in Selected Countries : 1990

	Per capita Health expenditure (official exchange rate dollars)		*Health expenditure as percentage of GDP*		
			Public Sector	*Private Sector*	*Total*
	1990		*1990*	*1990*	*1990*
Sub-Saharan Africa	US$	24	2.5	2.0	4.5
India	"	21	1.3	4.7	6.0
			(1.65)	(2.09)	(3.75)
China	"	11	2.1	1.4	3.5
Other Asia Islands	"	61	1.8	2.7	4.5
Sri Lanka	"	18	1.8	1.9	3.7
Philippines	"	14	1.0	1.0	2.0
Thailand	"	73	1.1	3.9	5.0
Malaysia	"	67	1.3	1.7	3.0
Korean Republic	"	377	2.7	3.9	6.6
Indonesia	"	12	0.7	1.3	2.0
Latin America and the Caribbean	"	105	2.4	1.6	4.0
Middle Eastern Countries	"	77	2.4	1.7	4.1
Formerly Socialist Economies of Europe (ESE)	"	142	2.5	1.0	3.6
Established Market Economies (FME)	"	1,860	5.6	3.5	9.2
FSE and EME	"	1,340	5.4	3.4	8.7
Demographically Developing group	"	41	2.3	2.5	4.7
World	"	323	4.9	3.2	8.0

Note : Figures within brackets are the estimates made by us.

Public Sector Expenditures include government health expenditure parastatal expenditure foreign aid, making the figures comparable with those for OECD countries. Private Sector expenditures for countries other than OECD members are based on household surveys carried out by the ILO and other sources, supplemented by information from United Nations National Accounts, World Bank Studies, and other studies prescribed in the scientific literature (World Bank, pp. 197-98).

"Health expenditure includes" outlays for prevention promotion, rehabilitation and care; population activities, nutation activities; Programme food aid; and emergency aid specifically for health. It does not include water and sanitation. Per capita expenditure are based on World Bank mid year population estimate.

Source : World Bank : World Development Report 1993, p. 200-201.

Therefore, answer to the question that whether India's expenditure on health care is low is self-explanatory. The reasons for its poor performance, in health status allocation. There could be in fact several reasons, for example (a) priorities in allocation of resources to different categories of expenditure by government such as preventive, curative / clinical and administration at the functional category level and current (wages and salaries and good and services) and capital expenditure at the economic categories level; (b) levels of literacy, nutrition, per capita income, water supply and sanitation; (c) extent of urbanization; and (d) role of non-economic factors, like religious beliefs, superstitions, and administrative inefficiency. According to a study made by us, per capita income and expenditure on health care (taken independently) has very little influences. This finding corroborates with the findings for other developing countries.

Summary and Conclusions

It has been seen that although India achieved considerable progress in health status, in comparison to other countries in Asia, its progress is not much to be proud of. Of the several reasons adduced for such a poor progress, inadequate or low amount of resources devoted to health care has been an important one. But to verify whether low amount of resource allocation was indeed the reason, estimate on the volume of resources devoted to health care has been made.

After careful examination of the methodologies followed by earlier studies on what constitutes health care expenditure, estimate has been made on expenditure in (a) public sectors, (b) private sectors, and (c) in the country as a whole. It has been found that (a) public and private sectors together had spent 3.75 per cent of GDP in 1990-91. Of this, the share of private sector (households, charitable and private hospitals and private enterprise hospitals) constituted about 56 per cent and the rest progress, inadequate or low amount of resources devoted to health care has been important one. But to verify whether low amount of resource allocation was indeed the reason, estimate on the volume of resources devoted to health care has been made. (44 per cent) accounted by public sector (*i.e.,* the Central, the State, the Union Territory and the Local governments and the public sector enterprises). An interesting aspect of this estimate is that the share of public sector turned out to be much higher than what others have estimated so far.

The allegation adduced for slow progress in India's health status seems to be incorrect. India did spend as much as other developing countries spent, and in fact more than what some developing countries in Asia — particularly China, Sri Lanka and Malaysia — had spent. The reason for poor progress in health status was not the lack of resources for health care, but something else. It could be inefficiency, misallocation of resources in the health sector, and misallocation of resources between health and other sectors. A detailed examination of resources allocation sector by sector, state by state may throw up clues for rectification.

NOTES

1. The number of years a person born in a given area would expect to live given the age specific mortality rates for the year.
2. Probability of dying by exact age 5.
3. Demogragraphically developing group includes the sub-Saharan Africa, India, China, other Asia and Islands, Latin America and the Caribbean and Middle Eastern Crescent regions.
4. For detailed description of the definition of health care and controversy surrounding it see K. N. Reddy and V. Selvaraju (1993).
5. See K. N. Reddy and V. Selvaraju (1993).

REFERENCES

Duggal, R. (1986a), *Political Economy and State Health Financing Radical Journal of Health*, Vol. I, No. 3, pp. 79-85.

Duggal, R. (1986b). *Health Expenditure of India*, FRCH Newsletter, Vol. I.

FRCH (1987), *Health Status of the Indian People*, A Supplement to the ICSSR/ICMR Report Health for All, An Alternative Streagy, Bombay.

Government of India, National Sample Survey Organisation, Department of Statistics, Ministry of Planning (1992), *Sarvekshana*, 51st Issue, Vol. XV, No. 4 April-June.

Indian Institute of Management (1987), Study of Health Care Financing in India, (Based on Case Studies in Maharashtra and West Bengal), Report Submitted to Asian Development Bank, Manila.

Ravishankar V. (1989), *India : Government Expenditure on Social Services 1976-77, 1986-87* (Background Paper for 1989 CEM), World Bank, New Delhi.

Reddy, K. N. and V. Selvaraju (1993), *Health Care Expenditure by Government in India*, National Institute of Public and Policy, New Delhi (mimeo).

Subba Rao, K. (1989), "Improving Nutrition in India—Policies and Programmes and Their Impact", World Bank Discussion Paper No. 49, World Bank Washington.

5

PATTERN OF FINANCING PRIMARY EDUCATION IN INDIA*

—Prof. K.N. REDDY

Introduction

The purpose of this paper is to analyse the pattern of financing primary education that includes, pre-primary, primary and middle school education in India by governments at the national and state levels. Under the Constitution of India, the primary education is the responsibility of the Government, more particularly of the State Governments. The Directive Principles of State Policy in the Constitution clearly mention that the "State shall endeavour to provide, within a period of ten years from the commencement of this Constitution, for free and compulsory education for all children until they complete the age of fourteen years" (Article 45) and "promote with special care the educational and economic interests of the weaker sections of the people, and in particular of the Scheduled Castes and the Scheduled Tribes and shall protect them from social injustice and all forms of exploitation; (Article 46). Unfortunately, as is wellknown, the Directive Principles of State Policy remain unfulfilled even after 44 years. It is feared that the Directives may still remain unfulfilled for many more years to come if proper direction is lacking. In the Eighth Plan document (1992-97) we are reminded that "India is away from the goal of universal enrolment and retention and to reach universalisation by 1997, an additional 5.61 crores children have to be enrolled." This is a tall order and the task of financing it is stupendous. Concerted efforts are needed to mobilise resources. Before attempting to think over mobilisation of resources, a

* Paper presented at the National Seminar on Financing Education for All held at the National Institute of Educational Planning and Administration New Delhi, September 5-7, 1994.

glance at the pattern of spending on primary education is warranted. In what follows, an attempt is made towards that end, based on available information.

Agencies Providing 'Primary' Education

Broadly speaking, primary education is provided (a) by government, and (b) non-government agencies. The former includes Central Government, State Governments, local bodies and their agencies, *e.g.*, public sector enterprises, autonomous bodies which get support directly or indirectly from general revenues of the budget. The non-government agencies include private schools, private sector industries, charitable institutions, philanthropists and external agencies outside the country. How much each of these agencies is providing for primary education is difficult to say, as little information is available on financing education by non-government agencies. It is presumed that the government is the principal fund-giver for primary education as the Constitution of India enjoins responsibility on it and huge sums are spent by the Central, the State and the Union Territory governments on the one hand and local bodies on the other. What is perhaps more relevant is the pattern of spending on primary education so that changes, if any, can be effected, through reprioritisation of resources.

Sources of Information

It may be noted that information on the pattern of spending at different levels of education is scanty, and whatever is available comes after a considerable time lag. One sources, usually referred to, is *A Hand Book of Educational Statistics* brought out by the Department of Education, Ministry of Human Resources Development, Government of India. It is a useful document, but the data it contains are pretty old and ignore the purposes for which the funds are spent. Another source of data is *Combined Finance and Revenue Accounts of Central and State Governments*, published annually, by the Comptroller and Auditor General of India. It provides information by the level of education and by the broad purposes, but suffers from the time lag, though not as much as the former. The latest year for which information on spending on education is available is for 1986-87; that is, nearly a lag of five years (assuming that actual can at best be available for 1991-92). The State and Union Territory budgets are more source of information. But, not much effort has been made to cull out information either by government or by specialised institutions in a comparable and consistent form. It would have been ideal had the Ministry of Human Resources Development itself taken up this task. While hoping that, some day, the ministry would wake up and realise its importance and disseminate information for dispassionate analysis, we shall make use of whatever data are available to us from the two sources cited above. The assumption is that the pattern of allocation of resources among different levels of education—elementary, secondary, pre-university, higher education, technical education, etc.—has not changed. It may be questioned on the ground that quite a few corrective steps have been taken during the seventh and the eighth plans. But, the reality is that the pattern does not change drastically in a period of just five years. If at all the pattern has changed, it must have changed marginally only, the reason being that commitments made for other levels of education cannot be brushed aside and have to be honoured somehow. Hence, the analysis of financing primary education—based on the aforesaid sources—in spite of time lag, it may be useful and provide guidance for policy making.

Pattern of Spending on Primary Education

Education may be broadly classified into eight categories: (1) Primary education; (2) Secondary education; (3) Special education; (4) Pre-university education; (5) University and higher education; (6) Technical education; (7) Sports and youth welfare; and (8) General. (It may be classified differently also depending on the purpose one has.) In our opinion, the above classification adopted by the Office of the Comptroller and Auditor General of India is fair and serves the purpose at hand.

As of 1986-87, true to the constitutional mandate, States financed 89.71 per cent of educational expenditure, while the Union and Union Territories together financed the rest. Both at the national level as well as at the states level, overriding priority was given to primary education. As of 1986-87, at the national level, primary education claimed 43.55 per cent of total education expenditure, while secondary education, university and higher education and technical education claimed 30.88 per cent, 13.37 per cent, and 5.59 per cent respectively (Table 5.1). The share of primary education came down from 46.41 per cent in 1974-75 to 43.55 per cent in 1986-87. At the state level too, primary education claimed a major share but declined from 50.06 per cent in 1974-75 to 47.42 per cent in 1986-87 (Table 5.2).

TABLE 5.1 : Relative Share of Expenditure by Major Categories at National Level for Selected Years

(Percentage)

	1974-75	*1979-80*	*1984-85*	*1985-86*	*1986-87*
Primary education	46.41	44.70	45.61	45.16	43.55
Secondary education	31.49	31.10	31.11	30.68	30.88
Special education	0.78	1.33	1.55	1.69	1.63
Pre-university education	0.42	1.35	1.50	1.55	1.57
University and higher education	12.90	14.24	13.70	13.14	13.37
Technical education	4.32	4.22	4.15	4.61	5.59
Sports and youth welfare	1.47	1.47	1.49	1.64	1.79
General	2.22	1.58	1.38	1.53	1.72
Total (1 to 8)	100.00	100.00	100.00	100.00	100.00

Source: See text.

As a percentage of GDP, resources devoted to education in the country increased from 2.10 per cent in 1974-75 to 2.98 per cent in 1986-87—a marginal increase. This phenomenon is contrary to the recognition given to the role of education in economic as well as in human development all over the world. It is of interest to know that the share of resources devoted to primary education increased very little—from 0.97 per cent of GDP in 1974-75 to 1.30 per cent in 1986-87 (Table 5.3). This being the case at the national level, what about the position at the states level? How wide are the differences among the states in their allocations to primary education? Are there any close associations between priorities accorded to primary education and literacy rates? What accounts for backwardness in literacy in some states? Is there any role for Union Government to minimise disparities in literacy between the states? What role did Planning and Finance Commissions play in improving literacy? What needs to be done by present (Tenth) Finance Commission? What steps are needed to achieve universalisation of elementary (primary) education by 2000 AD? Is it possible to make the Directive principles of state policy a matter of reality? A series of questions arise, but not all of them can be answered straight away.

There are wide disparities among the states, first, in the allocation of resources to education in general, and second, in the allocation of resources to primary education with which we are concerned. Barring the spécial category states of North-Eastern India, *e.g.*, Manipur, Meghalaya, Nagaland, Sikkim, which spent anywhere between 11 to 30 per cent of their SDPs, the major states spent 3 to 7 per cent of their SDPs on education in 1986-87. Among the major states, Kerala stood first,

TABLE 5.2 : Share of Primary Education in Total Expenditure on Education for Selected Years

(*Percentage*)

	1974-75	1979-80	1984-85	1985-86	1986-87
I. Union Government	6.25	6.41	7.13	5.66	5.63
II. Union Territories (Total)	38.35	45.56	45.26	43.41	42.30
Arunachal Pradesh	-	50.45	47.07	41.60	42.02
Goa, Daman & Diu	33.45	33.96	33.89	32.07	28.73
Mizoram	37.12	57.60	56.84	57.73	62.85
Pondicherry	49.40	50.17	49.91	47.00	42.00
III. States (Total)	50.06	48.16	49.14	48.94	47.42
Andhra Pradesh	42.71	43.65	48.88	45.86	45.56
Assam	48.50	51.23	61.29	58.14	60.01
Bihar	61.19	60.57	60.40	60.90	56.98
Gujarat	54.78	55.62	55.86	60.20	57.19
Haryana	40.20	37.07	39.37	38.77	38.64
Himachal Pradesh	48.31	49.48	57.50	36.54	37.06
Jammu & Kashmir	34.02	36.18	45.77	45.38	45.26
Karnataka	56.80	54.91	52.22	53.64	53.58
Kerala	57.70	55.34	51.70	50.76	51.21
Madhya Pradesh	50.50	46.96	46.79	45.74	46.30
Maharashtra	50.29	45.62	45.90	45.99	45.73
Manipur	57.89	48.42	46.29	48.40	25.98
Meghalaya	33.38	32.44	36.87	35.78	16.78
Nagaland	58.91	62.31	60.33	60.98	24.86
Orissa	44.53	38.43	42.25	40.47	40.90
Punjab	29.96	35.83	33.47	34.16	33.11
Rajasthan	56.58	55.22	52.98	53.06	52.94
Sikkim	-	30.59	17.49	26.27	10.47
Tamil Nadu	52.18	48.54	49.70	50.80	49.46
Tripura	39.94	37.26	35.79	41.73	39.73
Uttar Pradesh	55.79	47.15	50.77	49.05	51.54
West Bengal	41.54	40.95	40.39	39.79	36.30
Total (I + II + III)	46.41	44.70	45.61	45.16	43.55

Source: See text.

spending 7.33 per cent of its SDP on education, while Haryana and Punjab stood last, spending 2.93 per cent and 2.98 per cent of their SDPs respectively (Table 5.4). The so called BIMARU States—Bihar, Madhya Pradesh, Rajasthan and Uttar Pradesh, the proverbial low income states—spent higher percentages of their SDPs on education than the so called high income states (Punjab and Haryana) and as much as other middle income states, *e.g.,* Andhra Pradesh and Karnataka. The only exceptions are Kerala, Assam and Himachal Pradesh, which fall in middle income category, but yet spent relatively greater percentage shares of their SDPs on education. In regard to primary education also, the pattern is rightly the same (Table 5.4).

TABLE 5.3 : Expenditure on Education as Percentage of GDP by Major Categories at National Level for Selected Years

(*Percentage*)

	1974-75	*1979-80*	*1984-85*	*1985-86*	*1986-87*
Primary education	0.97	1.10	1.26	1.29	1.30
Secondary education	0.66	0.77	0.86	0.88	0.92
Special education	0.02	0.03	0.04	0.00	0.05
Pre-university education	0.01	0.03	0.04	0.04	0.05
University and higher education	0.27	0.35	0.36	0.38	0.40
Technical education	0.09	0.10	0.11	0.13	0.17
Sports and youth welfare	0.03	0.04	0.04	0.05	0.05
General	0.05	0.04	0.04	0.04	0.05
Total	2.10	2.46	2.76	2.86	2.98

Source: See text.

In terms of priorities accorded to different categories of education, the picture is different. As of 1986-87, Bihar, Uttar Pradesh, and Rajasthan allocated a little more than 50 per cent of educational expenditure to primary education, that is, they allocated as much as Kerala, Tamil Nadu, Karnataka, Maharashtra, Gujarat and West Bengal (Table 5.3). The irony is that their literacy levels have no relationship with expenditures made on primary education (Table 5.5).

It is interesting to note that some states, *e.g.,* Punjab, Haryana; West Bengal, Andhra Pradesh, Karnataka, Orissa, Madhya Pradesh, Maharashtra and Gujarat, accorded relatively low priority to primary education in spite of their relatively higher fiscal capacity and lower level of literacy. Therefore, would it not be relevant for the Union Government or the Planning and Finance Commission to earmark resources for primary education while transferring resources to the states? It is apparent that it was not the availability or otherwise of resources for education *per se* that was responsible for persistent illiteracy in these states, it was possibly on account of priorities accorded by them to different categories of education. Also, it is apparent that in spite of allocating higher percentage of resources to

TABLE 5.4: Expenditure on Education (Total) and Primary Education as Percentage of Net States Domestic Project by Major Categories at States' Level for Selected Years

States	*1974-75*		*1979-80*		*1984-85*		*1985-86*		*1986-87*	
	Total Education Expendr.	*Primary Education*	*Total Education Expendr.*	*Primary Education*	*Total Education Expendr.*	*Primary Education*	*Total Education Expendr.*	*Primary Education*	*Total Education Expendr.*	*Primary Education*
Andhra Pradesh	1.97	0.84	3.05	1.33	3.93	1.84	3.93	1.81	4.20	1.91
Assam	3.21	1.56	4.33	2.22	3.86	2.36	4.23	2.46	5.10	3.06
Bihar	2.15	1.32	3.24	1.96	0.39	0.23	4.42	2.69	4.66	2.65
Gujarat	2.44	1.34	2.73	1.52	3.50	1.95	3.91	2.35	4.32	2.47
Haryana	2.18	0.88	2.29	0.85	2.81	1.11	2.68	1.04	2.94	1.13
H.P.	5.08	2.45	6.13	3.03	6.57	3.78	6.24	2.28	7.15	2.65
J & K	4.15	1.41	4.57	1.65	4.32	1.98	4.49	2.04	5.02	2.27
Keranaka	2.57	1.46	3.02	1.66	3.14	1.64	3.45	1.85	4.18	2.24
Kerala	4.95	2.85	5.84	3.23	5.62	2.91	6.32	3.21	7.33	3.75
Madhya Pradesh	2.43	1.23	3.21	1.51	3.50	1.64	3.47	1.59	3.56	1.65
Maharashtra	2.19	1.10	2.60	1.19	2.97	1.36	2.97	1.37	3.54	1.62
Manipur	6.67	3.86	8.77	4.25	9.61	4.45	10.33	5.00	20.27	5.27
Meghalaya	-	-	4.90	1.59	5.84	2.15	6.24	2.23	14.86	2.49
Nagaland	8.82	5.20	9.20	5.73	9.57	5.78	11.12	6.78	30.07	7.48
Orissa	2.77	1.23	3.86	1.48	3.68	1.55	3.35	1.36	4.23	1.73
Punjab	2.30	0.69	2.39	0.86	2.86	0.96	2.80	0.96	2.98	0.99
Rajasthan	2.68	1.52	3.71	2.05	4.12	2.18	4.23	2.24	4.84	2.52
Sikkim	-	-	-	-	14.44	2.53	9.95	2.62	28.23	2.96
Tamil Nadu	3.10	1.63	3.26	1.58	3.61	1.79	4.04	2.05	4.38	2.17
Tripura	5.49	2.19	6.40	2.38	8.14	2.91	8.12	3.29	10.49	4.17
Uttar Pradesh	2.37	1.32	2.64	1.24	3.08	1.57	3.15	1.54	3.50	1.80
West Bengal	1.99	0.83	2.84	1.16	3.08	1.24	3.37	1.34	4.31	1.57

Source : See text.

primary education, the literacy levels in Bihar, Uttar Pradesh, Rajasthan, did not pick up much. It appears that inefficiency in the utilisation of resources must have been an important reason for such a sorry state of affairs. It is rumoured and has even appeared in the press that there had been considerable number of ghost schools and ghost teachers in some states. Another reason perhaps may be the imaginary belief that their low levels of literacy would depress their human development indicator (quite often taken into account in transfers), and thereby entitle them for larger transfers from the Centre through Finance Commissions awards.

TABLE 5.5 : Male and Female Literacy by States: 1981 and 1991

(per cent)

States	*Total*		*Male*		*Female*	
	1981	*1991*	*1981*	*1991*	*1981*	*1991*
Andhra Pradesh	35.66	45.11	46.83	56.24	24.16	33.71
Assam	—	53.42	—	62.34	—	43.70
Bihar	32.03	38.54	46.58	52.63	16.51	23.10
Gujarat	62.21	60.91	65.14	72.54	38.46	48.50
Haryana	43.85	55.33	58.49	67.85	26.89	40.94
Himachal Pradesh	51.17	63.54	64.27	74.57	37.72	52.46
Karnataka	46.20	55.98	58.72	67.25	33.16	44.34
Kerala	81.56	90.59	87.74	94.45	75.65	86.93
Madhya Pradesh	34.22	43.45	48.41	57.43	18.99	28.39
Maharashtra	55.83	63.05	69.66	74.84	41.01	50.51
Manipur	49.61	60.96	64.12	72.98	34.61	48.64
Meghalaya	42.02	48.26	46.62	51.57	37.15	44.78
Nagaland	50.20	61.30	58.52	66.09	40.28	55.72
Orissa	40.96	48.55	56.45	62.37	25.14	34.40
Punjab	48.12	57.14	55.52	63.68	39.64	49.72
Rajasthan	30.09	38.81	44.76	55.07	13.99	20.84
Sikkim	41.57	56.53	52.98	64.34	27.35	47.23
Tamil Nadu	54.38	63.72	68.05	74.88	40.43	52.29
Tripura	50.10	60.39	61.49	70.08	38.01	50.01
Uttar Pradesh	33.33	41.71	47.43	55.35	17.18	26.02
West Bengal	48.64	57.72	59.93	67.24	30.07	47.15
All India*	43.56	52.11	56.37	63.86	29.75	39.42

Note : * Excludes Union Territories.
Source: Registrar General of India, Census Reports.

Further, there are inappropriate allocations as between direction and administration on the one hand and government primary schools, non-government primary schools, local bodies schools, teacher training, minimum needs programme, tribal areas sub-plan and other items on the other. As of 1986-87 at the national level, 34 per cent of expenditure on primary education went to government schools while

24 per cent, 28 per cent and 21 per cent went to non-government schools, local bodies schools, and direction, administration and inspection respectively. Inter-state differences in these allocations are substantial. For example, of the total government expenditure on primary education Bihar spent about 2.5 per cent under these heads—direction and administration (0.02 per cent) and inspection (2.41 per cent) while Maharashtra and West Bengal spent less than 2 per cent of their expenditures on the same items (Table 5.6).

Suggestions for Transfer of Resources

In the light of not-so-good experience of the states regarding allocation of resources to primary education and the consequent effect on literacy, should not the Union Government take on itself the responsibility of financing primary education and monitor the same through the local bodies? This may be relevant at present, when decentralization is being effected through the 73rd and 74th Constitutional Amendments. Criticisms cannot be ruled out for this approach, but they have to be surmounted somehow. Vested interests have crept in continuing the *status quo*, and resources are allegedly being diverted to some other purposes. Primary education should be made the fundamental right of the people and it must become the obligation of the Union Government to fulfill it. For, illiteracy is a drag on the human and economic development and even a danger to the polity of the nation. Meeting basic needs—primary education, preventive and essential health care and allegation of poverty—should become the responsibility of the Union Government. If needed, a constitutional amendment should be thought of in transferring these functions to the Union Government from the State Governments. Perhaps even that may not be needed as the 42nd amendment to the Constitution (1976) has already placed education under Concurrent List. In our opinion, basic needs cannot be left to the State Governments as not all of them have matured enough to take a long term view and have a tendency to fritter away their limited resources on populist schemes. Moreover, their fiscal capacities are not uniform. And as long as their fiscal capacities are unequal, differences in their levels of literacy and other amenities would persist. The argument, quite often advanced, that citizens of all states, irrespective of their geographical locations, should have equal access to basic needs gains more support as the years pass by. The questions asked are—Why should a citizen of one state or region enjoy poor access to basic needs in comparison to other states or regions when the same

TABLE 5.6: Expenditure Pattern of Government on Primary Education : 1986-87

	Direction and Admn.	*Inspection*	*Govt. Primary School*	*Assistance to Non-govt. Primary Schools*	*Assistance to Local Bodies for Primary Education*	*Teacher Training*	*Minimum Needs Programme*	*Tribal Areas Sub-plan*	*Other Expendr.*	*Transfer to & from Reserved Funds & Deposit Account*	*Total*
1	2	3	4	5	6	7	8	9	10	11	12
A. Union Govt.	0.00	0.00	25.98	0.45	71.02	0.89	0.00	0.67	0.98	0.00	100.00
B. UTs	0.00	1.45	72.97	1.16	3.27	4.20	0.00	0.00	16.95	0.00	100.00
Arunachal Pradesh	0.00	0.00	97.04	0.00	0.00	0.00	0.00	0.00	2.96	0.00	100.00
Goa, Daman & Diu.	0.00	3.10	93.33	0.38	0.00	0.38	0.00	0.100	2.82	0.00	100.00
Mizoram	0.00	1.90	38.87	2.08	8.75	11.01	0.00	0.00	37.38	0.00	100.00
Pondicherry	0.00	0.00	89.83	1.44	0.00	0.00	0.00	0.00	8.73	0.00	100.00
C. States	0.31	1.58	33.73	24.28	28.15	1.13	1.67	1.24	7.57	0.36	100.00
Andhra Pradesh	0.31	1.65	4.31	6.78	82.14	0.44	0.00	0.27	4.12	0.00	100.00
Assam	0.40	2.15	47.53	33.66	9.90	3.42	0.00	2.82	0.12	0.00	100.00
Bihar	0.02	2.41	92.02	2.15	0.00	0.80	0.59	0.90	1.11	0.00	100.00
Gujarat	0.00	0.52	0.00	0.05	76.36	0.91	0.00	6.04	11.76	4.36	100.00
Haryana	3.06	0.00	95.03	1.14	0.03	0.00	0.00	0.00	0.73	0.00	100.00
Himachal Pradesh	0.61	3.51	78.41	0.03	0.00	0.52	11.44	5.49	0.00	0.00	100.00
Jammu & Kashmir	0.00	4.71	89.68	2.79	0.00	0.17	0.00	0.66	0.00	0.00	100.00
Karnataka	0.00	1.94	83.64	10.26	0.44	1.20	0.00	0.01	2.51	0.00	100.00
Kerala	0.00	3.36	35.96	55.12	0.00	0.03	4.85	0.00	0.68	0.00	100.00
Madhya Pradesh	2.74	1.51	86.68	3.17	0.14	3.99	0.00	1.75	0.03	0.00	100.00
Maharashtra	0.03	1.82	0.00	0.07	95.88	1.13	0.00	0.39	0.68	0.00	100.00

(Contd.)

TABLE 5.6 (*Contd.*)

1	2	3	4	5	6	7	8	9	10	11	12
Manipur	1.81	2.02	66.95	12.64	13.70	1.51	0.00	0.00	1.36	0.00	100.00
Meghalaya	0.00	0.82	0.47	8.32	85.11	5.28	0.00	0.00	0.00	0.00	100.00
Nagaland	0.00	0.00	94.52	0.22	0.00	0.77	4.48	0.00	0.00	0.00	100.00
Orissa	0.00	0.00	5.23	80.80	3.35	0.00	0.00	10.62	0.00	0.00	100.00
Punjab	0.00	1.69	97.10	0.82	0.23	0.00	0.00	0.00	0.16	0.00	100.00
Rajasthan	0.00	0.00	60.34	2.31	33.08	0.02	0.00	4.25	0.00	0.00	100.00
Sikkim	0.00	0.00	100.00	0.00	0.00	0.00	0.00	0.00	0.00	0.00	100.00
Tamil Nadu	0.00	0.00	1.87	28.46	3.56	0.42	0.00	0.00	65.70	0.00	100.00
Tripura	0.00	5.30	88.71	2.87	0.00	1.73	0.00	0.00	1.39	0.00	100.00
Uttar Pradesh	0.41	1.68	0.44	90.73	0.00	2.12	2.47	0.00	2.16	0.00	100.00
West Bengal	0.00	1.33	0.05	49.79	30.193	0.34	12.75	0.44	4.37	0.00	100.00
Total (A+B+C)	0.31	1.56	34.11	23.71	28.36	1.17	1.63	1.21	7.60	0.35	100.00

Source: Combined Finance and Revenue Accounts of the Union and State Governments, 1986-87, pp. 298-309.

citizens are asked to sacrifice equally for the nation? Are not the citizens, wherever they stay, entitled for a minimum level of social services? Would it not amount to double standards, for the preservation of sovereignty and for federal polity of the country?

Concluding Observations

Both at the national level as well as at the state level, primary education was given top priority by the government. But over a period of time (for which comparable data are available), its share in total expenditure on education declined from 46.41 per cent in 1974-75 to 43.55 per cent in 1986-87 at national level while at the State level it declined from 50.06 per cent in 1974-75 to 47.42 per cent in 1986-87.

Among the states also, the share of primary education in total expenditure on education in most of the states went down except in Andhra Pradesh, Assam, Gujarat, Jammu and Kashmir and Punjab where it went up from 42.71 per cent, 48.50 per cent, 54.78 per cent, 34.02 per cent and 29.96 per cent respectively in 1974-75 to 45.56 per cent, 60.01 per cent, 57.19 per cent, 45.26 per cent and 33.11 per cent respectively in 1986-87. The interesting feature is that, in the same period, in Bihar it went down from 61.19 per cent to 56.98 per cent, in Madhya Pradesh, from 50.50 per cent to 46.30 per cent, in Rajasthan, from 56.58 per cent to 52.94 per cent, in Orissa, from 44.53 per cent to 40.90 per cent, and in Uttar Pradesh, from 55.79 per cent to 51.54 per cent in spite of their low levels of literacy. In the years thereafter also (from 1986-87), the situation appears to have been more or less the same.

The point is that the so called backward/poor states have shown no different priorities as that of better off states (in terms of literacy). One may ask how-much of the states' resources of education should go to primary education. Should it be 40 per cent, 50 per cent, 60 per cent, 70 per cent, 80 per cent? There is no set norm at present. In fact, it is difficult to be exact about it, as the quantum of resources to primary education would depend upon the resources available to education sector on the one hand and the total resources available to the government on the other. Again, the issue is not that simple. Look at Table 5.7. On an average, the states had allocated one-fifth of their budgets to education sector, leaving four-fifth to the rest of the sectors, *e.g.,* medical and public health, housing, labour, agriculture, industry, general administration, etc. What is important is whether states have been utilising the, resources efficiently? Whether share to primary education should be raised to 70 per cent leaving other categories of education to private sector for further development? Indepth studies on these issues are called for.

TABLE 5.7: Share of Expenditure on Education in Total Expenditure on Revenue Account. 1992-93.

State	*Expenditure on Education (Rs. in lakh)*	*Total Expenditure (Rs. in lakh)*	*Expenditure on Education as Percentage of Total Expenditure*
Andhra Pradesh	1,14,978	6,45,156	17.82
Arunachal Pradesh	4,742	28.753	16.49
Assam	55,990	2,14,810	26,06
Bihar	1,27,295	5,73,869	22.18
Goa	7,496	33,175	22.60
Gujarat	1,06,806	5,23,820	20.39
Haryana	36,348	2,27,402	15.98
Himachal Pradesh	19,918	98,256	20.27
Jammu & Kashmir	22,384	1,52,140	14.71
Karnataka	96,139	4,95,412	19.40
Kerala	83,592	3,21,645	25.99
Madhya Pradesh	1,01,210	5,42,082	18.67
Maharashtra	2,09,699	10,04,872	20.87
Manipur	10,302	37,750	27.29
Meghalaya	7,179	36,805	19.51
Mizoram	5,301	32,107	16.51
Nagaland	5,289	48.880	10.81
Orissa	54,848	2,63,502	20.82
Punjab	56,857	4,19,671	13.54
Rajasthan	88,046	4,08,023	21.58
Sikkim	2,637	15,509	17.00
Tamil Nadu	1,45,415	8,67,952	16.75
Tripura	11,750	54,765	21.46
Uttar Pradesh	2,01,190	10,39,920	19.35
West Bengal	1,32,279	5,32,369	24.85
All States	17,07,690	86,18,645	19.81

Source: Reserve Bank of India—"Finance of State Governments, 1993-94", in *Reserve Bank of India Bullein*, February, 1994.

6

SOCIAL SECURITY FOR THE ELDERLY IN INDIA
Need for Reform

—Prof. K.N. REDDY

Need for Reform

In the past, thanks to the joint family system that existed, this problem was not of such concern. Now, the joint family system has almost gone, and with that, problems for the elderly have surfaced and are likely to increase further unless timely actions are taken by all concerned.

Basically, problems of the elderly (60 years and above) in India are four: (1) income security; (2) health care security; (3) personal (physical) security; and (4) social and emotional security. The last one is personal and has to be tackled through socio-cultural dynamics and hence left out of our purview. We shall confine ourselves to the first- three only here and discuss them in seriatim. Before doing so, a word about the number of elderly is warranted as it helps size up the magnitude of the problem and financial implications of it, if any, for the government.

As of 1991, there are 60 million elderly persons, of whom 7 million are in the organised sector (employees in public and private sector) and the rest, 53 million are in the unorganised sector. According to an estimate, the number of elderly is likely to reach 80 million by 2001 A.D. and 120 million by 2031 — thanks to the increase in life expectancy at birth and decrease in birth rate[1] (*see* Table 6.1 and 6.2). For those who retire from organised sector (Government and non-government sectors), there are some income security arrangements. Those who retire from government service, get pension and other retirement benefits, death-*cum*-retirement gratuity (DCRG), encashment of earned leave and facility to commute a portion of pension. Those who retire from non-government, or those from the government but opt for contributory provident fund (CPF) scheme, get CPF accumulations and cash equivalent of earned income. For those who retire from unorganised sector (largely workers in rural areas and others in urban areas), no retirement benefits are there. The only requirement benefits, to my knowledge, are those extended to poor and destitutes under "old age pension schemes" by some State govern-ments.[2] But benefits under such schemes are extremely small, not exceeding Rs. 100 per month, and that too, subject to the means test.

TABLE 6.1: Selected Social Indicators of Development 1950-51 to 1996-97

Item	*1950-51*	*1960-61*	*1970-71*	*1980-81*	*1990-91*	*1991-92*	*1996-97*
1. Population (million)	361.1	439.2	548.2	683.3	861.4	862.4	941.37
2. Annual exponential population growth rate	1.25	1.96	2.20	2.22	2.14	1.91	1.78
3. Sex ratio (number of females per 1000 males)	946	941	931	934	927	—	—
4. Urban population as % of total population	17.3	18.0	19.9	23.3	25.7	26.0	28.3
5 General fertility rate (live births per 1000 women of child bearing age)	—	201.0	192.0	154.0	140.9	130.3	113.0
6. Birth rate (number per thousand)	41.7	41.2	36.9	33.9	29.5	29.0	25.7
7. Death rate (number per thousand)	22.8	19.0	14.9	12.5	9.8	10.0	8.7
8. Infant mortality (per thousand live births)	182.5	135.1	129.0	110.0	80.0	79.0	68.0
9. Life expectancy at birth (overall years)	32.1	41.3	45.6	54.4	59.9	58.2	60.6
10. Total labour force (million)	140.0	188.7	230.4	270.8*	314.9	328.9	364.3
a) Rural	—	—	192.5	215.1*	249.3	—	—
b) Urban	—	—	38.0	55.6	65.6	—	—
11. Labour force proportion (per cent of total labour force) Total	—	—	67.3	71.5	71.0	—	—
a) Rural	—	—	83.5	79.4	79.2	—	—
b) Urban	—	—	16.5	20.6	20.8	—	—
12. Unemployment rates (per 1000 labour force)	—	—	—	—	—	—	—
a) Rural	—	—	—	—	13.0	20.0	—
b) Urban	—	—	—	—	45.0	30.0	—

* Refers to the year 1979-80.

TABLE 6.2 : Trends in the Growth of Elderly Population and Working Population : 1971 to 2031

Year	*Elderly population (60 years and above) (million)*	*Working population (20-59 years) (million)*	*Elderly population as percentage of working population (per cent)*
1971	32.8	236.9	0.138
1981	44.5	303.5	0.147
1991	59.7	384.3	0.155
2001	78.8	479.3	0.164
2011	87.1	500.3	0.174
2021	96.6	523.6	0.184
2031	119.1	569.3	0.209

Source : Estimated on the basis of Data available from Government of India, *Health Information of India,* 1992 and Data Compiled by E.P.W. Research Foundation, May 14, 1994.

So, a vast majority of elders, belonging to unorganised sector and particularly those belonging to lower middle income, middle income, upper middle income classes are exposed to misery. Some of the reasons for this situation are (1) break down of joint family system; (2) low level of income and custom dictated family responsibilities; (3) fatalistic philosophy. Many of the elders in this sector continue to work, until their last breath or enter the army of caste wars and politics or pray for their early exit from the world. Their conditions are pitiable. The so called obligations enjoined on the states in the Constitution, remained untouched. For example, Directive Principles of State Policy enshrined in Article 39(a), of the Constitution mentions that the State shall in particular, direct its policy towards security that the citizens have the right to an adequate means of livelihood'. Since the Directive Principles are not enforceable in the Court of Law, not much can be done except reminding the government, that it has obligations to elderly as well.

In regard to health care security, problems of elderly are no better. There is some assistance, to persons of government service, through Central Government Health Scheme (CGHS), Medical Reimbursement Scheme (MRS) under Central service rules, and Railway Medical Schemes (RMS). Employees, covered under CGHS get medical attention on payment of prescribed contribution. The facilities include out door as well as indoor treatment and are extended to dependent family members of the pensions[3]. But, the kind of treatment meted out to them in CGHS and public hospitals is not appreciative. A person experienced with CGHS narrated that "in recent times, there has been a noticeable and depressing deterioration in the services provided by the CGHS. Known doctors vanish without a trace and unknown new faces come in with whom one has to start all over again. So quick have been the transfers and changes in the dispensaries. The first signs of deterioration are right at the entrance. The outside of it, near the steps, is invariably blocked by motor cycles and assorted bundles belonging, significantly enough, to members of the staff..... Sometimes, I have gone for a dressing and found the person on duty missing for up to 15 or 20 minutes with no one in sight to inform on what is happening.... However, it is more the lack of kindness and courtesy sometimes on the part of the doctors on duty which stands out" (Amita Malik, 1992). Usually, there are long queues, and meager stock of medicines. It is almost a punishment to go to CGHS. Hence, they turn towards private hospitals. In unorganised sector, the situation is much worse. There is no insurance cover at all. Nor there are special facilities for priority treatment in government hospitals. They have to depend on private sector only.

In respect of personal (physical) security, elders are the easy targets for harassment and murders for petty gains. Their own relatives, sometimes own children gang up with thugs and get away with loot and murder. This problem has become a nightmare in cities like Delhi, Bombay, Calcutta, Madras, Hyderabad and Bangalore and has to be tackled with a human face. But, the role of the State in this respect is minimal, and confines itself to the tightening the law and order situation and policing. It is largely a problem of moral degradation and greediness in the society. The number of elderly facing this problem is extremely small and hence need not bother us any more here. Given, the adequate security of income, elderly themselves may insure against such problem.

What should be done with regard to each of the problems, income security, health care, security and personal (physical) security? Are they peculiar to India alone? How are they attended to in other countries, particularly in the developed and the most successful developing countries? For, it is from these countries that some lessons are possible for us to learn as they must have undergone these problems and solved them through trial and error. Even now, problems of the elderly in developed countries have not disappeared; in a sense they have increased. Developed countries, therefore are equally concerned about the problems of elderly. The only difference between the problems of developed countries and India is that ratio of elderly population to total population (or elderly population to active workers)—sometimes called dependent ratio — is relatively high in them. This is a plus point, for India — at least temporarily. Their worry has been increasing year after year at a fast rate. Look at the OECD countries. It is estimated that dependency ratio is to go up to 37.3 in Canada, 43.6 in Germany, 35.8 in France, 35.3 in Italy, 31.9 in Japan, 31.1 in U.K. and 31.7 in U.S.A. from their level of 20 or so in 1980. Their worry is about the low birth rates and consequent low level of active work force. For, it is the active work force who have to pay for the elderly or dependent aged population. The State has to promote a system that enhances productivity of the active work force to sufficiently high level or reduce the dependency ratio by raising the retirement age of elders. India's worry is of a different order. It is about the employment opportunities for the young and eradication of poverty — and not of those of the problems of elders — as these two are the most crucial for the political as well as economic stability of the country.

That is why, several programmes for the removal of unemployment and alleviation of poverty have been implemented. The chief among them are, Rural Development Programme (IRDP), Training of Rural Youth for Self-Employment (TRYSEM), Jawahar Rozgar Yojana (JRY), Nehru Rozgar Yojana (NRY), and the scheme for Self-Employment for Educated Unemployed Youth (SEEUY), Employment Guarantee Scheme (EGS) in Maharashtra, and the Self-Employment Scheme for Registered Unemployed (SESRU) in West Bengal. In the current year to give a filip to employment generation, Employment Assurance Scheme (EAS) and Prime Minister's Rozgar Yojana (PMRY) for the educated youth have been launched. The concern for the youth and unemployed is understandable. In fact, more innovative programmes should be brought in for them.

What is surprising is that no serious attention is paid to the problems of elderly as if their well being is no body's concern. In most of the developed countries governments have either operated or supported old-age pensions, and family income support (Robin Burgers and Nicholas Stern, 1989). Nevertheless, for the first time some reference is made into Eighth Plan towards the welfare of the elderly. I quote "The coverage of elderly persons without any means of support will be expanded through the schemes of old age pensions of the state governments. The main thrust of the programmes for the elderly will be non-institutional services which are family and community based. Financial assistance will be given to voluntary agencies to provide not only care but also help improve the incomes of the elderly besides involving them closely in the activities of the community so that they are not marginalised" (Government of India, Planning Commission, 1992).

Now, it is up to voluntary organisations to come forward with the programmes and help the elderly. But, the support coming forward from the government for the elderly seems to be limited to those who do not have any means of livelihood. What about those who have something, but their real income getting eroded on account of inflation, mounting health care expenditures, and incapacitation due to accidents? And what about those who are in the unorganised sector—particularly agriculture, construction, casual labour? As noted earlier, there is no social security — either income security or health care security—for the elderly in unorganised sector who constitute majority. As such the system is unjust, and elderly in unorganised sector too need some security in the event of unhelpful attitude from their families. Even for those employed in the organised sector, the system of security schemes such as pension, family pensions, contributory provident fund (CPF) accumulations — may not be sufficient as they grow older and older. Expenses on health care will mount, and in some unfortunate cases, their pensions may be insufficient to meet the costs of treatment. For example, treatment for cancer, cardiac surgery, paralysis, renal failure, kidney, prostate, and gall-bladder operations, respiratory diseases, may consume their entire pension and past savings. Therefore, alternative system of social security irrespective of their source of retirement (formal or informal sectors) should be thought of. The experience of the successful social security schemes in other countries may be drawn. To me it appears, that the social security systems of South Korea, Singapore, for income and health care security, and social security system of Japan and Germany for health care security alone are worth adapting. In what follows these systems are described.

In South Korea, there are two types of social securities which help elderly, (i) National Pension Programme, and (ii) National Medical Insurance. It seems both these programmes together are meeting the requirements of elderly without much strain on the government. A little elaboration of each of these programmes may be helpful.

In the Korean National Pension Programme there are four types of benefits: old age pension, invalid's pension, survivor's pension and lumpsum refund. A basic old age pension is payable to an insured person from the age of 60, if he or she has been in the programme for 20 years or more and ceases to be in a remunerative activity. If an insured person has been in the programme for a period ranging from

15 years to 20 years, however, he or she is eligible for reduced old age pension. An early old age pension is payable to a person without a remunerative job who has been in the programme for 20 years or more and wishes pension payment between the age of 55 and 60 years. Finally, a special old age pension is payable to a person whose age falls between 45 and 60, as of January, 1988, if he or she has been in the programme for more than 5 years. An invalid's pension is payable to a person in accordance with the degree of disability if he or she has fulfilled the minimum one year's requirement in the programme. When a person, who has been in the programme for more than one year, dies, his or her survivors are entitled to a survivors pension.

The level of benefits to the insured varies depending on the stay in the programme. The average amount of benefits payable to a person who has been in the programme for 20 years is approximately 40 per cent of his or her last monthly remuneration. A person whose income was below the national average could get more than 40 per cent of his or her last monthly remuneration, while the opposite holds true for a person whose income was above the national average. This feature shows the redistributive elements introduced in the Korean system. Benefits consist of two parts: a basic amount is related to the average amount of the monthly standard remunerations of all the insured persons as well as the average monthly standard remuneration of the insured individual.[6]

"The national pension programme is financed by contributions from the insured and their employers and the programme receives some support from the government to cover the administrative costs. Employers are required to contribute half of the total contribution payable by an insured person. However, voluntarily insured persons pay the total contribution by themselves" (Joon Koo Loo and Sang Dal Shim, 1992).

In Singapore, social security programme for the elderly is simple and somewhat similar to our CPF scheme, but combines with health care and housing. It is called Central Provident Fund (CPF) and is the most extensive component of Singapore's social security system. Its main role is to help its members provide adequately for themselves so that they do not slip into poverty in retirement. It is fully funded, and being fully funded, it is very flexible. it is administered by the CPF board under the CPF Act. As for financing part is concerned, four parties are involved:

(a) "*The Individual Himself.* The individual saves a portion of his income for future use. If employed, his employer will provide him medical relief, work injury compensation and joint contributions to the Central Provident Fund Scheme.
(b) *The Family.* Mutual care of family members and filial piety are encouraged.
(c) *The Community.* Insurance schemes pool resources to meet needs to those who fall into contingent need. Charities come in to meet requirements of the poor.
(d) *The Government.* Government subsidies and public assistance are given to the poor" (Leong Lick Tien, 1994)

Hence, the more capable individuals are more self-reliant. Those requiring help could turn to others and welfare organisations for assistance. Furthermore, desirable values such as self-reliance, keeping the family as the building block of society and filial piety, are continually being reinforced at the national level.

There are other success stories elsewhere in the world, particularly that of Chillian social insurance model—privatisation of social insurance which can be thought of. But the research findings are that it "has done little to reduce the overall costs of social insurance and is not geared to accommodate the acceleration of ageing projected for the next century" (Peter Lloyed - Sherdock, 1992). If for one reason or the other, the above described Korean model and Singaporean Model are not appealing to majority in India, a limited reform for health care security at least should be attempted for as health care costs to the elderly are the most burdensome. According to an estimate they may come up to 40 per cent of elderly survival expenses.

As noted earlier, health care security for the elderly is almost non-existent either in the organised sector or in the unorganised sector; the few benefits ensured under Central Government Health Scheme (CGHS) cannot be availed of without incuring substantial expenses. If a scheme is devised for health care, it will be of considerable help to them. In this respect, models of Germany and Japan may be of use and are described briefly below:

In Germay, coverage is comprehensive. There is freedom to choose the physician and hospital but no free market on prices. Equal access is guaranteed by a comprehensive statutory health insurance scheme, the "sickness funds", which cover more than 90 per cent of the population. Not only do these cover ambulatory, hospital and dental care with very little or no copyment, they also give cash benefits for maternity leave, "cure leave" and compensation for lost wages due to illness. The sickness funds are financed through contribution paid half by the employer and half by the employee. The amount of the contribution is determined individually be each sickness fund, as a percentage of the gross income of its members. If for instance, a sickness fund needs 13 per cent of gross income to finance its current cost, a member with an income of DM 4000 must pay 260 to the fund and the employer and additional and the employer and additional DM 260. The contribution to the statutory funds is unrelated to the size or health status of the employee's family. There is redistribution within a fund, from young and healthy to the elderly and ill, but since people must stay with one fund once they have enrolled, the redistributional effect is evened out over a person's life time. There is also a redistribution between single persons and employees on a pay-as-you-go basis, and the funds do not accumulate financial resources (Schulenburg, 1992).

Japan's health care is largely modelled on Germany's health care system. Nevertheless, it incorporates certain innovations suitable to native culture, tradition and environment. As in the German system, universal coverage is mandated by the government and achieved through a number of health insurance plans, carefully regulated by the government. The Japanese government takes a more active role than Germany's does, however, by providing the majority of the insurance coverage itself. The payment system is also similar to Germany's, since payments are made on national fee schedule with implicit limits on overall expenditure increases. The government negotiates the schedule with providers, and payments are made through a single channel. The schedule is a powerful tool, for the government, to use in controlling over all costs and in promoting the provision of certain services through higher fees. It is estimated that Japanese undergo an average of one screening a year. Annual screenings, which are provided at a nominal charge for all those over the age of forty, include a general examination, blood pressure, urine analysis, serum GOT and GPJ cholesterol examination and testing for various concerns. Mandatory screening for school children includes an electro cardiogram (Ikegami, 1992).

Health insurance system in Japan falls into three different systems. First, there is the insurance system for employees and their dependents. This can be subdivided into various plans. Government managed health insurance for those employed in small companies (which covers 28.9 per cent of the population). Society managed health insurance for those employed in large companies (25.5 per cent), mutual aid associations for government employees and private schools employees (9.7 per cent) seamen's insurance (0.4 per cent). Second, there is a system of community based health insurance to extend protection to the self-employed, unemployed, pensioners and their dependents. This segment of the population tends to have a lower than those covered under the employers' plan. The principal community based health insurance plan is the National Health Insurance (NHI) which covers 35.4 per cent of the population. Third, the Geriatric Health Act created an insurance pool in 1982 to cross subsidize the costs of the elderly (8.0 per cent) (*see* Tables 6.3 and 6.4).

TABLE 6.3 : Percentage of Health Care Funds from Government Insurance Premiums, and Private Sources, Japan, 1955-1989

Year	*Government*			*Insurance premiums*	*Patient charges, etc.*	*Total*
	National	*Local*	*Total*			
1955	11.6	4.2	15.9	45.5	38.7	100
1960	15.7	4.0	19.6	50.4	30.3	100
1965	22.1	3.9	25.9	53.5	20.6	100
1970	24.2	3.5	27.6	53.0	19.3	100
1975	28.9	4.6	33.5	53.5	13.0	100
1980	30.4	5.1	35.5	53.2	11.3	100
1981	30.3	5.1	35.4	53.5	11.1	100
1982	30.4	5.2	35.6	53.6	10.8	100
1983	30.6	5.7	36.4	52.5	11.1	100
1984	28.6	5.9	34.5	53.7	11.9	100
1985	26.6	6.8	33.4	54.3	11.3	100
1986	26.1	6.9	33.1	54.6	12.3	100
1987	24.9	6.7	31.6	55.6	12.7	100
1988	24.5	6.9	31.5	55.9	12.6	100
1989	24.7	6.7	31.4	56.1	12.5	100

Note : Figures for total government and private sources are rounded. Insurance premiums are not private, since contributions are part of social security and thus are compulsory payroll deduction.

Source : Kousei Tokei Kyokai 1991a, p. 236.

The insurance plans are self-financing. Contribution to employees' plan are at a fixed ratio to the income amounting to about 8 per cent of salary. Employers and employees each pay about half. The government subsidizes about one-sixth of the cost of government management health insurance but pays only the administrative expenses of the other employee plans. Contributions under the NHI plan are based on individual's income assets, with the government subsidizing about

50 per cent of its cost. The cost of Geriatric Health Act Plan is paid by the government and by a cross subsidy among the other insurance plans (Ikegami, 1992).

TABLE 6.4 : Health Insurance Plans, Japan 1991

Population insured	*Plan*	*Insurer*	*Number insured*[a] *(in 1000s)*	*Percentage of total*
Employees and dependants	Government-managed health insurance	National Government	35,694	28.9
	Day labourers' insurance	National Government	168	0.1
	Society-managed health insurance	1,814 health insurance societies	31,459	25.5
	Seamen's insurance	National Government	441	
	Mutual aid associations (MAAs)	27 national MAAs 54 local MAAs 1 MAA for private schools	12,045	
Self-employed and pensioners	National Health insurance (NHI)	3,262 municipal governments	39,729	32.1
	NHI associations	167 associations	4,060	3.3
Elderly[b]	Geriatric health act	Municipal governments	10,034	8.0

Notes: a. Include dependants.
b. Insured under provisions of Geriatric Health Act of 1982.

Source: Kousei Tokei Kyokai, 1991b, pp. 176-77.

Insurance, benefits cover most medical services. In addition, there are direct cash benefits paid to the insured for child birth, maternity leave, nursing and injury and sickness. Co-insurance is required under all the plans. Under the employees' plans, employees must pay 10 per cent of inpatient and outpatient costs, and employees' dependents must pay 20 per cent and 30 per cent of in-patient and out-patients costs, respectively. Under the NHI plan, both the insured and their dependents must by 30 per cent of inpatient and out-patient costs. The differences in contributions and coverage of the different plans reflect the evolutionary nature of Japan's insurance system, and cause some concern about equity. For all patients however, there is a limit of 60,000 (about $400) per month to the maximum amount of co-payment which must be paid. In addition, the elderly do not have to pay any co-payment and instead pay a nominal deductible of 800 per month for out-patient care and 400 per day for in-patient care (Ikegami, 1992).

It is evident from the foregoing, that the system of social security for the elderly in India is devoid of respect, compassion, and gratitude to the elderly who gave their best during their productive career in the country. It needs reform. The present confusing system has to go—lock stock, and barrel. Leaving aside the unorganised sector, for the present, for whom no security worth the name is available, even the organised sector, for whom some security is available—as mentioned earlier—have to think twice to continue with the present system. In case, reform of social security suggested above is not favoured, pensions, gratuity, CPF contributions need the indexing for inflation. If indexation is not possible they must be delinked from Government Management, and must be put in charge of a Trust—say National Pension Board or Central Provident Fund—and be managed like any commercial organisation. For, these funds are contributions from employers and employees, for the welfare of elderly.

TABLE 6.5 : Pensions and Other Retirement Benefits as Percentage of Expenditure and Revenue (Centre and State Governments Combined)

Year	*Total expenditure* (Rs. crore)	*Pension and other retirement benefits* (Rs. crore)	*Total revenues* (Rs. crore)	*Pensions and other retirement benefits as percentage of*	
				Total expenditure	*Total revenue*
1988-89	116138.96	4127.03	76234.94	3.55	5.41
1989-90	138450.65	4837.04	90944.35	3.49	5.31
1990-91	155708.81	5183.75	98018.82	3.33	5.28
1991-92	177700.94	6138.66	119878.27	3.45	5.12
1992-93	204356.45	7190.35	139388.76	3.52	5.15
1993-94	218205.80	7731.16	151363.23	3.54	5.10

Source : Government of India, Ministry of Finance, Department of Economic Affairs (1993), *Indian Public Statistics*, pp. 3 and 6.

In my opinion, such a delinking may help government in its stabilisation and structural adjustment goals. As of now, pensions and retirement benefits as a percentage of total revenues and as a percentage of total expenditures are hovering around 3.5 per cent and 5.20 per cent respectively for the past five years (Table 6.5). Now, with the Fifth Pay Commission's recommendations coming—hopefully on the higher side—the share of pensions in total expenditures may go up, which means expenditures on vital developmental heads may come down. That is not what is expected from the government, committed to growth with justice. It may also help employees in getting better return for their accumulations in the trust fund. With a little bit of business acumen on the part of the trust they (employees) can obtain concessions for their travel in road and rail transport, concessions for their housing and concessions for their medical care. With assured flow of income and health care facilities, their chances of staying with their own families with dignity may brighten up.

NOTES

1. Life expectancy at birth (years) increased from 32.1 in 1950-51 to 59.9 in 1990-91 and likely to go up to 60.6 by 1996-97.
2. Birth rate (number per thousand) declined from 41.7 in 1950-51 to 29.5 in 1990-91 and likely to decrease to 25.7 in 1996-97.
3. For detailed explanation of these schemes see Government of India, *Fourth Pay Commission Report* (1986), Part II, p.86.
4. Svend Erick hougaard Jenson and soren Bo Nielson — "Aging, Generational Conflicts and Adjustment of Pension Systems", Paper Presented at 48th Congress of International Institute of Public Finance, Seoul, Korea, August 24-27, 1992.
5. For detailed discussion of these programmes, see Government of India Finance Ministry, Economic Division, *Economic Survey*, 1993-94, p.157.
6. To be more specific calculation of the basic amount can be achieved by the following formula:

   $$\text{Basic amount} = 2.4\,(A+B)\,(1+0.05n)$$

   where

   A = Average amount of the monthly standard remuneration of all the insured persons for the year preceding the pension payment year.

   B = Average amount of the monthly standard remuneration during the insured term of the insured individual.

   n = Number of years over of 20 years. This formula shows that an insured person benefit would be larger as he or she stays in the programme longer than 20 years (adapted from Joon Koo Lee and Sang Dal Shim, 1992, pp. 106-24).
7. It is highly facilitative as far as the withdrawals and pensions are concerned. "Members can withdraw their CPF savings when they attain 55 years of age. They have to retain a Retirement Minimum Plan (S $ 34, 600) with the CPF for old age annuity payments from age 60, and a Medisave Minimum Sum (S $ 11,000) for hospital expenses. The balance left in their ordinary, special and Medisave Accounts can then be withdrawn. Subsequent withdrawals are allowed once every 3 years (at age 58, 61 and so on), if a member has continued to work and contributed to the CPF. Members are expected to invest their withdrawn CPF savings prudently for their old age needs for their permanent disability. On their death, a member's savings are released to their nominees, or in the absence of nominees, to their family members as determined by the law. When the member reaches Age 60, The Board will provide him a monthly income of at least S $ 230 from the account until the sum is exhausted. A member can alternatively deposit his Minimum Sum (S $ 34,600) with an

approved bank which will likewise provide him a monthly income, or he can buy a life annuity from a private insurance company. The monthly income provides for subsistence living and is safeguarded against a member's savings running out prematurely. Members who do not have the full S $ 34,600 in their Retirement Account at age 55 can have the account tapped-up through tax deductible cash deposits or transfers of CPF savings from their children. Members can at any time invest their CPF savings themselves in trusted stocks, convertible loan stocks, unit trust, and gold; for better returns, but have to be returned to members CPF account when these investments are sold. All members can use their CPF ordinary shares for several purposes, subject of certain conditions (for details see Leong lick Tien, 1994, pp. 216-28).

8. There were about 1214 statutory sickness funds in 1992 and covered 90 per cent of population. All money spent on medical care is financed ultimately by the people, whether through contributions to sickness funds, insurance premiums to private insurers, taxes or direct payments. The share of private health insurance is relatively modes, for more details regarding organisational and delivery aspects of health care see Schulenburg, 1992).

7

NEED FOR REFORM IN HEALTH SECTOR

Can National Health Insurance be an Alternative?

—Prof. K.N. REDDY

"Health is wealth" and is an essential requirement for the enjoyment of every aspect of life. A chronically sick person, in spite of his high income and high education, cannot enjoy his life and would contribute very little good to the society. This has been recognised, at the time of launching of the Five Year Plans — 42 years ago — and echoed in the Eighth Five Year Plan too. A few months ago also, it has been mentioned in the Economic Survey that "human development is the ultimate goal of our development and is also crucial for the long run success of economic reforms. Sound, long-term development of social sectors, such as education, and health, is crucial for sustaining economic growth in an increasingly integrated world economy" (Government of India, 1994).

Given this importance, what efforts have been made by the government during the past several years? What has been achieved so far? Where does India stand in comparison to other comparable developing countries? Is health care system in India satisfying? Is it equitable? Is it cost effective? Should the same system continue? Is there no alternative system that improves accessibility, reduces cost escalation, and speeds up health status? If yes, what should be the alternative? Can the national/public health insurance be the alternative? In what follows, an attempt is made to discuss these briefly.

It may be gratifying that during the past three decades, considerable progress has been made in improving the health status, be it in terms of life expectancy at birth or in terms of child mortality rate (the most commonly used indicators of health status). But that achievement, when compared with other developing countries, looks humble and not much to be proud of. For example, during 1960-90,

(a) life expectancy at birth in India increased by 23.40 per cent only (from 47 to 58 years), as against 60.46 per cent in China (from 47 to 58 years), as against 23.40 per cent only (from 43 to 69 years), 30.76 per cent in Thailand (from 52 to 68 years), 28.26 per cent in Indonesia (from 46 to 59 years), and 36.96 per cent in demographically developing group (from 46 to 63 years); and (b) child mortality rate decreased by 45.96 per cent in India (from 235 to 127), as against 79.52 per cent in China (from 210 to 43), 84.29 per cent in Sri Lanka (from 140 to 22),75.84 per cent in Thailand (from 149 to 36), 48.13 per cent in Indonesia (from 214 to 111), and 53.10 per cent in demographically developing group (from 226 to 106) (Table 7.1).

This lack-lustre improvement in health status has quite often been defended on the count that resources spent on health care had been low and inadequate. This is not convincing. As of 1990, according to the World Development Report (World health care — 1.3 per cent by the private sector — as of 1990, according to the World Development Report (World Bank 1993), India spent 6 per cent by the private sector — as against China's 3.5 per cent of GDP (1.8 per cent by the public sector, and 1.9 per cent by the private sector), Thailand's 5 per cent of GDP (1.1 per cent by the public sector, and 3.9 per cent by the private sector Indonesia's 2 per cent of GDP (0.7 per cent by the public sector, and 1.3 per cent by the private sector), Malaysia's 3 per cent of GDP (1.3 per cent by the public sector, and 1.7 per cent by the private sector), and demographically developing group's 4.7 of GDP (2.3 per cent by the public sector, and 2.5 per cent by the private sector (Table 7.2).

Several reasons may be cited for such a poor progress and high cost health care, but not all of them can be mentioned on account of complex factors — medical care, water supply, sanitation, nutrition, child care, women welfare, per capita income, education, housing, marital status, personal habits, like smoking and drinking, air pollution, occupation, climate, religious beliefs, culture, and economic structure, etc. — that go into the determination of the health status. We shall confine ourselves to those reasons which are institutional in character and come under the purview of the Ministry of Department of Medical, Public Health, and Family Planning of the Central and the State governments.

Institutional Factors

Resources have been misallocated all along. Contrary to the world opinion, a major chunk of the resources have gone to the curative

TABLE 7.1: Health Status Indicators for Selected Countries

	General mortality Life expectancy at birth		*Percentage increase in 1990 over 1960*	*Median age at death 1990*	*Child Mortality rate*		*Percentage decrease in 1990 over 1960*
	1960	*1990*			*1960*	*1990*	
Sub-Saharan Africa	43w	52w	20.93	5w	251w	175w	30.28
India	47	58	23.40	37	235	127	45.96
China	43	69	60.46	64	210	43	79.52
Other Asia & Islands	50w	62w	24.00	42w	182w	97w	46.70
Sri Lanka	58	72	24.13	73	140	22	84.29
Philippines	59	64	8.47	49	103	62	39.81
Thailand	52	68	30.76	71	149	36	75.84
Malaysia	58	72	22.41	63	106	20	81.13
Korean Republic	53	70	3208	71	133	31	76.69
Indonesia	46	59	28.26	47	214	111	48.13
Latin America and the Caribbean	54w	70w	29.63	55w	161w	60w	62.73
Middle Eastern Countries	44w	61w	38.64	24w	242w	111w	54.13
Formerly Socialist Economies of Europe (FSE)	66w	72w	09.09	72w	68w	22w	67.65
Established Market Economies (EME)	70w	76w	08.57	75w	36w	11w	69.44
FSE and EME	69w	75w	08.70	74w	46w	15w	67.39
Demographically Developing Group	46w	63w	36.96	39	226	106	53.10
World	53w	65w	22.64	35	195w	96w	50.77

Source : World Bank. World Development Report 1993, pp 200-1.

services rather than to the preventive health services. As of 1990-91, a little more than 60 per cent of the resources had gone to curative services, namely, medical relief, medical education and training, the Central Government Health Scheme and Employees State Insurance Scheme, etc. However, only 26 per cent had gone to preventive service, namely, prevention and control of diseases, prevention of food adulteration, drug control rural and urban family planning, maternity and child health, etc., and the rest to miscellaneous and administrative services. Similarly, very little had been allocated to facility creation (hospital buildings, beds, machinery and equipment), and too much had been allocated to consumption expenditures. To be specific, as much as 97.02 per cent of the resources had gone to salaries (58.97 per cent), office expenses (2.58 per cent), and others (35.47 per cent), as against 2.97 per cent to machinery and equipment (Table 7.3).

There has been an urban bias in the allocation of resources. As of 1990-91, 66.96 per cent of the resources spent on health care had gone to the urban sector which accounts for 25.7 per cent of the total population, while only 33.04 per cent of the resources has gone to the rural sector, which accounts for 74.30 per cent of the total population. In terms of per capita allocations, the biases are substantial. The per capita expenditure on health care of the urban sector was Rs.152, against Rs. 26 of the rural sector. In other words, the allocation of resources to the urban sector in terms of per capita was 5.86 times more than what the rural sector had received (Reddy Selvaraju, 1994). The point is, the rural areas were already far behind in terms of water supply (50 per cent of the rural population, and 24 of the urban population has no access to potable water in 1985-87 — UNDP, 1990), sanitation (98 per cent of the rural population, and 69 per cent of the urban population had no access to sanitation in 1985-87, UNDP, 1990), maternity care, child welfare, etc. and if, on top of it, the health care also was neglected, what would happen except slow progress in health status that had been witnessed so far.

The system is accessible to the elite and well-off, and not so to the poor and the rural sector. A study conducted in 1989 for Andhra Pradesh revealed that the per household benefits to the poor were Rs. 20.42 only, against Rs. 39.97 to the middle income, and Rs. 726.17 to the high income group (Reddy, Sudhakar, 1989). Perhaps for this and other reasons, a wellknown physician and social worker, lamented that "the fault in our health system lies not in the inadequacy of human or financial resources but in their skewed utilisation and distribution. This failure in the health scene is due to deliberate distortions by

TABLE 7.2 : Health Expenditure in Selected Countries : 1990

	Per capita health expenditure (official exchange rate US dollars)	*Health Expenditure as percentage of GDP*		
		Public Sector	*Private Sector*	*Total*
Sub-Saharan Africa	24	2.5	2.0	4.5
India	21	1.3	4.7	6.0
		(1.65)	(2.09)	(3.75)
China	11	2.1	1.4	3.5
Other Asia & Islands	61	1.8	2.7	4.5
Sri Lanka	18	1.8	1.9	3.7
Philippines	14	1.0	1.0	2.0
Thailand	73	1.1	3.9	5.0
Malaysia	67	1.3	1.7	3.0
Korean Republic	377	2.7	3.9	6.6
Indonesia	12	0.7	1.3	2.0
Latin America & the Caribbean	105	2.4	1.6	4.0
Middle Eastern Countries	77	2.4	1.7	4.1
Formerly Socialist Economies of Europe (FSE)	142	2.5	1.0	3.6
Established Market Economies (EME)	1860	5.6	3.5	9.2
FSE and EME	1340	5.4	3.4	8.7
Demographically Developing Group	41	2.3	2.5	4.7
World	323	4.9	3.2	8.0

Note : Figures within brackets are estimates made by us.

The public sector expenditures include the government health expenditure, parastatal expenditure, foreign aid, making the figures comparable with those for OECD countries. The private sector expenditures for countries other than OECD members are based on household surveys carried out by the ILO and other sources, supplemented by information from United Nations National Accounts, World Bank studies, and other studies prescribed in the scientific literature (World Bank 1993, 197-8).

"Health expenditure includes" outlays for prevention, promotion, rehabilitation and care; population activities, nutrition activities; Programme food aid; and emergency aid specifically for health. It does not include water and sanitation. Per capita expenditure are based on the World Bank mid-year population estimate.

Source : World Bank, World Development Report 1993, 200-1.

TABLE 7.3 : Structure of Health Care Expenditure* by Government by Economic Categories in Nominal Terms: 1974-75 to 1990-91 (Central, State and Union Territory Governments combined)

(*Percentage*)

Year	*Salary*	*Office expenses*	*Machinery and equipment*	*Others** (1+2+3+4)*	*Total*
	(1)	(2)	(3)	(4)	(5)
1974-75	39.93	4.37	2.85	52.86	100.00
1978-79	40.11	3.61	3.20	53.09	100.00
1982-83	51.14	4.58	2.91	41.37	100.00
1986-87	52.41	3.55	3.34	40.70	100.00
1990-91	58.97	2.58	2.97	35.47	100.00

Notes :

* Health care expenditure here refers to expenditure on medical relief, hospitals and dispensaries, and family welfare only as data for other items are not available.

** Others include materials and supplies, travel expenses, motor vehicles (purchase maintenance, cost of fuel) accessories, medicines, rent and taxes, festival advance, petroleum, oil lubricants, stores and equipment, scholarships and stipends, cost of textbooks to the children of low paid government servants, etc. They vary from State to State.

Source: Reddy K.N., Selvaraju V (1994).

control resources. In consequence, health has been converted into a major business in illness and human suffering, where consumer resistance is at its lowest, and now poses a new threat to the health of our people. The timings of hospitals are such, that the poor and manual workers can have treatment for themselves and their dependents, only at the expense of their day's earnings" (Anita, 1993).

The system discriminates between the employees in the organised sector and the employees in the unorganised sector. The former constitutes a very small group and yet enjoys hospital facilities disproportionately to their extremely small contributions. Look at the services available under Central Government Health Scheme (CGHS) and the Employees State Insurance Scheme (ESIS). CGHS provides comprehensive medical care, that is, free medical care through the network of allopathic dispensaries as well as ayurvedic, homeopathic, unani, sidha, dispensaries/units and supply of medicines, laboratory and X-ray investigations, domiciliary visits, emergency treatment, ante-natal care, confinement and post-natal care, advice on family welfare, specialist consultation and hospitalisation facilities in government hospitals as well as in hospitals recognised under CGHS, to the Central Government employees, the employees of autonomous organizations, the retired Central Government employees, the Members of Parliament, ex-MPs, ex-Governors, retired Judges of the Supreme Court and High Courts, freedom fighters, and members of public in 14 specific areas, in Delhi, numbering about 40 lakhs. Similarly, ESIS provides for sickness, medical care, maternity and employment injury benefits to the employees of all factories — other than seasonal factories and establishments in the notified class of establishments, in which 10 per cent or more employees are employed and in part of which a manufacturing process is being carried on with the aid of power or is ordinarily so carried on or in which 20 or more employees and in part of which a manufacturing process is being carried on without the aid of power or were working on any day in the last 12 months, shops, hotels, restaurants, cinemas including preview theatres, road motor transport, and newspaper establishments employing 20 or more persons — by contributions from their employees, employers, and State governments (with a major share for medical care from the State governments) numbering about 65 lakh persons. About Rs. 241 crore were spent on their medical care in 1991-92. In other words, the State governments spent Rs. 370 per employee on medical care, which is five times more than the per capita benefit received by persons in the unorganised sector. The point is why should there by a discrimination, as between the employees of the organised sector and the employees of the unorganised sector. Painful questions arise in this context. Is it the fault of the persons not being employed in the organised sector? Is it the right of a fortunate few who are elected to run the country, or employed in a government or public enterprise or employed in a factory to corner the resources — contributed by all — for their own benefit?

Too much attention (and as a result too much resources) has been paid to family welfare with too little effect. Of the total health care expenditure (medical, public health and family welfare) in the country, a little more than 18 per cent of it was spent on family welfare during 1974-75 to 1990-91 without any significant impact incurring the population growth. This is not to say that population control is unimportant. What is urged is that population control must be cost effective? As much as 11 per cent of the Ministry's resources had gone to medical education (1990-91) not directly related to health, and benefit the upper strata of the society. Indirectly, it is a subsidy to better-off sections. Can India afford such allocations?

There is a colossal wastage in expenditure on the national health programme — malaria eradication programme, filaria control programme, leprosy eradication programme, tuberculosis control programme, programme for control of blindness, iodine deficiency disorders control programme, sexually transmitted diseases (STD) control programme, blood safety programme, Aids control programme, mental health programme, etc. — due to lack of proper monitoring and evaluation system. It is suspected that the funds have been diverted to the purposes unconnected with health care by the states. Perhaps, for this reason, incidence of cases in these programmes have not markedly come down in some states (Orissa), in spite of considerable resources transferred to them under the national health programmes. To what extent this impression is correct needs empirical verification, State by State. The pity is neither the Central Government—the provider of funds—nor the states—the users of the funds—had paid attention to this issue. Sometimes the distinction between plan and non-plan expenditures had played its role in mismanagement and/or misallocation of funds.

There is a mismatch between the supply of and demand for, health services, both at the Central and the States' levels. Under the Constitution of India, the states are responsible for the provision of health care, but are not able to cope with demand for health services. The devolutions made, at the behest of the Finance Commissions and the Planning Commission are not able to meet their requirements. Nor are the states able to allocate higher percentage of their resources to health care. A glance at the allocation pattern of expenditure on health care will reveal marginal decline, and in some states significant decline too. The paradox of the national policies is that when it comes to the question of political stability and safeguarding the sovereignty of the country, the states are treated as Union of the States, and when it comes to the provision of basic services, such as health, sanitation, and nutrition, the same states are asked to fend themselves. To my knowledge, no other federations pursue such awkward national policies. For example, federations like Canada, Germany, Australia, and Switzerland are having national (social) insurance with accessibility to every one. The United States of America, another well-known federal country, the hard core believer in private competition, provides accessibility to the poor under medic-aid programme and to the old and disabled under medicare programme. It needs no reiteration that in most of the federations, health care (up to a particular point) is the concern of the Centre as well as the States, and not completely the responsibility of the states.

The quality of service in public hospitals (government hospitals) has been deterorating fast, partly because of the lack of adequate supply of medicines and equipment and partly because of the faulty manpower planning and selection procedures. The delivery system has become bureauratic and unaccountable. It is more so in primary health centres and sub-centres in rural areas. According to the findings of some researches, whether at the sub-centre or at the primary health centre, the health workers remain unaccountable to the community which they are supposed to serve. "Doctors posted at PHC have no proper training they are more thorough in recongnising and treating of rheumatic fever. Medical officers posted at primary health centres do not have adequate experience in simple tasks like giving injections, IV fluids, and resuscitation" (Muley, 1993). In the words of a journalist : "going to a public hospital remains a nightmarish experience, big crowds, long queues, confusing maze-like layouts, incomprehensible instructions, tedious procedures, casual diagnosis, rough handling by sullen staff, rude physicians, bribe, taking touts, complete absence of accountability, and unconscionable delays. Most working people think twice about visiting hospital OPD, simply because it means missing a day's work and wages. . . . Most public hospitals are inherently patient-unfriendly and hopelessly mismanaged" (Praful Bidwai, 1992).

Finally, the system lacks dynamism and innovation. The same old system, "rationing by queue" inherited from the British Raj, with a few modifications, here and there in organisational structure, is being continued. Neither is there innovations in the financing side, nor any deviations in the delivery system. As a result, shortage of resources had become a perennial problem and help encourage physicians to become inactive. The government is unable to do anything to increase the supply of services except forcing the people to obtain health care from the private sector. A more important thing is that the present system of health care is not cost-effective. A comparison with China, Japan, and the UK reveals how expensive our health care system is. As mentioned earlier, China, Japan, and the U.K. had ensured health care to their people by spending 3.5 to 6.0 per cent of GDP, and whereas we in India with the same percentage of GDP (6 per cent) could not ensure. It is a sad reflection on the model India is following. This system has to give way to a more efficient one, and reforms in health care have got to be introduced, as done in the fiscal, financial, trade, and industrial sectors during the past three years.

Alternative Models

Then, on what lines should the reforms be brought in? A debate should be encouraged on this, and a consensus be arrived before choosing an alternative, for, the issues involved are quite contentious. Theoretically, four alternatives are possible: (i) public financing and public delivery; (ii) private financing and public delivery; (iii) public financing and private delivery; and (iv) private financing and private delivery.

The first three are in practice in one country or the other, but the last one is nowhere in practice, nor is likely to be. The first is the famous Beverdige model, national health service practiced in the UK until its recent reforms. The second one is the idealised US model, ignoring the major role played by the government in that country for the moment, or a model practised in Singapore, and Taiwan. The third-one is the Bismarck Model, idealised national (public or social) health insurance scheme practised in Canada, Germany, France, Japan, and China with minor differences in the mode of funding and delivery systems.

International evidence suggests that the combination of public financing and private delivery — the third model — is superior to the other approaches. The argument for the public financing arises from the recognition that single-payer systems tend to have lower costs than do public-private mixes. A multiple array of funding sources gives rise to two key policy dilemmas. First, it is easier to shift costs than cut them, there is a tendency for each founder to attempt to avoid those clients likely to generate high costs. Second, monopsony bargainning power over the providers is harder to achieve in multi-payer system. According to William C. Hsiao (1992) of the Harvard University, who made a comparative study of the UK, the US, Canada, Germany, Japan, and Sweden, the public financing and private delivery system of health care, practised in Canada scored highest from the point of view of performance, health outcome, public satisfaction, and access to health. The system of public financing and public delivery (the first model), practised in the UK, produces social equity and low-cost health care, but suffers from rigidity, over centralisation and inadequate responses to patients' demands. On the other hand, the system of private financing and private delivery, coupled with public financing and private delivery for the old and infirm, and the indigent, practised to a large extent in the US, produces innovations and high quality services for those who can pay, but suffers from high costs and social inequity.

Doubts may arise whether India can go in for the best of the systems, namely, public financing and private delivery (model 3), for, (a) the size of the population is far more than any of the countries mentioned, (b) the level of the per capita income is far lower than the others, and (c) the type of its federal setup is far different from others. But these doubts do not stand the test of scrutiny. In fact, India has the necessary infrastructure—sizable public hospitals, not-for-profit hospitals, private hospitals, medical associations, enlightened charitable trusts, voluntary organisations—and experience in running public insurance schemes (such as, CGHS and ESIS) and the private delivery of health care which help implement the national health insurance scheme. The costs of implementing the scheme may not be more than what health care is costing now at all-India level (3.75 per cent of GDP, public and private sectors combined, according to our estimates—Reddy, 1994). Details of public financing or the mix of private financing or payment of premiums to the Centre, State, and Local governments and delivery by the public and private agencies can be worked out, once the choice of alternative is clearly known. If necessary, the experience of China—not much different from Canada, Japan, Germany in form, and slightly different in structure—can be made use of.

Conclusion

To sum up, health care by the Government in India has lost its efficiency thrust. Nor has it encouraged any innovation. It has become a paradise for those who matter in political and bureaucratic circles, and organised sectors and for those who have expenses accounts. It is a hell to the poor and the people in unorganised sectors. Economic reforms, leading to prosperity and social justice, will have less meaning, if they are not backed up by health care system, that takes care of illness and sickness — a foundation for prosperity and enjoyment of life. The sooner the health care by the government is reformed, in terms of financing, organisation, and delivery, the speedier would be the improvement in the health status, and faster would be the increase in the human development index in the comity of nations. There is ample scope to reform health care in the direction of the national health insurance. What is urgently needed is a detailed study on the feasibility of the national health insurance.

REFERENCES

Antia, N. H. (1993): Shortage of the Existing System. In. Anita N. H., Bhatia Kavita. Eds. *People's Health in People Hands*. FRCH, p. 61, 71

Government of India (1994): Economic Survey, 1993-94. New Delhi. Planning Commission.

Hsiao, W.C. (1992): Comparing health care systems: What nations can learn from one another. *Journal of Health Politics, Policy and Law* 17 (4), Winter.

Muley, Y.P. (1993): Experiences of Medical Officer in a Primary Health Centre. In. Anita N.H., Kavita Bhatia *Eds. op.cit.* p. 29.

Praful, Bidwai (1992): Public hospitals turn into illness factories. *Times of India* (Bombay), August 3.

Reddy, K. N., Sudhakar S. (1989): Who benefits from Government expenditure? A case study of Andhra Pradesh. *Journal of Political Economy.* 1, Jan-June, 114-37.

— —, Selvaraju V. (1994): *Health Care Expenditure by Government of India: 1974-75 to 1990-91.* New Delhi, National Institute of Public Finance and Policy.

Reddy, K. N. (1994): Health Expenditure in India: Is it low? *Finance India* 8(2), June.

UNOP (1990): *Human Development Report*, New York, UNIDO, p. 47.

World Bank (1993): *World Development Report* 1993. Washington, World Bank.

8

FACTORS AFFECTING RURAL POVERTY IN INDIA
A Review

—Prof. K.N. REDDY

Studies on poverty in India goes back to the early sixties with a study made by Planning Commission in 1962. Since then, the problem of poverty has been a subject of extensive research and intense debate. At the outset, it must be mentioned that, the exercise concerning poverty is constrained by the availability of the relevant data. The principal source of data on poverty are the various consumption expenditure surveys conducted by the National Sample Survey (NSS) organization which report the distribution of population in India and the states across per capita monthly expenditure classes (PCME). The consumption expenditure surveys have been conducted since 1951 practically every year until 1973/74. A decision was taken to suspend the annual surveys (with the exception of 1973/74) in 1972/73 and start quinquennial surveys (with a considerably large sample). Four quinquennial surveys have so far been conducted for the years 1972/73, 1977/78, 1983 and 1987.[1] Therefore, in the literature on poverty in India, two separate analysis can be identified on the basis of period—one using the time series consumption data from 1951 to 1973/74 and the second covering four points data for 1973/74, 1977/78, 1983, 1987/88. Corresponding to these two periods, there are two norms or poverty lines which have been worked out for two reference years, *i.e.,* 1960/61 and 1973/74. The earliest 1960/61 norm or poverty line of Rs. 20 PMCE at 1960/61 prices was recommended by working group set up by the Planning Commission in July 1962. The Rs. 20 PMCE norm has formed the base for spate of studies undertaken by the researchers during the sixties and seventies.[2] The 1973/74 poverty norms of Rs. 49 with reference to year 1973/74, was also fixed by the Planning Commission and it served as a base for number of subsequent studies on poverty for four quinquennial survey years. For the years 1977/78, 1983/84, and 1987/88 poverty line have been work out by using relevant price indices[3]. Generally most of the studies used Head-Count Ratio (HCR) which gives measure of prevalence of poverty (*i.e.* number or proportion of people living below poverty line). However, such a measure is quite insensitive to *depth* of poverty, *i.e.*, how far below the poverty line the poor are situated. So some studies also used Sen index or other measures which capture the depth of poverty.

Studies on rural poverty in India have addressed two basic analytical issues: one concerning the pattern of long term trend in rural poverty and second relating to the explanation of inter-temporal change either in India as a whole or in different states. Clearly the second group of studies particularly those focusing on the agricultural growth and poverty linkages are more relevant for the present discussion.

Studies based on the time series analyses raised three closely related questions. First, was there a secular change in the incidence of rural poverty over the period under study? Secondly, to what extent can the movements in the incidence of rural poverty be explained by the movements in agricultural income and prices? Thirdly, after controlling for changes in agriculture output, did the nature of development process in agriculture unleash secular, immiserising forces?

The first precise statement on the agricultural performance and poverty linkage was presented by Ahluwalia (1978) in which relationship between indices of rural poverty (*i.e.*, head-count ratio and Sen-index) and net domestic product in agriculture per capita (NDPPC) was worked out covering time series between 1956/57 to 1973/74. He also used time variable "*t*" in the equation. Ahluwalia observed an inverse relationship between over-time movement in the extent of rural poverty and per capita real agricultural income for India and in seven states. Secondly, he observed no significant time trend in rural poverty operating independently of the effect of agricultural output per head at all-India level. In eight states, however, the estimated coefficient on the time term shows significantly positive coefficient which means that there were factors at work in rural economy which by themselves operate independently and tend to increase rural poverty. In Ahuwalia's opinion, decrease in average size of holding due to increasing population pressure on land, and labour displacing technological change in agriculture could be some of the factors which tend to raise rural poverty. Ahluwalia argued that inverse relationship between rural poverty and agricultural income per capita point to the working of some 'trickle down' associated with agricultural growth.

Ahuwalia's exercise has been criticized and modified in various ways by several others. His conclusions on trickle down have been questioned by Griffin and Ghose (1979). They argued that if the period of study (of Ahluwalia's series) was to be restricted to 1960/61 and 1973/74 (*i.e.,* if the first-two observations are dropped) there would be a positive relationship between rural poverty and agricultural performance at state level. There is also no statistically significant co-relation between rural poverty and time trend, when dependent variable was taken as the percentage annual trend rate of growth of poverty and trend growth rate of per capita agricultural production and food production taken separately. But when the percentage change in rural poverty (from 1960-64 to 1970-74) was used as dependent variable, there was an inverse relationship with trend rate of growth of output per capita; both agricultural production and food production taken separately.

In a state level analysis Madle (1983), confirmed Ahluwalia's results as he observed statistically significant inverse relationship with growth in per capita foodgrain production and rural poverty (head-count ratio) during 1963/64 to 1973/74 in six states. Secondly, the state-wise coefficient of correlation between incidence of rural poverty and time variable shows that barring the exception of Assam with high positive correlation, Punjab and Haryana with high negative correlation and Tamil Nadu with moderate correlation, there is no statistically significant correlation between rural poverty and time trend.

Since in nine out of fifteen states there is no statistically significant co-relation, Mandle argued that "the production performance of agriculture was not decisive factor underlying the incidence of rural poverty although improved performance does help to ameliorate poverty. Other factors such as land distribution, wage rates, and unemployment would appear to be more important."

Dharm Narain (1986) expanded Ahluwalia's (1978) specification by including additional explanatory variable, *i.e.,* nominal consumer price in addition to agricultural income with same time series data (*i.e.,* 1956/57 to 1970/71) and observed a negative coefficient between agricultural income per person but a positive coefficient with price variable (*i.e.,* consumer price index of agricultural labour) and rural poverty. Time has a negative coefficient indicating a downward trend in the incidence of rural poverty.

Dharm Narain believed that downward trend was due to the influence of other factors, such as, employment generated through socio-economic overhead in rural areas, support to traditional cottage and village industries, growth of tertiary sector in rural area resulting from agricultural development, land reform, development of co-operative institutions and growth in health and education and other services.

Saith (1981) analyzed the relationship between rural poverty prices and agricultural production as well as time using Ahluwalia's data but with modified form and also with a truncated time series covering the period 1960/61 to 1970/71.[4] Saith used agricultural production and price variable as percentage deviation from their respective fitted trend curve. He observed that rural poverty is directly related to prices, fluctuations and inversely to agricultural production. In terms of explaining the fluctuations in the level of poverty, Saith observed that, price deviations are considerably more important than product deviation around their respective trend values. Additionally, the incidence of poverty displays a reasonably strong tendency to increase over time, taking into account the influence of price and production fluctuations. (While Ahuwalia observed no trend) Saith believed that several features accompanying the agricultural growth generated by new technology, such as increasing subdivision of holdings (which reduce overall demand for hired labour), use of labour-saving mechanization, wide spread resumption of land from small tenants by the large farmers could be some of the factors responsible for raising time trend in rural poverty during the period under study (p. 205).

Mathur (1985) made a notable attempt to reconcile the differences in the results obtained by Ahluwalia (1978) and Saith (1981). Like Ahluwalia and Saith, he also observed an increased relation between rural poverty and agricultural growth, whether this growth is measured by gross output or by value added. (He however, observed that value-added indicator underestimates the effects of agricultural growth) the analysis supports Saith's contention that inflationary pressure increases rural poverty. But Mathur's results differs from that of Ahluwalia and Saith on time trend, as he obtained a declining trend (Ahluwalia observed no trend and Saith observed raising trend). Mathur observed that with conventional linear specifications, after taking into account price and production effect—not their fluctuations, there is no evidence of a positive time trend in rural poverty, if at all there is any trend, it is negative (p. 426). Thus, the differences in the results of Ahluwalia and Saith were largely due to differences in the data used for the dependent variable or by the choice of variables but mainly due to their specifications of estimating equation (p. 427).

Ahluwalia (1978), Saith (1981), and Mathur, however, generally agreed on one point that is, population size does not influence poverty independently of per capita agricultural output. In other words, population growth only matters in so far as it affects average food availability. Walle (1985) argued that there are reasons for believing that rural population growth does affect rural poverty independently of agricultural output per capita income. Walle worked out the relationship between rural poverty (head-count ratio) and agricultural output, real agricultural wages and population growth rate (rural) using Ahluwalia's data for 1959/60 to 1970/71. A pooled model with variable slope coefficients demonstrate that poverty in India during 1960s was a function of both agricultural production and population. In particular, an adverse effect of population growth on poverty is found to exist independently of output per capita and real wages[5]. The results also show strong negative relationship between poverty and real wages which is to be expected considering the growing number of households who depend on the agricultural labour market.

In the second round, Ahluwalia (1985) analyzed the impact of current as well as lagged agricultural income and the prices on rural poverty by covering the period 1956/57 to 1977/78. The expanded data base confirmed Dharma Narain's results of positive relation of rural poverty with the level of the prices and an inverse relation with agricultural income per head at all India level. Ahluwalia observed further that an inverse relation of agricultural income with rural poverty is strengthened considerably if it is also lagged.

Gaiha (1989) improved the specification of Ahluwalia (1986) and Saith (1981) with respect to the price variable. His specification employs a measure of (level of) agricultural production per capita and a measure of fluctuations in consumer price index of agricultural labour and variable "t" representing time (Ahluwalia took level of both agricultural income per capita and prices and Saith took fluctuations in both agricultural income per capita and the prices)[6] and work out the association with head-count ratio and Sen index for two different time series, *i.e.,* 1957-77 and 1957-73 separately. Gaiha argued that it is the short-run fluctuation or suddenness of an increase in the consumer prices (not matched by increase in the wage rate as typically wages 1 kg behind the price rise which is relevant for measuring the impact on rural poverty. He observed that the effects of fluctuation in consumer price index of agricultural labour was consistently positive and statistically significant, indicating that short term unanticipated changes in prices aggravated rural poverty. The rural poverty and agricultural production were inversely related, the effect of the latter in some cases, especially at the state level was either weak or absent. Gaiha maintained that his results (for the period 1956-77 differs from Ahluwalia's (1985) insofar as he reported a strong price effect, but a weak output effect.

Yet another improvement was made in Ahluwalia's (1986) specification by Bhattacharya and others (1991) by extending his 1956/57 to 1977/78 series up to 1983/84. At all-India level, the researchers narrowed down the focus on output of cereals, relative price of cereals (*i.e.,* price of cereals relative to the price of manufacturers) and marketable surplus from rural to urban area as factors affecting rural poverty (head-count ratio). They observed that while the rise in per capita output of cereals reduces rural poverty, rise in per capita non-agricultural real income aggravate the incidence of rural poverty.[7] The relative price of cereals in previous years also raises rural poverty in current year. The government policy of procurement-*cum*-distribution, however, tended to somewhat reduce the incidence of rural poverty.

Bell and Rich (1994) sought to improve on the earlier studies of the movement in and determinants of rural poverty in India in three ways by using data from 1952/53 to 1977/78 at all-India level. Like the earlier studies, they also observed a stronger favourable connection between the levels of poverty and sustained growth in per capita real output over the long period. The estimated coefficient of real per capita output and poverty is always negative and statistically significant. They also found no support for the hypothesis that after controlling for movements in real output per head, there was an underlying upward trend in the extent of poverty and concluded that the growth process over the period in question was distributionally neutral. They also found support for the hypothesis that unanticipated inflation exacerbated poverty.

In a recent study, Ravallion and Datt (1995) used consumption, agricultural yield and wage rate data for the years 1958-90 to measure the effects of agricultural growth on rural poverty. They found that measure of absolute poverty (head-count ratio) responded favourably to changes in mean consumption over the period 1958-90. The absolute poverty measures responded in the short run to changes in agricultural wages as well as to average yields. And wages responded to farm yields presumably through effects on labour demand, such as due to multiple cropping. Higher yield thus, helped reduced poverty through induced wage effects, as well as the more direct channels including effects on both employment and own-farm productivity. In short-run, there was also a strong adverse impact of inflation on real agricultural wages and in turn on poverty.

Among the initial responses, Bardhan was perhaps the first to develop a comprehensive and forceful critique of Ahluwalia's (1978) "trickle down" hypothesis. Bardan's analysis also makes departure from earlier studies in another way as he examined the role of technological, institutional, and demographic factors in addition to agricultural growth and prices.

Bardhan, analyzing the National Sample Survey (NSS) data at three levels of disaggregation, *i.e.,* (i) at the level of individual households in about 550 sample villages of West Bengal in 1977/78; (ii) at the level of fifty-five NSS agroclimatic regions (below the state level) for early 1970s; and (iii) at more aggregate state level for 1971/72, came to a different conclusion. He is skeptical of an inverse relationship between rural poverty and agricultural performance, in fact, he argues that certain type of agricultural growth processes can have the opposite impact of aggravating rural poverty.[8]

In an exercise relating to 550 households in Bengal, Bardhan analyzed factors affecting poverty separately for agricultural labour households and primary cultivator households. He observed that the risk of poverty is associated with households and village specific characteristics. The results of logic analysis suggest that the probability of falling below poverty line is lower for an agricultural labour household with a large area to cultivate, a smaller number of dependents, greater participation in non-farm work, and higher educational level. Similarly, it is lower for an agricultural labour household that belongs to a village where the wage rate, irrigation level, rainfall, fertilizer use is greater and villages where alternative opportunities to work on public work programmes are higher. The probability of falling below the poverty line is greater if, the village is remote, household belongs to the scheduled castes (there are fewer "connection" and greater deprivations in access to resource and job opportunities and low bargaining power), and the current period is in an agriculturally slack season.

The unexpected finding is the highly significant positive coefficient of growth rate of agricultural production. Hence, Bardhan argued "other things remaining the same, the probability of an agricultural labour households' sliding below the poverty line seems to be higher if it is in a district where agricultural production has gone at a faster rate" (p. 84). According to him, it is difficult to identify the factors but the results are certainly consistent with the significant rise in the proportion of agricultural labour households to total rural households and reported increase in tenant eviction in highly advanced areas of Bengal.

Similar results obtained for primarily cultivating households (or self-employed households). The additional variables, *i.e.*, proportion of area irrigated by canals and tube wells at village level have a negative association with probability of poverty. The agricultural growth is again significantly associated with likelihood of poverty. Bardhan argued that "possible growth-induced mechanisms of pauperization of small farmers may be relevant for primary-cultivated households" (p. 86).

In a regional level analysis in the absence of direct estimate of poverty, Bardhan used two alternative surrogate indicators of poverty: the per capita monthly expenditure level of non-cultivating wage-earner households and the proportion of rural households that were poor in terms of the value of assets owned for the year 1970/71. The linear regression analysis of regional variations in per capita monthly expenditure of non-cultivating households shows that, it is higher in regions with better rainfall, more irrigation, greater proportion of worker in manufacturing and smaller proportion of scheduled castes and scheduled tribes households (suffering from special social disadvantages in access to opportunities). Unlike West Bengal, "growth" rate of crop production in a region seems to have a positive impact on the level of living of wage-earning households. The number of oil engines and electric pump sets per hectare of cropped area in a region and the proportion of large farmer households have a negative effect. Bardhan, therefore, argued that "agricultural growth in general seems to be helpful, but larger farmer-dominated growth dependent on private ownership of modern equipment (*i.e.,* certain type of growth) may not be" (p. 88). In second exercise, Bardhan observed that proportion of asset in poor rural households was lowest in better-irrigated (particularly well-irrigated) and high growth regions and in regions where the scheduled caste households make up the lowest percentage of total household. Again, the number of oil engine and electric pump set (per hectare) has a significant positive association with poverty.

Lastly, in a state level analysis using a third measure of poverty, *i.e.,* calorie-deficient households, the linear regression results show that it is negatively associated with the value of agricultural production per male workers and positively associated with the concentration of rural assets ownership and with consumer price index of agricultural labour;

which suggests that there is less rural poverty in more productive states, but more in areas with greater unequal distribution of ownership of assets and higher prices.

Bardhan's general conclusion is that "agricultural growth and productivity improvement tend to help raise incomes all around, but certain types of growth processes generate negative forces for the poor, particularly in an institutional setting of highly unequal distribution of assets and access to resources" (Bardhan, 1986, pp. 90-91).

In a broadly similar exercise of NSS regional level data for 1972/73, Rao *et al* (1986) obtained more or less identical results. They observed that level of rural poverty (measured in terms of percentage of person with a calorie-intake less than or equal to the minimum) was negatively associated with growth rate of crop-output, level of irrigation, canal irrigation,[9] and rural electrification but positively associated with percentage of Scheduled Castes and Scheduled Tribes population, proportion of agricultural labour and consumer prices of agricultural labour.

Yet in another exercise based on same NSS regional level data for 1972/73, Sundaram and Tendulkar analyzed link between rural poverty and unemployment rate. They observed that asset per households, agricultural productivity per hectare, and per capita consumption expenditure helped to reduce the incidence of rural poverty (head-count ratio) but inequality in the distribution of consumption expenditure and unemployment rate (daily status) aggreviate the prevalence of rural poverty. They discovered also that higher unemployment rate was largely the result of widespread existence of wage labour households. The higher proportion of wage labour households in turn was the outcome of inequality in the distribution of assets per household and density of population per hectare of operated area. Among the variables used, the availability of income generating assets at household level was the most important variable in explaining inter-regional variations in the incidence of rural poverty in India.

The critique and major extension of Bardhan's (1985) analysis of immiserizing effects of growth was, however, made by Gaiha [1987(a) and 1987(b)]. He argued that Bardhan's overall conclusions "that certain types of growth process tend to generate negative forces for the poor, particularly in an institutional setting of highly unequal distribution of assets and access to resources was intuitively appealing, but was some what ambiguous." Such an analysis to be persuasive it has to be based on a panel survey in which a sample of household is observed over a period of time. Gaiha's analysis is based on a panel survey of 4,118 cultivating households each of which was interviewed in 1968/69, 1969/70, and 1970/71.[10]

He observed that the effects of the new technology were not altogether favourable. Specifically, while substantial number of both poor and non-poor cultivating households benefited, smaller but non-negligible subsets of households also experienced income losses during 1968/69, 1969/70, and 1970/71.[11] The decline in income was both due to loss of cultivable area and lower yield rate, the latter reflecting the effect of reduction in the area under HYVs (together with other complementary inputs), a hike in tenancy obligation. The reduction in income from cultivation was not compensated fully through alternative sources of income—especially casual agricultural wage employment. A feature of the growth process was the dominance of large cultivator which resulted in the impoverishment of subset of cultivating households. Gaiha argued that profitability of new technology—especially on large farms—could not, by itself, justify this causal link. For transfer of cultivable land, charging of excessive rents, etc. to occur role of interlinked transactions in credit, land, and labour market in rural area, with asymmetrical economic power relation were important. Author also considered whether such income losses persisted in subsequent years. Based on the 1970/71 and 1981/82 panel survey data comparison of the same households, Gaiha observed that the nature of the growth process has altered somewhat in more recent years and as a result, there has been a weakening of some of the earlier mechanism causing absolute impoverishment.[12]

Studies reviewed so far (*i.e.,* up until the end of 1972/73) analyzed mainly the impact of agricultural output and prices on the long term trends in rural poverty during 1956/57 and 1972/73 (except few papers based on NSS regional level one point data). Such an analysis was possible due to the availability of consumption data on annual basis. However, due to discontinuation of annual surveys in 1972/73 and its replacement by the quinquennial survey, the studies after 1972/73 are confined to four points of time, *i.e.,* 1973/74, 1977/78, 1983/84, and 1987/88. Studies after 1972/73 differs also from the earlier ones in another way. While the studies based on time series data analyzed the role of agricultural growth and prices, the mechanism through which the process of growth suppose to improve the income of poor did not receive much attention. Studies after 1972/73 in addition to growth and prices also examined the impact of labour related outcomes (of growth process), such as employment (on-farm and off-farm sectors), wages, job diversification of rural economy and the impact of poverty alleviation programmes.

Mahendra Dev (1988) for instance analyzed the inter-relation between labour productivity (*i.e.,* value of crop-output per agricultural worker) and rural poverty for all rural households and separately for self-employed and wage labour households in agriculture. The cross-section (state level) regressions for 1964/65, 1972/73, 1977/78, and 1983 revealed a significant inverse relationship between labour productivity and incidence of rural poverty of all households. Regression exercise on the pooled cross-section data shows that the poverty reducing impact of labour productivity has increased after introduction of new technology as compared to the pre-HYV period. However, comparisons since 1972/73 shows that the poverty reducing impact of labour productivity has been maintained but not strengthened. The results indicate also that both types of households namely; self-employed and wage labour employed in agriculture benefits from the higher level of labour productivity. In a separate regression exercise, Mahendra Dev, observed that higher labour productivity helps to reduce the poverty of agricultural labour households by raising the wage rate and employment. Through a decomposition exercise, he observed that yield growth was a major source of rise in labour productivity. The conclusion that emerges from this analysis is that agricultural development based on yield increasing technology generally helped to reduce rural poverty through increase in labour productivity of agricultural classes.

Ghose (1994) using cross-section state-level data for three points of time, *i.e.* 1970/71, 1977/78, and 1983/84 examined the impact of selected factors upon the incidence of rural poverty. He observed a favourable impact of foodgrain production per hectare and foodgrain production and state domestic product from agriculture per capita (rural) on rural poverty during three years under study. Similarly, real wage rates (male labour) and unemployment rate have an expected sign as the higher real wage rate and the lower unemployment rate (irrespective of the level of wages) help reduce poverty.

Ghose also observed an inverse relationship between rural poverty and average size of the marginal and the small farm holdings, but statistically significant only in one year (*i.e.,* 1983). High value of significant coefficient indicates that small increase in average size of smaller holdings would reduce poverty substantially. Since foodgrain productivity turn out to be an important factor affecting rural poverty in all years, Ghose analyzed the factors underlying variations in foodgrain productivity. He discovered that irrigation and fertilizer have a significantly positive effects upon foodgrain productivity, so does the agricultural credit as supporting factors for technology adoption. The average size of operational holdings is inversely related with foodgrain productivity. The finding is in conformity with inverse relationship between farm size and productivity of land which is very often generalized in Indian agriculture.

In a cross-sectional state level analysis of poverty of rural labour during 1977/78, 1983, 1987/88, Alok Kumar (1994) obtained identical results, *i.e.,* an inverse relationship of agricultural performance, real wage rate, land-labour ratio and sources and type of debt but a positive relationship of consumer price index and unemployment rate with level of poverty among rural labour in India.

Tendulkar *et al* (1993) have probed the relationship between the measures of poverty prevalence (head-count ratio) with various combinations of factors such as labour-market related outcome (*i.e.,* unemployment rate, wage rate, and wage income) access to credit, prices, and Gini-ratio of per capita consumption[13] for rural area using state-wise cross-section data from 1983 and 1987/88. The results show that per capita monthly wages income is an important determinant of prevalence of poverty in rural area. Since the per capita monthly wage income is derived by multiplication of person days at work per capita, and wage rate in casual employment, it reflects the combined effect of both employment and wage rates.

The cereals prices paid by rural households also turn out to be significant factors.

Tendulkar *et al.* (1983) also highlighted the positive impact of public employment programmes (including the supply of cereals at subsidised price through PDS) in alleviating poverty in short-run. Authors noted that compared to the peak year 1983 the level of rural poverty was distinctly lower in a drought year 1987-88.

Using the state-wise poverty estimates of Tendulkar *et al.* (1983) Sen and Ghose (1993) analyzed the poverty employment link for the years 1972/73 and 1987-88. They also discussed the impact of rural non-farm employment and public work programmes in the determination of wages and rural poverty. The first equation revealed that while higher unemployment (daily status) increases the rural poverty, the rise in per capita consumption help in alleviating the same. The person days employment per rural person (taken separately for agriculture and non-aricultural) have a favourable impact on the prevalence of rural poverty. In second equation, replacing the per capita consumption variable with two income variables, *i.e.*, per capita (rural) agricultural income and wage rate, observed a strong favourable impact of both on rural poverty. About half of the impact of higher agricultural employment and entire effect of higher non-agricultural employment on prevalence of poverty, however, operates not directly, but through their effect on wage rate. This implies that expansion of employment particularly in non-agricultural activities is unlikely to reduce poverty unless it pushes the real wage rates.

According to authors, in fact, the mechanism for poverty reduction in India has been arising trend in real agricultural wages, since the mid-seventies (*i.e.,* after 1974/75).[14] And the improvement in wage rate in rural area was largely due to tightening of the labour market because of job diversification (and hence the movement of workers) in favour of non-farm sector. Authors argued that there is an evidence that since the mid-seventies (1974-75) a rise in non-agriculture's share of employment has actually been accompanied by raising real wage in agriculture and non-agriculture. Higher real wages and sectoral shift would suggest that the shift was largely determined by 'pull factors' and hence dynamic in nature. However, according to them actual picture is more complicated as both "pull" as well as "push" factors were at work.

The tightening of labour market in rural area was mainly due to movement of rich groups out of agriculture for better jobs created in government and other sectors which helped to raise the real wages for remaining workers in rural area. In case of rural rich, thus, the shift was largely determined by higher earnings. Among the poorer households, however, employment diversification into non-agriculture continued to reflect a distress situation as they increasingly entered into casual work in sectors like construction and mining where the incidence of poverty was relatively high (Bhalla, 1993).

Shiela Bhalla's (1993) earlier analysis for 1983/84 seems to support the findings of Sen and Ghose (1993). Bhalla (1983) works out the incidence of poverty for households engaged in nine occupation groups, analyzed the relationship between level of poverty in each group and agricultural development and in a separate exercise also examined whether or not variations in rural non-farm work force, growth rates were caused by push and pull factors.

Incidence of rural poverty (head-count ratio) was found to be greatest among the agricultural households followed closely by mining and construction. The electricity, gas, and water supply categories are conspicuous for having the lowest incidence of poverty.

Bhalla observed that variations in level of poverty across states among the households engaged in agriculture, construction were explained by crop-labour productivity and value of cultivating households assets. Thus, households employed in the construction industry were better off in regions where labour productivity in agriculture was high. Similarly, level of poverty of households engaged in the services and trade was lower in region of high agricultural labour productivity. This suggests that services and trade activities in rural areas depend most severely on demand generated by agricultural activities. The factors behind interregional variations in poverty among rural manufacturing households were both farm labour productivity, rural and cultivating household's assets and the development of rural-urban infrastructure.[15]

In an analytical exercise which was carried out to determine whether or not observed variations in non-farm work-force growth rates were caused by "push" (as indicated by direct positive relationship of poverty in household industrial categories with growth rate of non-farm work force), or by "pull" (as reflected in low degree of poverty in household industrial categories where high work force growth had been registered), an anticipated inverse relationship between poverty and state level work force growth rate of non-farm employment appeared for agriculture, manufacturing, electricity, transport and services. But in some states high work force growth rates in mining, construction tend to be positively associated with poverty, which implies that work force growth particularly in construction activities may reflect distress diversification of work force.

Thus, Bhalla concludes that the high work force growth rate in sectors like construction or mining may indeed be partly the product of "push factors" while in the remaining non-farm industrial categories work force growth is in response to opportunities for a distinct improvement in level of living. This supports the results of Sen and Ghose (1993) for recent years, 1987/88.

Studies reviewed so far focused mainly on linkages of rural poverty with agricultural income, prices, employment, and wages. Few studies highlight also the association of rural poverty with land distribution. Aspects of land distribution used in the analysis were, land concentration, farm size, incidence of landlessness, and marginal holdings and access to land in lease market and term of lease.

For instance, among other factors, Dharm Narain (1986), attached great importance to land reform's measure undertaken during the 1950's and the 1960's (which include distribution of surplus land to landless households and protection to tenants) for declining trend in proportion of persons below poverty (head-count ratio) at all India level during 1956/57 to 1972/73. Ahluwalia (1978) attributes the raising trend in rural poverty during 1956/57 to 1972/73 in eight states to decline in average farm size. Mudale (1983) believed that the lack of downward trend in ratio of rural poor in nine states during 1963/64 to 1973/74 may be due to adverse distribution of land. Similarly Saith (1981) argued that raising trend in rural poverty (head-count ratio) during 1960-61 and 1971/72 in India could be attributed to increasing subdivision of landholding (which reduces over all demand for hired labour) and widespread resumption of agricultural land from small tenants by large farmers. None of these time series studies however, have worked out a casual link between rural poverty and land distribution variables in rigorous manner. The lack of time series data on the land distribution perhaps restrict the observation to general conjecture only.

Some researcher, however, analyzed the casual link between incidence of rural poverty and one or the other variables associated with land distribution by using state-level or NSS regional level data for selected years.

In an exercise relating to households data in West Bengal, Bardhan (1986) observed that during 1971/72, possibility of falling below poverty line for agricultural labour household was lower with larger area to cultivate and smaller proportion of scheduled castes and tribe households. In a regional-level analysis for 1972/73, (NSS) Bardhan observed that per capita monthly consumption expenditure of non-cultivating wage earner households (proxy for poverty ratio) in 1972/73 tend to be lower if the proportion of large farm households and proportion of scheduled caste and scheduled tribe population was high (reflecting suffering from special social disadvantages in accessible to opportunities). The proportion of "assert-poor rural households" (alternative proxy variable for poverty rate) was also lowest in a region where scheduled caste households make up the lowest percentage of total household. In a state-level regression analysis for the same year, Bardhan observed a positive association of calorie deficient households and concentration of rural assets.

Interlocked factor markets which affect their production efficiency, net income and ultimately the incidence of poverty, Shergill (1989) in a separate exercise for 1971/72 found that these two tenancy variables have very low correlation with the poverty in 1971/72 and conclude that extent of tenancy as such does not seem to influence the incidence of rural poverty.

Shergill (1989) also observed a negative regression coefficient for Gini-ratio of operational holdings with rural poverty for 1971/72, which suggests that higher land concentration is associated with lower incidence of poverty. The negative coefficient of land concentration was confirmed by Chadha and Sharma (1991) for 1961/62, 1971/72 and 1981/82 as well. Both Chadha and Sharma (1991) and Shergill (1989) seems to agree on the common explanation for negative coefficient of land concentration with rural poverty which clashes with received notions on the regressive role of inequitable distribution of land. Shergill argued that, "Where capitalist development of agriculture followed a relatively more normal pattern, land concentration, use of modern technology, high land and labour productivities go hand in with fast growth of class of agricultural labourers, in such a socio-economic situation the class of agricultural labour and its capitalist employers in agriculture having emerged and grown simultaneously, land concentration is more likely to be associated with more and regular employment and higher wages for rural labours and consequently with lower incidence of poverty....on the other hand where—the growth of a numerous class of rural proletarians was not accompanied by emergence of technologically more progressive large farms ... in such a scenario mass rural poverty then is a likely outcome; most of the cultivators themselves being poor, fail to provide regular employment and reasonable wages to the mass of rural proletarians" (P. All).

For more recent years, *i.e.,* 1970/71, 1977/78, and 1983/84 Ghose (1994) however, observed a negative association of rural poverty and average size of marginal and small holdings in India. The high value of significant coefficients indicate that a small increase in average size of marginal holding would reduce poverty incidence substantially.

Summing Up

This extensive review of studies on the rural poverty provides several useful insights into the dynamics of poverty in India — particularly concerning the effects of agricultural growth. One group of studies tried to explain the overtime movement in the incidence of rural poverty at an all-India level using time series data. Others tried to explain the variations and changes in rural poverty across the states and regions using data for selected years.

In the first group, the discussion was initiated by Ahluwalia (1978) who obtained and inverse relationship between agricultural income per capita and rural poverty during 1956 to 1977/78. This led him to conclude that improved agricultural performance can help reduce the incidence of rural poverty. Most of the latter studies followed Ahluwalia in using agricultural income per capita. Few used value of crop output (Mathur, 1985) foodgrain output (Mundal, 1983) or cereal output per capita (Bhattacharya and others, 1991).

All these exercises which used Ahluwalia's time series data up to 1977/78 and others who worked on his extended data base up to 1983/84 (Bhattacharya and others) and further to 1990 (Ravallion and Datt, 1995) have confirmed Ahluwalia's results at an all-India level. The only exception was that of Griffin and Ghose (1979), who drop three observations from Ahluwalia's time series and fail to reproduce any significant links between poverty and agricultural performance.

Saith (1981), Narain (Desai, 1985), Ahluwalia (1986), Gaiha (1989), Bhattacharya and others (1991), Bell and Rich (1984), and Ravallion and Datt (1995) added the price variable to the variable of agricultural output. They employ various selections of prices levels, nominal prices, short-term fluctuation (deviation from the trend) and relative prices (relative cereals prices to manufacturing). All these modified price variables shows positive coefficient and hence poverty aggravating impact. Among the whole lot, only Mathur (1989) and Ravallion and Datt (1995) work out the relation of variables other than agricultural output and prices; they worked out the relation between wage rate and poverty and discovered a favourable impact of higher real wages on rural poverty.

Ravallion and Datt (1995) also observed that higher wages were largely induced by higher yield rates. Since the yield ratio has a favourable impact on rural poverty, it implied that good agricultural performance help to reduce poverty by improving the wages and employment level of rural labourer.

The state level cross-section exercises generally support the all-India time series results concerning the favourable impact of agricultural growth and adverse impact of prices on rural poverty. Number of studies have observed that variations in crop output or income per worker (and also per hectare) explain the large part of inter-regional variations in prevalence of rural poverty. In a separate exercises, Bardhan (1986), Mahendra Dev (1988), and Ghose (1994) obtained an inverse relation of output-per-worker with the incidence of rural poverty during 1972/73, 1977/78, and 1983/84. Ghose (1994) also observed identical relation between rural poverty and foodgrain output per capita and per hectare during three periods. Ghose's results clearly revealed that inter-state variations, the levels of rural poverty, were mainly caused by variation in the yield rates of foodgrain, which were in turn induced by the higher use of inputs like fertilizer, irrigation, and credit. The favourable impact of irrigation, both canal and wells, and of rainfall was identified by Bardan (1986) and Rao, *et al* (1986) for 1972/73.

Mahendra Dev (1988) added that lower level of poverty (due to higher output-per-worker) was the results of higher real wages rate and employment rate, which in turn was induced by higher yield rates. This implies that growth in agricultural output in excess of labour force can improve the labour productivity which in turn improves the wages and employment. For recent years (*i.e.,* 1977/78, 1983/84, and 1987/88) Alok Kumar (1995) also confirmed that foodgrain production per hectare and per capita (rural) was closely associated with lower level of poverty of rural and agricultural labour.

In a separate exercise, the positive impact of real wages and employment was also confirmed by Tendulkar and others (1995) for 1983/84 and 1987. Tendulkar and others, observed that per capita monthly wage income (which is a reasonable proxy for total income accruing to poor rural households) was an important detriment of poverty in rural areas.

Sen and Ghose (1995) in the cross-section regression exercise also observed a positive impact of wages and employment on rural poverty in 1983/84 and 1987/88. In fact they argued that higher wage rates has been a major factor for the decline in rural poverty in India since the mid-1970's. Higher real wages in turn was a result of tightening of the rural labour market caused mainly by the movement of rural labour to non-agricultural sector. Sen and Ghose however, argued that the shift towards non-farm sector was mainly induced by employment generated by the external agency of the state rather than forces internal to rural economy. They thus, highlighted the role of the state programmes in creation of non-farm employment. Tendulkar and others (1995) also observed the importance of states' measures to generate employment in alleviating poverty in the short-run-particularly during drought years.

The state level cross-section regression exercises also confirmed the adverse impact of higher prices on rural poverty. Bardhan (1986), for 1972/73 and Alok Kumar (1995) for 1977/78, and 1983/84 obtained a positive coefficient for consumer price index of agricultural labour households. Similarly, Tendulkar and others (1993), also obtained a positive coefficient for cereal prices and ratio of overall rural poverty.

Few studies also highlight the favourable impact of rural infrastructure like availability of road and electricity, on the prevalence of rural poverty (Bardhan, 1985; Rao and others, 1985). The higher education level (increasing the non-agricultural opportunities available to the persons or households) and non-farm employment were generally associated with lower poverty. Some studies however, noted an adverse impact of higher population growth and higher family size on poverty of rural household (Mathur, 1985 and Bardan, 1985).

While most of the studies based on both all-India time series and state level data (for selected years) confirmed the favourable impact of agricultural performance on rural poverty. We have also seen that Bardhan (1986), Ghose and Griffin (1979) and others expressed reservation about the poverty alleviating impact of some types of growth processes and institutional settings. Bardhan (1986) argued that agricultural growth and productivity improvement seems to be helpful but large farmers dominated growth dependent on private ownership of modern equipment may not, particularly in an institutional setting, skewed distribution of assets and access to resources. This observation was based on a positive coefficient of oil engines and electric motors, proportion of large farmers and of proportion agricultural labour households, and concentration of rural asset ownership with prevalence of rural poverty during 1972/73. Few studies examined the linkage of land distribution and rural poverty for latter years (Sau, 1971; Rao and *other*, 1985; and *Shargill*, 1989) and observed that higher level of rural poverty was closely associated with greater proportion of agricultural labour and landless agricultural labour household during the early 1970's. Chadha and Sharma (1991) also obtained a positive coefficient for proportion of agricultural labour households as well as proportion of marginal and small farmers with rural poverty for 1961, 1971, and 1981. They have observed a positive coefficient for percentage of leased—in area obtained and the lease—in area cultivated under share crop. In their opinion, the latter was mainly due to impact of adverse terms and conditions (such high rent, short term lease, and interlocking of factor markets) under which the marginal and small farmers generally operate land of the large farmer.

NOTES

1. Annual consumer expenditure surveys (with smaller sample) have been resumed since 1986/87 while continuing with the programme of quinquennial survey (Tendulkar, *et al*, 1993).
2. Although the Rs. 20 PMCE at 1960/61 prices has been used by many, since each one of them adopted a somewhat different method to workout this norm, the poverty line varied between the studies. For instance, as against the Planning Commission, norm of Rs.20 PMCE, Minhas (1970), Ojha (1970), Bardhan (1973), Rudra (1971), Dandekar and Rath (1971), Ahluwalaia (1978), Datta (1980) and Vaidyanathan (1974) have preferred Rs. 16.67, Rs. 18.00, Rs. 14.00, Rs.15.63, Rs.15.00, Rs.15.00, Rs.15.00 and Rs. 20.00 PMCE, respectively.
3. Research have used different price indices: whole sale price indices (Dandekar and Rath, 1988 and Gupta, 1984 both rural and urban areas). Consumer price index for agricultural labourer in respect of rural poor (Bardhan, 1973, Ahluwalia, 1978 and 1986, and Datta, 1980) and consumer price indices for industrial workers in respect of urban poor or a combination of the consumer price indices for industrial workers and urban poor (*Minhas, et al,* 1987) and more importantly separate all-India and state specific price indices for rural and urban poor (Minhas et al, 1990 and 1991).
4. Saith (1981) provides justification for deleting the first three observations and last observation from Ahluwalia's (1978) time series data (pp. 199-200).
5. Saith (1981) argued for inclusion of consumer price variable, but the estimating equation used fluctuation in both indices of agricultural production and consumer price. Gaiha argued that this specification is problematic because fluctuation in prices may reflect fluctuations in production and in that case one of the two explanatory variables is redundant. In contrast, Ahluwalia (1985) used both current and lagged level of agricultural production and level of prices as explanatory variables is redundant. In contrast, Ahluwalia (1985) used both current and lagged level of agricultural production and level of prices as explanatory variables. Apart from the difficulty that the use of consumer price as casual factor implies that there is no catching up (or in other words, inflation perpetually aggravate poverty). The fact that the level of current and lagged agricultural production and the level of consumer price are collinear suggests that there is a certain redundancy in this specification too. In view of this, Gaiha's specification employs a measure of (level of) agricultural production (per capita) and measure of fluctuation in consumer price ...p. 336.
6. Walle (1985) emphasized that the identified population effect on poverty cannot be properly viewed as a "Malthusian effect" since by assumption the test used have held agricultural output per capita constant. Most probably, the result reflects an association between population growth and adverse changes in the distribution of income due to increased rural unemployment (p.438).
7. Bhattacharya and others (1991) argued that underlying mechanism is rather simple. Give the output of cereals, a growth in non-agricultural or urban income would lead to an excess demand for cereals and hence, would push up the relative prices of cereals, adversely affecting the consumption of those rural people who were dependent on the market. As a consequence, the incidence of rural poverty would rise (p. 187).
8. Bardhan identifies eight possible ways through which agricultural growth led by new agricultural technology may counteract the positive impact and immiserized some people (p. 77).
9. Rao et al (1986) observed that the canal irrigation should result in reduction of rural poverty due to rise in employment and wage rate associated with such development.

Also benefit of canal irrigation can be expected to the distributed widely among different class of farmers (p. 98).

10. The data are drawn from Additional Rural Income Surveys carried out by the National Council of Applied Economic Research (1975) of 4,118 households from the Intensive Agricultural District Programme (IADP) and Intensive Agricultural Area Programme (IAAP).
11. The poverty cut-off point was taken to be Rs.16.00 per persons per month at 1960/61 prices. With the help of this cut-off points, a classification of cultivating households by poverty status for 1968/69, 1969/70, and 1970/71 was worked out. The categories were (a) poor who remained poor without becoming poorer; (b) poor who became poorer; (c) poor who became not poor; (d) not poor who remained not poor; and (e) not poor who become poor (Gaiha, 1986, p. 571).
12. Gaiha mentioned that "the panel data indicates that (i) land owned per household increased in the bottom four deciles; (ii) there was a reduction in concentration at the upper end of the distribution; and (iii) there was an improvement in the land owned by landless and marginal land owners as a result they experienced an increase in the share of agricultural income in total household income. Gaiha argued that this could be partly due to the government programmes (p. 43).
13. Tendulkar, *et al.* (1983) took six variables to capture the impact of labour market outcome, *i.e.,* (i) per capita monthly aggregate person days at work (ii) average wage rate of male and female for casual labour; (iii) per capita monthly wage of cereals paid by rural labour; (iv) person days unemployment; (v) price of cereals paid by rural labour; and (vi) Gini coefficient of size distribution of per capita total consumption expenditure.
14. Sen and Ghose (1993) observed that an important point to be noted in this context is that both raising real wages and falling poverty are trends observable after the mid-seventies in almost all the states, whereas, the phenomena of agricultural prosperity is only true for a few regions (p. 47).
15. Bhalla (1994) observed that the improvement of the conditions of those engaged in rural manufacturing in infrastructurally backward state would thus, depend on overall infrastructure development at the state level and not just in rural areas. It was concluded that this finding could be related to non-rural input supplies or to the overall level of development of transport, communication, and banking networks (p. 613).

9

REFORM OF DIRECT TAXATION IN INDIA

—Prof. B.S. SREEKANTA RADHYA

Tax reform has received a new impetus since 1991 as an important component of economic reforms. The post-1991 period has witnessed a major departure in the approach to taxation in India. The purpose of this lecture is to highlight the reform measures introduced since 1991 in the area of direct taxation and to analyse their significance.

Objectives of Tax Reforms

Broadly speaking, the following are the objectives of tax reforms in India :

(a) Revenue augmentation;
(b) Enhancing the income—elasticity of tax revenue;
(c) Minimising the efficiency cost or excess burden;
(d) Designing an appropriate policy of tax incentives;
(e) Ensuring equity, *i.e.,* justice or fairness in taxation;
(f) Making the tax system as simple as possible;
(g) Ensuring a combination of flexibility and stability;
(h) Improving the tax administration.

New Philosophy of Taxation

The post-1991 tax reform is tailored to meet the requirements of new economic policy launched in July 1991 which envisaged liberalisation of both domestic and external sectors of the economy. It advocated a market-oriented approach to development. This approach is based on the supply-side Economics. The tax policy has to be in conformity with the new economic policy and therefore a supply-side tax policy has been envisaged.

The supply-side tax policy basically aims at overcoming the negative substitution effects of taxation. As pointed out by

V.P. Gandhi, "supply-side economists stress minimising the distortions that taxes, in general, and high and progressive taxes, in particular, inject into market decisions and believe that reforming the tax structures, in general, and lowering the rates of taxes, in particular, would encourage savings and production by allowing the economic incentives of a free market to work." (Gandhi, V.P. 1987) There are two versions of supply-side tax policy namely basic supply-side tax policy and popular supply-side tax policy. While the former lays emphasis on reform of the tax system in all its aspects, the latter focuses on reform of income taxation in particular especially by reducing the top marginal income tax rates. The advantage of reducing the top marginal rate is that the negative substitution effect will disappear and work effort, supply of savings and capital will all increase and the rate of growth of the economy gets accelerated. The best-known exponent of this view is Arthur Laffer according to whom as the income-tax rates are raised, the revenue will increase as long as the tax rates are in the normal range and then reach a peak and thereafter further increase will take the rates to a prohibitive range resulting in a fall in revenue.

The argument that the burden of debt should be kept low to stimulate development is not new. As pointed out by R.M. Bird, "Tax more, said Kaldor; tax less, said Bauer. Increase public spending to encourage development, said Kaldor; reduce public spending to encourage development, said Bauer. Tax the rich especially heavily, said Kaldor; tax the rich if at all, with great care, said Bauer, who in this and other ways should perhaps be considered the modern father of supply-side taxation in developing countries". (Bird, R.M. 1992) Bauer's views which were not taken seriously in those days are now receiving a lot of attention.

Since the tax reform in the post-1991 period is part of stabilisation and structural adjustment policy based on IMF prescription, the standard tax policy advice of IMF seems to have its influence on the tax reform undertaken in recent years. In respect of direct tax system, the IMF policy advice is as follows: (Parthasarthi Shome, 1995)

1. To overcome the problems like inefficiencies, inequalities, high compliance costs and tax evasion created by a complicated tax system, the existing tax system must be simplified.
2. Personal income-tax must lay emphasis on lowering the marginal rates and broadening the tax base. Top marginal rates

should not be more than 40 per cent and tax incentives must be minimised.

3. Adoption of a single, proportional rate for the corporate income-tax within the range of 30-40 per cent is desirable. It is also desirable to have the same top marginal rate for both personal income tax and corporate income tax. All domestic enterprises whether private or state-owned should be treated alike and similarly there should be equal treatment of domestic and foreign enterprises. There should be a minimum corporate tax wherever revenue is eroded because of too many concessions.

The overall approach till mid-eighties was such that the stress was on high rates and on using tax policy as an instrument of reducing inequalities. The outcome was neither more revenue nor reduction in inequalities and only more and more evasion. The expectation that higher taxation will increase public sector saving and investment also did not come true. While Kaldor, Lewis and others felt that increased taxes fuel increased development, Bauer, Please and others felt that increased taxes lead to decreased development and it is the latter view that has gained currency of late. Against this background, we may now turn to the reform measures introduced in the area of direct taxation in the post-1991 period.

Reform in the Post-1991 Period

Reforms in the post-1991 period are all based on the recommendations of the Tax Reforms Committee. Recognising the need for removal of the negative substitution effect of a highly progressive tax system, the TRC said ". . . our general approach is that the best results, in terms of compliance (and therefore, revenue), efficiency and equity are obtained through a system incorporating moderate rates on a broad base". In accordance with the opinion expressed by this Committee, attempts have been made to lower the rates and to broaden the tax base.

Until mid-eighties, the top marginal rate was very high. In 1973-74 it was as high as 97.75 per cent and it was reduced to 75 per cent in 1974-75 and to 67 per cent in 1976-77. It was in 1985-86 that it was brought down to 50 per cent and in the reform years, there has been further reduction in the marginal rate. In 1992-93 it was brought down to 40 per cent and to 30 per cent in 1997-98. In fact the prevailing marginal rate is even lower than what was recommended by the TRC which had recommended a rate of 40 per cent for income above Rs. 2 lakh.

In respect of Corporation tax also, the rates have been considerably reduced. In 1984-85, the rate for closely held companies was 68.25 per cent and for widely held companies it was 57.75 per cent and for non-domestic companies it was 77.5 per cent. In 1991-92, the rate for closely held companies was reduced to 50 per cent and for widely held companies it was reduced to 40 per cent and for non-domestic companies it was reduced to 65 per cent. In 1994-95, the distinction between closely held companies and widely held companies was removed and for both of them the rate was fixed at 40 per cent and in respect of non-domestic companies the rate was reduced to 55 per cent and further in 1997-98, for closely held and widely held companies the rate was reduced to 35 per cent and for non-domestic companies it was reduced to 48 per cent and thus in the post-1991 period, Corporation tax rates are much lower than the rates which prevailed prior to 1991.

Regarding the impact of lower tax regime on tax compliance and revenue collection, it is rather too early to make any judgment because it takes some time for the new policy to yield results. The impact of the new policy would be felt only in the long run. It should also be noted that revenue realisation in any given period depends on a number of factors and not just on the tax rates.

With regard to the widening of the tax base, the measures that have been introduced are :

1. *Presumptive Taxation* : Introduced in 1992-93, the scheme was intended to bring under tax net retail traders with a turnover of Rs. 5 lakh or less. They were expected to just pay Rs. 1400 per annum and filing of return was not required. The scheme was abolished as it was not a success and in its place in 1997-98, a scheme for retail traders with a turnover between 8 and 40 lakhs was introduced according to which 5 per cent of the turnover would be presumed as their income and taxed accordingly.

2. *Estimated Income Scheme* : An estimated income scheme was introduced in 1994-95 for contractors and truck owners. In the case of contractors with turnover up to Rs. 40 lakh, 8 per cent of gross receipts would be assumed as their profit and in case of truck owners, the profit would be presumed to be Rs. 2000 per truck per month in the case of heavy transport vehicles and Rs. 1800 per vehicle per month in the case of light commercial vehicles.

3. *Tax deduction at Source* : In 1991-92, a scheme of deduction of tax at source in respect of bank interest, income distribution by UTI,

etc., beyond Rs. 2500 per annum was introduced It was soon abolished because of the pressure brought on the Government on the ground that it causes a lot of inconvenience to those getting interest income. But it was reintroduced in 1995-96 with an enhanced limit of Rs. 10,000 per annum. In the case of interest on bank deposits held by individuals, deduction at source is at the rate of 10 per cent and in the case of domestic companies it is at the rate of 20 per cent and in the case of UTI, deduction is at the rate of 20 per cent for domestic companies and at the rate of 15 per cent for individuals.

4. *Economic Criteria Scheme* : One more scheme for widening the base of personal income-tax introduced in 1997-98 budget is the Economic Criteria Scheme, according to which those who satisfy any of the two following criteria have to file the income-tax returns :

* ownership of a four-wheel vehicle
* occupation of immovable property
* meeting certain prescribed criteria
* ownership of a telephone
* foreign travel in the previous year

5. *Minimum Alternate Tax* : For widening the base of the Corporation Tax it was necessary to bring under the tax net all those companies which were managing to get into the category of zero-tax companies by making use of all the permitted deductions and concessions. For this purpose, in 1984 section 80VVA had been introduced according to which deductions were to be restricted to 70 per cent of the pre-incentive total income so that at least 30 per cent of the income of the company could be taxed. In 1987, this was modified by introducing section 115J according to which provision, to levy corporation tax of 30 per cent of the book profits as computed under the Companies Act was made. In terms of this provision, wherever the income of the companies as computed under the Income Tax Act was less than 30 per cent of the book value, the tax was to be levied on 30 per cent of book profit. In 1990 this was given up when investment allowance was scrapped and further reduction in incentives was contemplated. Since the need for bringing the zero-tax companies under the tax net was again strongly felt in 1996, the 1987 scheme was revived under the name; Minimum Alternate Tax. This was opposed on the ground that exports would suffer and investment flow to backward areas would suffer and also on the ground that in general this would be a disincentive for the growth of the corporate sector. The demand for

scrapping the MAT was not conceded, but only some modifications were made in the budget for 1997-98. Exports were exempted and a system of credit was introduced according to which as pointed out by the Finance Minister in his Budget Speech " When a company pays MAT, the tax credit learned by it shall be allowed to be carried forward for a period of five assessment years and in the assessment year in which regular tax becomes payable, the difference between the regular tax and tax computed under MAT for that year will be set off against the MAT credit available."

In respect of Wealth Tax also important changes have been brought about. The exemption limit has been raised to Rs. 15 lakh and for wealth in excess of Rs 15 lakh the tax rate is 1 per cent of the value. The basis of tax has been shifted from wealth to unproductive asset and this is a very desirable change in Wealth Tax.

To sum up, the direct tax system in India has undergone a big change in the post-1991 period. Tax less to fuel development is the new philosophy of taxation and in accordance with this we have moved to a low tax regime with wider tax base. A welcome change that has taken place is that the share of the direct taxes in the total tax revenue is increasing and it has now reached 20 per cent. The reform, however, is incomplete since some of the measures suggested by the TRC such as rationalisation of taxation of perquisites, and taxation of agricultural income of non-agriculturists have not been implemented. The objective of widening of the tax base would have been better served if these recommendations also had been implemented. Nevertheless, the present direct tax system is much better than what it was prior to 1991.

REFERENCES

Bird, R.M, *Tax Policy and Economic Development*, The Johns Hopkins University Press, Baltimore, 1992.

Gandhi, V.P., *Supply-Side Tax Policy : Its Relevance to Developing Countries*, IMF, Washington, 1987.

Government of India, Report of the Tax Reforms Committee, New Delhi, 1992.

Government of India, *Economic Survey*, 1995-96 and 1996-97.

Parthasarthi Shome, *Tax Policy Handbook*, IMF, Washington D.C. 1991.

World Bank, *Lessons of Tax Reform*, Washington D.C. 1995.

10

REFORM OF INDIRECT TAXATION IN INDIA

—Prof. B.S. SREEKANTA RADHYA

India has a very complex system of indirect taxation mainly because of its federal nature. Tax jurisdiction of the Centre and the states are no doubt demarcated. But still there is a lot of overlapping in the case of commodity taxation and this has given room for serious problem in indirect taxation. Each one of the indirect taxes of the Centre and the states has its own deficiencies. But taking the indirect tax system as a whole, certain major deficiencies can be identified. The purpose of this lecture is to analyse these deficiencies and to look for solution for them.

Deficiencies

1. Indian indirect tax system is a highly unintegrated tax system. The Centre and the states have their own independent policies and even among states there is no common approach.
2. States' sales tax system lacks harmonization. There are wide differences in the tax rates, exemption, etc. There is also tax competition leading to trade diversion. This has distorted the tax system and instances are not lacking where the luxuries are taxed at a lower rate than the necessities and consequently justice or fairness in taxation is not ensured.
3. Cascading effect is perhaps the most important problem of indirect tax system. In a system of taxation, where the same tax base is used by different layers of Government, input is repeatedly taxed the cumulative effect of all the indirect taxes that fall on the same commodities is what is know as cascading effect, the consequence of which is high cost of production for the producer and high price for the consumer. The other problems associated with cascading are that exports become uncompetitive and vertical integration is encouraged

and nobody has control over the final incidence of indirect taxes.

Reform of indirect taxation should primarily aim at removing the deficiencies mentioned above. Certain reform measures within existing system are possible. One, to bring about uniformity in commodity taxation, the Additional Duties of Excise levied on sugar tobacco and textiles in lieu of sales tax can be extended to more commodities. But the state governments are not prepared to agree for this proposal since they are not happy with the scheme of Additional Duties of Excise. This possibility has already been explored and rejected. Two, an attempt towards harmonization of sales tax has been made through inter-state councils without much success. There reform of Union Excise Duties has been tried through MODVAT. Since this is confined to manufacturing stage only, the cascading effect is not eliminated completely.

Since reform within the existing system is not really helpful, a drastic change in the system is needed and the real solution in the introduction of full-fledged VAT. This system is so popular that as many as sixty countries of the world have gone in for VAT of which forty are developing countries. France was the first country to apply the value added principle in 1954 and Brazil was the first to adopt VAT in its comprehensive from in 1967.

Value Added Tax

As pointed out by Carl S Shoupo "The VAT is a tax on the value added by a business firm through its own activity to the goods and services it buys from other business firms" (Malcolm Gills and others 1990). There are various stages in the production and distribution cahin and the tax is levied and collected at each stage value is added. Tax credit is given for what is paid at the earlier stages and the input is taxed only once and the cascading. This brings about instant harmonization in commodity taxation and evasion is also difficult.

There are three variants of VAT namely consumption variant, income variant and gross product VAT and there are three alternative methods of VAT computations namely credit method, subtraction method and addition method.

In India modified value added Tax has been there since 1985-86. Its coverage has been expanded over the years and about 80 per cent excise revenue comes from this. But as pointed out earlier, this is confined to only the manufacturing stage and full benefit of VAT is not derived. The question now is how to go further to derive full benefit and the various possibilities have been examined by experts. The Study Team on the Reform of Domestic Trade Taxes in India (NIPFP 1994) has examined the following four options in this regard:

1. A National VAT;
2. State VATs;
3. Dual VAT systems;
4. Independent Dual VAT systems.

After a careful examination of all the above options, the Study Team came to the conclusion that the fourth option is the most appropriate one for India. Under the independent dual VAT system there would be an independent central VAT and an independent state VAT for each state. When the present MODVAT is extended to all the commodities and some of the services, it will become a central VAT at the manufacturing level. State VATs would come into existence when the sales tax levied by the state is converted into state VAT incorporating the value added principal in a harmonized environment.

While conversion of the present MODVAT into a central VAT poses no problem, converting sales tax into state VAT requires some extra effort on the part of the states. Certain misgivings that the states have in this regard must be removed. One fear is that administrative burden will increase and the cost of collection will increase and the cost of collection will increase and other fear is that the set-off given to inputs under the state VAT would lead to loss of revenue and this is unlikely to be compensated by bringing the value added in subsequent stages under the tax net. However, the Committee of Stage Finance Ministers on Sales Tax Reforms (NIPFP 1995) has supported the idea of converting the sales tax into state VAT and a few stages have made a modest beginning in this direction and the result of these experiments will provide valuable guidance to the other state.

In sum, the archaic system of India's indirect taxation needs to be reformed very urgently. Good lot of thinking has gone into this in recent year and there seems to be a consensus about what needs to be done. But the progress is very slow and a lot more attention need to be given to bring about the required changes in the system on the above lines.

REFERENCES

Government of India (1978), Report of the Indirect Taxation Enquiry Committee, Part II, New Delhi.

Government of India (1992), Report of the Tax Reforms Committee, New Delhi.

Government of India, *Economic Survey*, 1995-96 and 1996-97.

Malcolm, Gillis, Carl S Shoup and Gerardo, P. Sicot,(ed) (1990) Value added taxation in developing countries, The World Bank, Washington D.C.

National Institute of Public Finance and Policy (1994), Report of the Study Team on the Reform of Domestic Trade Taxes in India, New Delhi.

— —, (1995), Reports of the State Finance Ministers on Sale Tax Reforms, New Delhi.

11

INDUSTRIAL GROWTH IN INDIA

Measurement Through Chain Index

—Prof. D.U. SASTRY

India's faltering industrial growth since mid sixties after an impressive performance during the first decade and half, has been a subject of debate. A number of explanations have been suggested to explain this phenomenon. Those who have contributed to this debate have invariably used index of industrial production to measure industrial growth. Many recognize the limitations of the index of industrial production. Some suggest using alternative bodies of data. In all this debate, the focus has been more searching for explanations than for precisely measuring production movements. It is important, therefore to begin by measuring industrial growth as accurately as possible before searching for explanations.

The objective of this paper is to construct a chain index of industrial production to study industrial growth in India over the three decades, 1950-80. The official index of industrial production is a Laspeyres Index with fixed base year weights which may not portray production movements faithfully. The current official index is based on gross value added weights of 1980.Of course, there have been revisions of index from time to time with different base year, but such revisions have been by and large infrequent. For instance, the gap is 10 years between the index with 1980 base and 1970 base; similar is the gap between the index with 1970 base and the previous one with 1960 base. The current index is nearly 15 years old. The fixed base index numbers assume unchanging industrial structure. This is not a very realistic assumption to make over such long time intervals. Structural change is a phenomenon continuously taking place under a variety of influences such as changes in technology, output composition and emergence of new products. In the present context structural change is taken to mean changes in value added proportions of individual industries in the total value added of industry. This could occur as much during the period of industrial growth as during the period of industrial retardation. For these reasons, it is necessary to incorporate changes in the weighting pattern in the production index every year in order to take account of the structural change. The chain index is meant to incorporate such changes.

A Critique of Official Index

The first systematic and comprehensive index of industrial production was put out in early 1950s with 1951 base. There were, however, two earlier indices, an interim index with 1946 base and a pre-war index with 1911-14 base. The 1951 index covered 88 items from mining, manufacturing and electricity. This was revised in July 1962 with base 1956 covering 201 items, the increase was partly the result of a more detailed classification and partly due to new additions. In 1967 a revised index with 1960 base appeared. While the monthly index covered 307 items, the annual index covered a much smaller number of 142 items for which annual data were available. This series was again replaced in March 1975 with 1970 base covering 352 items. Both 1951 and 1956 indices used Census of Manufacturing Industry (CMI) data for generating weights whereas 1960 and 1970 indices used data of Annual Survey of Industry (ASI). The ASI has a large industry coverage (63) as compare to CMI (29). In all these cases net value added weights have been used.

The index with 1970 base is in fact based on value added weights of 1968, the latest year for which the census data were then available. Items for which regular monthly production data are available and whose annual production is Rs. 1 crore or more or alternatively value added of Rs. 25 lakh or more, are included in the index. Physical output data are available for 335 items and for the remaining 17 consisting mostly of machinery, data are available only in value terms. In such cases, they are converted into real terms by using appropriate price deflators. The Director General of Technical Development (DGTD) collects monthly production returns through its 47 Directorates for 261 items on a voluntary basis. For nearly 30 items, data are collected from several statutory bodies like textile commissioner, iron and steel controller, coal controller, etc., whose coverage is almost complete. In mining and electricity, net value added figures are supplied by concerned authorities. In case of sugar, salt and tea, monthly indices are adjusted for seasonality. The annual index is an average of monthly indices and relates to calendar year.

That the index of industrial production suffers from several limitations is wellknown. There have been several lines of attack. The revised index number series with 1960 weights exaggerates the growth rate for the first plan period and minimizes the importance of faster growth rate observed during the later year as a result of assuming constant weights of 1960 for the entire period 1951-60 (Shetty 1969). It is suggested that a way to correct this is to chain the index number with different base years, *i.e.*,1951,1956 and 1960, assuming that the pattern of weights which is being periodically revised with an interval of four to five years is representative of the period for which they are applicable. Thus, the series with 1951 base is the best indicator of growth for the period up to 1956, the revised series with 1956 base is true for the period up to 1960 and so on. The links are provided by annual percentage changes in the index number series with different base years. first of all this is not a chain index. If 'structural changes in industrial output are of a continuous nature and occur practically every year', then what is required is to change the weighting pattern every year in constructing the index and then link them. This is not the procedure followed.

Some have argued that periodic revisions of the index with four to five years interval will help to capture changes in industrial structure, as pronounced changes are observed in value added proportions even over such short time intervals (Krishna 1972 and Somayajala 1975. 1976). Periodic changes in the base year will undoubtedly help to some extent. But if change is a continuous phenomenon we may do better by changing the base every year and link it through the chain index.

Srinivasan and Vaidhyanathan (1975) have argued that there is no bias in using the base year shares as weights as long as we are interested in the growth of total value added by the industries included in the index at constant prices. 'The change in the relative shares in the aggregate value added of the industry by itself should not be the reason for changing the base year—in fact, in this case, changing the base year will achieve nothing. Growth rate will remain the same. This is true under certain conditions like no change in prices, no change in value added proportion to gross output, no new commodities and no change in the composition of output. But these are restrictive conditions. Prices are changing, gross output/value added proportion are changing, output composition is changing and new commodities are continuously emerging. In a sense, their note which was intended to clarify the nature of the official index, appears to have deflected the issue.

Recently the limited coverage of the index due to the voluntary nature of data supplied by producing units to DGTD and lack of representativeness of the items covered in specific industry groups has been highlighted (Isher Ahluwalia 1982). for example, for the group covering footwear, other wearing apparel and made up textile goods, the index is based on two items only, indigenous type of footwear and western type of footwear which constitute only 30 per cent of the value of output of the group in 1970-71. In industries like beverages, basic metal industries and metal manufactures the coverage is 18 per cent, and between 20 to 25 per cent respectively. For more than half the industries at two digit level, the coverage is more than 50 per cent. Thus, it is inadequate coverage and lack of representativeness of the items included that limits the accuracy of the index.

Another aspect of coverage which seems to be serious is the exclusion of the unorganised small sector which produces roughly half the industrial output from the purview of the index. Some efforts have been made recently to fill this lacuna in the new index with 1980 base, although these efforts were not entirely satisfactory. There are no two opinions about improving the coverage of the index and its representativeness in order to improve the accuracy. However, if one is looking for monthly index, there is no other alternative except to depend upon CSO series. ASI output data pose measurement problems. Some non-response, also existing ASI data, though less server. The choice, therefore, is not either using ASI data or the official index. Both are valuable sources of information.

Method of Construction

The construction of the chain index of industrial production involves a number of steps: (1) generating value added weights for every year, (2) obtaining quantity relatives for each industry group, (3) calculation of primary indices and finally, and (4) constructing the chain index. These are discussed below:

1. The weights are generated for each industry group for the period 1950-78 as follows:

$$W_{it} = \frac{V_{it}}{\Sigma V_{it}}$$

where,

W	=	weights
V	=	value added
i	=	industry
t	=	time

We have considered gross value added weights. The official indices have all used net value added except the index with 1980 base. Our choice is dictated by two considerations. First, the quantity index is based on the movements of physical output which itself is gross output.

Second the choice of net value added assumes that depreciation actually measures capital consumption, which may not be the case. In fact, recorded depreciation figures are more accounting entities governed more by tax laws than by actual wear and tear of machinery.

2. Quantity relatives for each industry are calculated for the period 1950-78 as follows :

$$\frac{q_{it}}{q_{it-1}} \times 100$$

where,

q	=	quantity index of industrial production
i	=	industry group (two digit level)
t	=	time

We do not have commodity index of industrial production with common base year for each individual industry for the entire period. For the period under consideration, four different series of index of industrial production with 1951, 1956, 1960 and 1970 as base, exist. These series have been linked by the following procedure. Year to year growth rates of the production index have been calculated. The splicing is done by taking the geometric mean of the common year between the series with different base years.

3. The primary indices are constructed by using gross value added weights and quantity relatives. The primary indices are:

$$Q_{01};\ Q_{12};\ Q_{23};\ \ldots\ldots\ldots\ldots\ldots\ldots\ldots\ldots\ldots\ldots\ Q_{t-1,\,t}$$

where,

$$Q_{01} = \Sigma W_o \frac{q_1}{q_0}$$

$$Q_{12} = \Sigma W_1 \frac{q_2}{q_1}$$

$$Q_{23} = \Sigma W_2 \frac{q_3}{q_2}$$

$$Q_{t-1,\ t} = \Sigma W_{t-1} \frac{q_t}{q_{t-1}}$$

Q_{01} is the primary index of the first year with previous year as base. Q_{12} is the primary index of the second year with the first year as base and so on. The base year is always with respect to the previous year of the index. W_0, W_1' W_2, . . . W_{t-1} are weights of the respective years denoted by the subscript. V_0, V_1' V_2, . . . V_{t-1} are gross value added of individual industries. Although the two digit level industry grouping has remained the same over the period the number of commodities included is the index has been changing over time both due to the emergence of new commodities and due to more detailed and finer classification. Therefore, the Q_s, *i.e.* Q_1' Q_2, Q_3 . . . Q_{t-1}, Q_t include changes in the number of commodities.

4. The chain index is finally obtained as a product of these primary indices of individual years, *i.e.*

Q_{01} = 100
Q_{02} = $Q_{01} + Q_{12}$
Q_{03} = $Q_{01} + Q_{12} + Q_{23}$
Q_{04} = $Q_{01} + Q_{12} + Q_{23} + Q_{34}$
Q_{0t} = $Q_{01} + Q_{12} + Q_{23} + Q_{34} \ldots\ldots\ Q_{t-1,\,t}$

The chain index has obvious merits. It makes efficient use of all price and quantity information. The weights are continually updated and hence the index would reflect more faithfully changes in industrial structure. Since, the weights are continuously changed, the chain index provides a rolling comparison because the primary indices which are linked together have previous year as their base. The chain index is a discrete approximation to the continuous Divisia Index numbers (Allen 1975). Divisia Index numbers have certain desirable properties. It is invariant to the choice of the base year (time reversal test). The product of price and quantity indices equal to the value ratio (factor reversal test). The theoretical superiority of the chain index which is a practical realisation of Divisia Index rests on such desirable properties. For these reasons, it is more precise than the Laspeyre index. However, the construction of a chain index is computationally laborious, time consuming and demanding in terms of data requirement. But if precision were the objective, the chain index is the obvious choice.

The Data

The construction of chain index is based on the quantity index numbers of industrial production published by the Central Statistical Organisation (SCO). The CSO index consists of three major groups : (1) mining and quarrying, (2) manufacturing and (3) electricity. The manufacturing group accounts for a little over 80 per cent of weights in the aggregate index. Within the manufacturing sector, there are eighteen groups at the two digital level. Our interest in this study is primarily with this dominant group.

Some of the individual industry groups had to be combined for a variety of reasons such as the absence of continuous series of index of industrial production for the entire period 1950-78, and due to different industry classification between CMI and ASI sources which constitute the basis for generating weights. The manufacture of beverages has been combined with tobacco and tobacco products because the index for beverages is available only from 1970. Similarly, the manufacture of wood and cork except furniture has been combined with furniture and fixtures as the index for the latter is not available. The two ASI groups, namely, manufacture of electrical machinery have to be combined into one single group to establish correspondence with the CMI group of general engineering and electrical engineering. For the miscellaneous group, production index is available only from 1960.

The weights generated from CMI for the period 1950-58 and from ASI for the period 1959-78 are based on gross value added. Both census sector of ASI and sample sector of SSMI have been considered for generating weights. Differences in the classification of industries between ASI and SSMI sources exit. ASI industry is much more detailed than CMI classification and re-grouping has been done to establish correspondence between them. Apart from the lack of correspondence between the two sources, there are definitional differences in the units covered.* Furthermore, ASI industry classification has itself changed from 1973-74 to suit the National Industrial Classification and has been suitably adjusted to make the two digit industry group comparable with the earlier period. Besides, ASI reports for 1972 are not released although census was conducted. This data gap has been filled by taking not value added from *National Accounts Statistic*. Gross value added figures have been obtained by considering the average depreciation of two years, 1971 and 1973. The CMI and ASI data are on a calendar year basis up to 1965 and thereafter changes from April to March.

Analysis of Results

The two indices of industrial production, *i.e.,* the official index and the chain index are presented in Table 11.1. Before we examine the production movements of these alternative series, it would be useful (1) to compare value added weights for the official index with our value added weights for common years and (2) to examine changes in value added weights over the period 1950-78.

Some Comparisons

The value added weights underlying the official index for 1951, 1956, 1960 and 1970 are generally lower as compared to our value added weights and differences are considerable for some industry groups (Appendix II). One possible reason could be that value added weights used in the official index are not of depreciation while ours is gross of depreciation.

Changes in value added proportions are supposed to reflect changes in industrial structure.† Structural change may be continually taking place due to a variety of reasons and one possible way to capture it is to study changes in value added proportions over short time intervals. An examination of the data reveals (Appendix III) that changes in value added proportions are considerable in food

* The CMI covers all registered factories with 20 or more workers using power, while ASI covers factories with 50 or more workers using power and 100 or more workers without power.

† This is not a sufficient condition for structural change. One should also examine changes in input output coefficients. It is possible to conceive a situation where changes in input output coefficients may neutralize each other leaving value added proportions unchanged.

manufacturing and textiles for a number of periods. For some industry groups such as chemicals and chemical products, basic metals, machinery, rubber and rubber products changes are observed only in some periods. Most industry groups, however, show perceptible changes over 1957-60. If attention is focused on the recent decade of the seventies, five industry groups have lost their position while seven have improved their share over 1970-74. The picture is not very different for 1974-78. Value added proportions have changed considerably in four industries, *i.e.,* food manufacturing, textiles, chemicals and machinery if the whole period of 1950-78 is considered. The important point that emerges from this examination is that value added proportions have been changing over the period and such changes are perceptible for certain industry groups even over short intervals. It is this finding which markets the fixed base Laspeyres index of industrial production very inadequate to study the production movements. The obvious choice seems to be the chain index which takes into account such continually changing structure.

Trends in Production Indices

The official index of industrial production increased from 100 in 1952 to 415 in 1978 in contrast to 421 according to chain index (Table 11.1). The chain index thus, shows a somewhat faster increase over the period. Within this broad period. two distinct phases are discernible. The first two decades up to 1970 shows that the official index rises such faster than the chain index and thereafter it lags behind the chain index.

The same picture emerges for the period 1952-665 and 1966-78. The correlation between the official index and the chain index over the period in very high, 0.99.

Annual percentages growth in the index for the alternative series presented in Table 11.2 indicate striking similarity with peaks and troughs occurring in the same years. However, a closer scrutiny would several that perks are generally higher in the chain index as compared to the official index barring 1955. Although the troughs generally occur in the same years except for 1957, three out of six troughs are higher and the remaining three lower in the official index as compared to chain index. The 1967 trough is not as deep in the chain index as it is in the official index.

TABLE 11.1 : Alternative Indices of Industrial Production

Year	*Official Index*	*Chain Index*
1952	100.0	100.0
1953	102.3	102.8
1954	109.5	109.2
1955	120.2	116.8
1956	130.9	124.7
1957	134.8	126.2
1958	137.2	131.2
1959	148.8	144.0
1960	172.3	162.8
1961	186.9	177.5
1962	203.2	194.1
1963	219.8	210.2
1964	237.7	229.4
1965	252.2	247.6
1966	253.5	247.4
1967	248.1	244.8
1968	266.8	263.2
1969	286.8	284.2
1970	300.7	297.9
1971	300.9	305.1
1972	319.8	327.2
1973	325.9	332.3
1974	328.3	332.8
1975	337.3	342.6
1976	370.3	376.4
1977	388.7	397.2
1978	415.1	421.0

Growth Rate Comparisons

The growth rates for the alternative indices of industrial production have been estimated by fitting semi-logerthermic trend equation for the period 1952-78 and for several sub-periods (Table 11.3). The results are presented in Appendix IV. The fix is uniformally good and all coefficients are highly significant.

Industrial productions has grown at the rate of 5.6 per cent per annum over the period 1952-78 according to the official index as against 5.8 per cent according to the chain index. Since industrial development under the plans really began from the Second Five Year Plan it would be more meaningful to study growth from 1956 onwards. The official index shows a growth rate of 5.2 per cent per annum over 1956-78 as against 5.6 per cent according to the chain index. That is to say, the official index of industrial production seems to understate somewhat the growth of industry as compared to the chain index and such underestimation appears somewhat sharper for the period 1956-78. These differences although appear quite small are important because they are compound growth rates.

TABLE 11.2 : Annual Growth Rates

(Percentage)

Year	*Official index*	*Chain Index*
1952		
1953	2.3	2.8
1954	7.1	6.2
1955	9.7	7.0
1956	8.9	6.8
1957	3.0	1.2
1958	1.8	4.0
1959	8.4	9.8
1960	11.6	13.1
1961	8.5	9.0
1962	8.7	9.4
1963	8.1	8.3
1964	8.2	9.1
1965	6.1	7.9
1966	0.5	–0.1
1967	–2.1	–1.1
1968	7.5	7.5
1969	7.5	8.0
1970	4.9	4.8
1971	0.1	2.4
1972	6.3	7.2
1973	1.9	1.5
1974	0.7	0.2
1975	2.7	2.9
1976	9.8	9.9
1977	5.0	5.5
1978	6.8	6.0

TABLE 11.3 : Trend Growth Rates of Industrial Production

(Percentage)

Periods	*Official index*	*Chain Index*
1952-78	5.6	5.8
1956-78	5.2	5.6
1952-65	7.7	7.8
1966-78	4.1	4.4
1952-60	6.7	5.8
1961-70	4.8	5.3
1971-78	4.4	4.4

The period 1952-78 consists of two distinct phases. The first phase from 1952-65 is a period of industrial expansion and the second period from 1966-78 is a period of industrial deceleration. The official index shows a growth rate of 7.7 per cent per annum for the first period and 4.1 per cent annum for the second. The chain index on the other hand shows 7.8 and 4.4 per cent respectively for the two periods. two points stand out clearly in this comparison. First, both the chain index as well as the official index show high rates of growth for the period of expansion and low rates of growth for the period of deceleration. Second, the official index exaggerates somewhat the low growth rate for the second period. The official index indicates a bigger fall in the growth rate in the second over the first as compared to the fall in the chain index.

Variability defined as the absolute deviation of residuals as a percentage of the estimated trend value is somewhat higher in the chain index as compared to the official index for the period 1952-65 as compared to 1966-78. That is to say, higher growth rate observed for the phase of expansion is accompanied by greater variability and lower growth rate for the period of deceleration is accompanied by smaller variability.

	Variability	
	1952-65	*1966-78*
Official Index	0.056	0.026
Chain Index	0.069	0.023

An examination of the decadal growth rates reveal 6.7 per cent per annum for the first decade, 4.0 per cent for the second and 4.4 per cent for the third according to the official index as against 5.8, 5.3 and 4.4 per cent respectively according to the chain index. Except for the decade of the seventies, the decennial growth rates are different between the two indices of industrial production. The growth rate of 6.7 per cent per annum for the first decade is higher in the official index as compared to 5.8 per cent in the chain index, whereas, the opposite picture of a lower growth rate of 4.8 per cent per annum in the second decade and a higher growth rate of 5.3 per cent according to chain index, is suggested. Nevertheless, both the official index and the chain index series show a fall in the growth rate from the fifties to the sixties and then to the seventies, but the extent of fall is different between the two series and between the two decades. The official index shows a decline of 38 per cent in the 1960s over the 1950s whereas, the chain index shows a fall of only 7 per cent. For the decade of the seventies while the official index shows a decline of 8 per cent over the sixties, the chain index shows a decline of 18 per cent. That is to say, the actual fall in the growth rate of industrial production is substantial in the seventies which the official index does not reveal.

In a recent study (Isher Ahluwalia 1982) industrial growth has been estimated using ASI output data at 1970 prices. For the manufacturing sector as whole, the growth rate of 6.1 per cent per annum over the period 1959-75 is indicated according to ASI output data as against 4.8 per cent according to the official index of industrial production. Thus, the growth rate is lower according to the official index. For the two sub-periods 1959-65 and 1966-75 the growth rates are 8.4 and 5.6 per cent per annum whereas, the official index shows 8.6 and 4.0 per cent respectively. For sub-periods, both series show significant fall in the growth rate after 1966 'but the extent of deceleration is more marked if index of industrial production data are used rather than ASI data. These results are dimensionally in the same ball park as ours although the two data sets and periods covered are different. However, the marked deceleration in the growth during the second period has been attributed to inadequacy and shortcomings of the index of industrial production. While this may be so, our analysis with the same index of industrial production reveals that deceleration is much less marked according to the chain index as compared to the official index.

Summary and Conclusion

We have attempted in this paper the construction of the chain index of industrial production to study the growth of Indian Industry over the broad period 1950-80. Unlike the official index, the chain index incorporates the continually changing pattern of weights for every year in the series.

The results suggest that the growth rate of the industry over 1952-78 is 5.8 per cent per year according to the chain index as compared to 5.6 per cent according to the official index. Apparently, this difference is small. It is possible to argue on this basis that it is not worth the time and effort to go in for the construction of the chain index. But if one looks at the period 1956-78 as well as the sub-period 1966-78, the difference widens between the chain index and the official index. The difference is 0.4 per cent per year for the period 1956-78 and 0.3 per cent per year for the sub-period 1966-78. These are trend rates of growth. Over a period of 5 years, the difference is 2 per cent and over a period of 26 years the difference will be over 10 per cent. These are not small by any stretch of imagination. Furthermore, if precision is the objective of measurement, the chain index is the inevitable choice.

Industrial declaration over 1966-78 period is somewhat exaggerated according to the official index. The fall in the growth rate is 4.1 per cent for the period 1966-78 from 7.7 per cent over 1952-66 according to the official index, whereas, the fall is 4.4 per cent from 7.8 per cent to the corresponding periods according to the chain index. That is to say the extent of declaration is exaggerated in the official index thanks to the method of construction of the index. The official index is Laspeyres index with fixed base year weights which assumes unchanging structure.

Despite these shortcomings, the official index is useful and in some respects even better than the index based on ASI output data. ASI output data are in value terms and all deflation procedures are at best approximations and introduce its own distortions. The official index on the other hand uses physical output data for most industry groups except for machinery and therefore, somewhat free from such distortions.

Finally, it would be prudent to work with alternative indices which will provide a check on each other.

REFERENCES

Allen, R.G.D. Index Numbers in the or and Practices, Macmillan 1975.

C.S.O. "Notes on Index Number of Industrial Production". *Monthly Abstract of Statistic*, July 1979.

Isher Judge Ahulwalia, Industrial Growth in India : *Stagnation Since the Mid Sixties*, Oxford University Press, 1985.

Krishna, K.L. "Industrial Capacity and Production", In C.R. Rao (Ed.) *Data Base of the Indian Economy*, Vol., 1. 1972.

Mudget, Bruce D. *Index Number*, John Wiley & Sons, 1951.

Shetty, S. "Index Number of Industrial Production : Chain Series". *Economic and Political Weekly*, 26 April 1969.

Srinivasan, T. N. and Vaidyanathan, A. "A Note on the Index of Industrial Production", in C.R. Rao (Ed.) *Data Base of the Indian Economy*. Vol., 1, 1972.

Somayajulu, V.V.N. "Strucural Changes and Growth in Indian Industries : 1946-70". *Asian Economic Review*, December, 1974.

—— "Structural Changes in Indian Industry, 1960-65". *Economic and Political Weekly* November, 1976.

APPENDIX I

VALUE ADDED WEIGHTS IN CURRENT PRICES

(*per cent*)

Year	*Food Manufacturing*	*Beverages and Tobacco*	*Textiles*
1	2	3	4
1951	11.12	0.43	61.89
1952	12.65	0.48	56.46
1953	12.23	0.42	56.01
1954	11.97	0.37	54.42
1955	13.31	0.45	51.69
1956	12.93	0.43	50.40
1957	14.00	0.51	46.38
1958	13.95	0.47	44.18
1959	15.17	2.95	30.14
1960	14.25	2.72	30.59
1961	13.44	2.73	30.08
1962	12.23	2.43	28.68
1963	10.66	2.45	27.23
1964	10.50	2.33	26.66
1965	10.58	2.72	24.42
1966	11.52	2.68	23.08
1967	9.92	2.77	23.50
1968	8.69	3.21	23.90
1969	11.38	3.59	21.10
1970	9.53	3.19	20.51
1971	8.44	3.35	20.17
1972	8.98	3.16	18.79
1973	7.89	2.21	23.76
1974	8.15	1.65	21.55
1975	8.38	2.49	18.53
1976	8.65	3.40	16.91
1977	9.42	2.35	18.48
1978	7.96	2.76	19.52

(*Contd.*)

APPENDIX I (*Contd.*)

(*per cent*)

Year	*Leather and Fur Products*	*Rubber Products*	*Chemical Products*
1	2	3	4
1951	0.39	0.00	8.28
1952	0.36	0.00	9.62
1953	0.42	0.00	9.76
1954	0.37	0.00	9.82
1955	0.33	0.00	9.39
1956	0.37	0.00	10.89
1957	0.31	0.00	12.11
1958	0.31	0.00	13.25
1959	0.55	2.25	8.37
1960	0.47	2.53	8.77
1961	0.77	2.55	9.52
1962	0.37	2.50	9.72
1963	0.29	2.42	9.77
1964	0.33	1.93	9.68
1965	0.32	2.09	10.17
1966	0.45	2.26	10.17
1967	0.36	2.08	11.08
1968	0.41	2.52	12.42
1969	0.31	2.48	13.09
1970	0.35	2.51	14.01
1971	0.32	2.42	15.29
1972	0.30	2.08	14.86
1973	0.28	1.56	14.44
1974	0.33	1.80	15.29
1975	0.33	2.07	15.04
1976	0.42	1.71	14.68
1977	0.37	1.67	15.16
1978	0.42	1.88	16.28

(*Contd.*)

APPENDIX I (*Contd.*)

(*per cent*)

Year	*Non-Metallic Mineral Products*	*Basic Metal Industries*	*Retail Products Except Machinery and Transport*
1	2	3	4
1951	3.91	10.35	0.00
1952	4.28	12.27	0.00
1953	4.46	12.70	0.00
1954	4.79	14.11	0.00
1955	5.30	14.51	0.00
1956	4.65	14.51	0.00
1957	5.11	15.77	0.00
1958	5.57	15.67	0.00
1959	4.68	9.57	2.45
1960	4.71	9.15	2.82
1961	4.56	9.61	2.84
1962	4.74	12.26	3.06
1963	4.50	13.66	3.44
1964	4.31	14.65	2.96
1965	4.44	14.04	3.52
1966	4.66	12.95	3.26
1967	4.63	12.10	3.04
1968	4.13	12.75	2.02
1969	4.06	11.88	3.03
1970	4.19	12.31	3.25
1971	4.01	11.30	3.19
1972	3.99	11.24	3.09
1973	3.64	12.06	2.06
1974	3.40	12.68	2.68
1975	3.92	13.35	2.63
1976	3.82	13.21	2.69
1977	4.22	11.19	2.69
1978	3.85	12.54	2.35

(*Contd.*)

APPENDIX I (*Contd.*)

(*per cent*)

Year	*Machinery (36+37)*	*Transport Equipment*	*Petroleum Products*	*Miscellaneous Industries*
1	2	3	4	5
1951	0.68	0.31	0.00	0.00
1952	0.73	0.39	0.00	0.00
1953	0.87	0.48	0.00	0.00
1954	0.68	0.67	0.00	0.00
1955	0.91	0.80	0.00	0.00
1956	0.81	0.86	0.00	0.00
1957	0.98	1.01	0.00	0.00
1958	1.17	1.09	0.00	0.00
1959	6.98	8.71	2.57	1.69
1960	7.38	9.70	1.88	1.34
1961	8.29	8.68	1.95	1.39
1962	8.24	9.31	1.63	1.43
1963	9.37	9.08	1.82	1.64
1964	10.39	9.57	1.39	1.67
1965	11.26	9.97	1.28	1.68
1966	11.55	10.17	1.97	1.67
1967	12.54	10.24	2.21	2.05
1968	12.00	9.49	2.35	1.82
1969	12.28	9.09	2.19	1.91
1970	13.27	8.44	2.07	2 11
1971	13.83	9.33	2.42	2.04
1972	14.00	8.78	2.09	5.03
1973	14.63	8.59	1.72	2.38
1974	14.74	8.25	2.39	2.06
1975	15.76	8.13	2.55	2.45
1976	15.75	8.19	3.60	2.96
1977	15.51	8.03	3.78	3.00
1978	14.53	8.98	2.73	2.37

APPENDIX II

COMPARISON OF CSO VALUE ADDED WEIGHTS WITH OUR VALUE ADDED WEIGHTS

(per cent)

	Industries	*1951*		*1956*		*1960*		*1970*	
		CSO	*OURS*	*CSO*	*OURS*	*CSO*	*OURS*	*CSO*	*OURS*
	1	2	3	4	5	6	7	8	9
1.	Feed manufacturing	11.85	11.12	13.99	12.93	12.09	14.25	7.74	9.53
2.	Beverage and Tobacco	1.50	0.43	1.49	0.43	2.22	2.72	2.90	3.19
3.	Textiles	48.01	61.89	41.76	50.40	27.06	30.59	17.43	20.51
4.	Footwear & Other Wearing Apparel	0.85	0.00	0.28	0.00	0.21	0.26	0.34	0.39
5.	Wood and Cork	0.21	0.28	0.24	0.42	0.80	1.30	0.49	1.03
6.	Paper and Paper Products	1.57	2.36	1.39	2.85	1.61	2.13	2.24	2.85
7.	Leather and Fur Products	0.27	0.39	0.18	0.37	0.43	0.41	0.32	0.35
8.	Rubber Products	3.35	0.00	3.04	0.00	2.22	2.53	2.22	2.51
9.	Chemical & Chemical Products	4.16	8.28	3.58	10.89	7.26	8.77	10.90	14.01
10.	Non-Metallic Mineral Products	3.31	3.91	2.47	4.65	3.85	4.71	3.33	4.19
11.	Basic Metal Industries	8.04	10.35	9.25	15.41	7.38	9.15	8.84	12.31
12.	Metal Products Except Machinery & Products	2.57	0.00	0.99	0.00	2.51	2.82	2.77	3.25
13.	Machinery (36+37)	2.07	0.68	3.51	0.81	6.43	7.38	10.85	13.27
14.	Transport Equipment	2.92	0.31	2.86	0.86	7.77	9.70	7.39	8.44
15.	Petroleum Products	–	0.00	3.79	0.00	1.34	1.88	1.62	2.07
16.	Miscellaneous Manufacturing Industries	–	0.00	-	0.00	1.23	1.34	1.70	2.11

APPENDIX III

CHANGES IN VALUES ADDED PROPORTIONS OVER SHORT TIME INTERVALS

Industries	*1951-54*	*1954-57*	*1957-60*	*1960-63*	*1963-66*	*1966-68*	*1968-70*	*1970-74*	*1974-78*
1	2	3	4	5	6	7	8	9	10
Food Manufacturing	0.85	2.03	0.25	3.59	0.86	0.14	2.40	0.60	0.42
Beverage and Tabacoo	0.06	0.14	2.21	0.27	0.23	0.91	0.43	0.67	0.27
Textiles	7.47	8.04	13.79	2.36	4.15	2.18	2.31	0.26	0.99
Leather and Fur Production	0.02	0.06	0.16	0.18	0.16	0.14	0.01	0.03	0.09
Rubber Products	0.00	0.00	2.53	0.11	0.16	0.22	0.48	0.01	0.19
Chemicals and Chemical	1.54	2.29	3.34	1.00	0.04	0.92	1.77	0.18	1.24
Non-Metallic Mineral Production	0.08	0.32	0.40	0.20	0.16	0.60	0.07	0.07	0.07
Basic Metal Industries	3.76	1.66	6.42	4.51	0.71	1.07	0.64	2.11	0.81
Metal Products Except Machinery & Transport	0.00	0.00	2.82	0.62	0.18	0.23	0.16	0.46	0.28
Machinery (36+37)	0.00	0.03	6.40	1.99	2.18	0.73	1.72	1.76	1.23
Transport Equipment	0.36	0.34	8.61	0.62	1.09	1.08	0.31	0.65	0.85
Petroleum Products	0.00	0.00	1.88	0.06	0.15	0.22	0.10	0.46	0.18
Miscellaneous Manufacturing Industries	0.00	0.00	1.34	0.30	0.03	0.24	3.12	2.58	0.08

APPENDIX IV

TREND GROWTH RATES OF INDUSTRIAL PRODUCTION

Years	*Official Index*	R^{-2}	*Chain Index*	R^{-2}
1952-78	5.6 (27.8)	0.98	5.8 (28.2)	0.97
1956-78	5.2 (21.8)	0.96	5.6 (20.5)	0.95
1952-65	7.7 (30.1)	0.99	7.8 (18.4)	0.96
1966-78	4.1 (18.1)	0.97	4.4 (20.6)	0.97
1956-65	8.4 (20.2)	0.98	9.3 (17.1)	0.97
1952-60	8.4 (20.2)	0.98	9.3 (17.1)	0.97
1961-70	4.8 (10.8)	0.93	5.3 (6.5)	0.92
1971-78	4.4 (9.5)	0.93	4.4 (9.0)	0.95

Growth rates are estimated by Semi-Log Trend Equation :

Log Tax+bt.

Note : Figures in the packers are t Values.

INDEX